# THE
# FIFTY-YEAR
# SEDUCTION

## ALSO BY KEITH DUNNAVANT

*Coach: The Life of Paul "Bear" Bryant*

*Timeout: A Sports Fan's Dream Year* (with Edgar Welden)

# THE
# FIFTY-YEAR
# SEDUCTION

How Television Manipulated College Football, from the Birth of the Modern NCAA to the Creation of the BCS

# KEITH DUNNAVANT

THOMAS DUNNE BOOKS
ST. MARTIN'S PRESS ☙ NEW YORK

THOMAS DUNNE BOOKS.
An imprint of St. Martin's Press.

www.stmartins.com

Design by Phil Mazzone

ISBN 0-312-32345-X
EAN 978-0312-32345-5

First Edition: October 2004

10 9 8 7 6 5 4 3 2 1

To my mother, Marjorie Dunnavant, who taught me, among other things, the value of perseverance

# CONTENTS

# ACKNOWLEDGMENTS

During my days as a college football writer, I covered many of the latter-day events described in this book as they were happening, including the aftermath of the *Board of Regents* decision, the rise and fall of the College Football Association, the bowl-sponsor revolution, and the conference realignment frenzy. Because of this, dozens of college administrators, coaches, network executives, bowl leaders, and conference officials who were my sources—on and off the record— played a role in my understanding of the forces roiling the sport, which provided the foundation for this book.

I conducted dozens of interviews directly for this book, and I would like to take this opportunity to express my gratitude to all who so graciously gave of their time to share their views on various subjects and helped me place important events, issues, and personalities in the proper context. Several of the notable characters who appear in these pages deserve special mention because they were kind enough to indulge several long interviews, not to mention countless follow-up phone calls, and their significant participation in the process helped bring it to life in more ways than one. Special thanks to Wayne Duke, Chuck Neinas, Father Edmund P. Joyce, Wiles Hallock, Father William Beauchamp,

Tom Hansen, Mike Tranghese, Franny Murray, and the late Jeff Coleman.

The participation of several key television-industry executives and talent enriched this work beyond words. Thanks to Jim Spence, Chuck Howard, Donn Bernstein, Keith Jackson, Chris Schenkel, Loren Matthews, Ken Schanzer, Tony Verna, Chet Simmons, Andy Sidaris, and the late Lindsey Nelson. Several books on the TV business proved invaluable, especially *Beating the Odds* by Leonard Goldenson, *Roone* by Roone Arledge, and *Up Close and Personal* by Jim Spence.

My family, friends, and business associates, scattered in Alabama, New York, Georgia, Florida, and elsewhere, have been incredibly supportive of this project, and they all have my thanks.

I feel very fortunate to have the opportunity to work with David Black, one of the best literary agents in the business, who pushes me to reach for my true potential.

Most important, I would like to acknowledge the man who made this book possible in a very real sense—Pete Wolverton, the associate publisher of the Thomas Dunne imprint at St. Martin's Press. Pete, who shares my passion for college football, pounced on a rather causal comment I made over lunch one day in the spring of 2003, and subsequently rescued this book from the ashes. He got it when many others didn't, which is to say, Pete is a guy with significant vision. He believed in this book, he understood why the subject matter was important and timely, and he played a major role in shaping the finished product. Thanks also to associate editor John Parsley, publicity manager Joe Rinaldi, and the entire team of dedicated professionals at St. Martin's Press.

# PREFACE

Like countless boys who learned their ABCs and memorized their multiplication tables during the era of Vietnam and Watergate, I never experienced a world without television. It was always a part of the context of my life. In fact, I barely remember life before the wonders of color television. The medium influenced everyone and everything in American culture, even those adults who came of age without it, but for baby boomers like me, the sum of television's importance far exceeded the content of our favorite shows. It was a window to the outside world that informed the way we developed in a variety of ways.

Now, from the vantage point of creeping middle age, it seems clear that television played an undeniable role in making sports a powerful force in my life. Many Saturday afternoons, I escaped the blistering summer heat while watching Major League Baseball's game-of-the-week, and blockbuster events like Hank Aaron's record-setting home run and Billy Jean King's historic grudge match victory over Bobby Riggs are indelibly marked in my memory. Without television, I probably would not have been exposed in any meaningful way to the NBA Finals, the Super Bowl, or the Final Four, and it's doubtful whether I would know the name Evil Knievel, much less carry to this day a vivid image of him parachuting into the Snake River Canyon on ABC's *Wide World of Sports*.

The power of television motivated me to try to slide head-first into second, just like Pete Rose. The power of television left me struggling in vain to throw the long bomb like Joe Namath, sink the jumper from the top of the key like Jerry West, and serve from the baseline like Jimmy Connors. Watching sports on TV filled my head with a million dreams shattered by the reality of my extremely limited athletic ability.

It would not be entirely accurate to say television made me a college football fan. Culture and geography took care of that. Growing up in a small Alabama town during the Bear Bryant era, I gravitated to the Crimson Tide at some point between my first steps and my first day of kindergarten, influenced greatly by the fevered passions of my father—who spent many of his years in radio as a sports announcer—and my five older brothers. We planned our autumn Saturdays around listening to the 'Bama games on the radio—broadcast throughout the Tennessee Valley over my dad's sports-oriented FM station—and it was during those formative moments converting John Forney's descriptions into mental pictures that I learned how to add and subtract in my head under pressure, trying to beat Forney to the punch on down and distance.

But if culture, geography, and radio conspired to make college football an important part of my life, television allowed me to experience the sport's sights and sounds in a much more powerful way. Amazing runs. Bone-crushing tackles. Perfectly thrown bombs. They all came to life during ABC's NCAA game-of-the-week, which always seemed like a big event. TV took hold of my senses and allowed me to understand the drama and feel the sensation of the moment in a way that radio could not touch.

Even though my favorite team could be seen only two or three times per season, television introduced me to a great big world of pageantry and tradition. It was Chris Schenkel and Keith Jackson who first welcomed me to exotic places like Ann Arbor and

Lincoln; taught me to appreciate great rivalries like Notre Dame–Southern Cal and Texas–Oklahoma; schooled me on innovations like the Student Body Right and landmarks like Touchdown Jesus.

In those pre-*SportsCenter* days, before we all took instant highlights for granted, the true mark of a serious college football fan in my part of the country was whether you made the very conscious decision to preempt coverage of the NFL games on Sunday afternoons to watch the *Bear Bryant Show, The Auburn Football Review,* and *College Football Today* with Bill Fleming. We were all so hungry. Day-old game films seemed as precious as video from the moon. When ESPN came along and started showing complete games on tape delay on Sunday nights, we finally knew why God—or was it Ted Turner?—had invented cable.

Measured against the backdrop of this era's incredible abundance, when the average fan can watch a dozen or more games live in a single day—and view highlights from just about any game in the country almost instantaneously on the various scoreboard shows—those days seem quaint, even deprived.

But all these years later, it's difficult for me to overestimate the impact of those precious moments in front of the tube, especially when that experience was closely linked to my subsequent career as a sportswriter, which inevitably led to this book. Like millions of people from all walks of life, all across the country, I'm living proof of the immense influence television has wielded in expanding the reach of college football, because it ensnared me, captured my imagination, affected my life, which makes me yet another product of The Fifty-Year Seduction.

In fact, anyone who has invested their time and passion in the sport over the last half-century is inexorably linked to this tale of power, greed, compromise, and unintended consequences. Ultimately, we are the source of all the power and everything it produces, because we are the ones who watch the games and buy the tickets.

While providing a showcase for the sport, television has

dramatically multiplied the number of people who care about it, significantly enlarged the role it plays in their lives, and harnessed the result of all that collective passion for the benefit of the networks and colleges. Television has also simultaneously raised the stakes, heightening the tension in the historic struggle between higher education and commerce.

This book is about the increasingly symbiotic relationship between television and college football, and it is also about the consequences of their partnership. This book is about the clout produced by television, and it is also about the various battles to control that power. This book is about how television helped shape the modern sport, and it is also about how the medium became the common denominator in the game's rise as a big business.

Over the last half-century, televised college football has manufactured money, greed, dependence, and envy; altered the recruiting process, eventually forcing the colleges to compete with the irresistible force of National Football League riches; aided the National Collegiate Athletic Association's explosion from impotent union to massive bureaucracy; manipulated the rise and fall of the College Football Association; fomented the realignment of conferences; and seized control of the postseason bowl games, including the formation of the lucrative and controversial Bowl Championship Series.

At the dawn of the television age, most colleges feared the medium's ability to create free tickets. Now it is impossible to imagine the modern sport without television, which is precisely the point.

# THE
# FIFTY-YEAR
# SEDUCTION

# 1

## THE BIG BLUFF

Inside a crowded, smoke-filled Dallas hotel ballroom on a dreary day in January 1951, retired Admiral Thomas J. Hamilton grabbed a mike and rallied his troops. "We are dealing with a terrific force like a powerful wind of gale velocity," he thundered. "We are already feeling the first breezes of this hurricane." After speaking for several minutes about the danger looming on the horizon, the decorated Naval aviator urged his colleagues to "act now" or risk "serious harm" from being "caught in the path" of the "great threat" to their way of life.

As he looked around the room, Hamilton saw the fear in many eyes.

Facing an unprecedented crisis, the college sports officials gathered for the forty-fifth annual convention of the National Collegiate Athletic Association (NCAA) listened to Hamilton—the University of Pittsburgh's athletic director—with an alarming sense of urgency. The need to act boldly was nearly unanimous.

Gripped by a sense of gathering hysteria, the delegates seemed resolved to harness their collective strength to save college football . . . from the menace of television.

. . .

On Saturday, September 30, 1939, as the Nazi blitzkreig of Poland plunged Europe into war and isolationist America, still recovering from the Great Depression, tried desperately not to notice, announcer Bill Stern welcomed a tiny audience of viewers to the first televised college football game, a contest between powerhouse Fordham—home of the fabled Seven Blocks of Granite—and lightly regarded Waynesboro State at Triboro Stadium on an island in the middle of New York City's East River. Early in the first quarter, the single camera positioned high in the stands panned wide to capture Waynesboro's Bobby Brooks rambling for a sixty-three-yard, history-making touchdown as the small crowd of fans who had made the 400-mile journey from western Pennsylvania cheered with great enthusiasm. But Fordham was too good. The Rams, a perennial top-twenty team in those early days of the Associated Press rankings, overwhelmed the Yellow Jackets to claim a 34–7 victory.

The telecast represented yet another first for the National Broadcasting Company's (NBC) experimental New York station, following by one month the first televised Major League Baseball game between the Brooklyn Dodgers and the Cincinnati Reds and preceding by three weeks the first televised professional football game between the Brooklyn Dodgers and Philadephia Eagles of the National Football League. The forerunner of WNBC-TV—a division of David Sarnoff's giant Radio Corporation of America (RCA) conglomerate, which controlled two national radio networks and dominated the manufacturing of sets—also broadcast the first live news event, the first boxing match, the first scenes from a Broadway play, the first musical performance, and the first man-on-the-street interview.

With a tower and transmitter located atop the Empire State Building, the world's tallest manmade structure and one of the marvels of the age, located some fifteen blocks south of the RCA Building in Midtown Manhattan, NBC beamed a signal capable of being received throughout the greater New York City area. However, television remained a novelty. Only a few hundred primitive black-and-white sets with tiny screens measuring $7.5 \times 10$ inches existed and the hefty price tag of about $500 rendered them a luxury enjoyed mostly by the wealthy or purchased by tavern owners looking for a way to attract customers.

When the Philco Corporation introduced television to Philadelphia during the same period, just a step behind RCA, many of the earliest TVs ended up in the homes of the company's employees, especially the engineers trying to work the kinks out of the technology. In 1939, Philco's station became the first affiliate of the NBC television network, and the following year, the two stations cooperated to provide coverage to both cities of the 1940 Republican National Convention. From the start, the forerunner of KYW-TV Channel 3 gravitated to sports programming. On October 5, 1940, when about 700 TVs were scattered around the area, the station broadcast the University of Pennsylvania's 51–0 victory over the University of Maryland at Franklin Field—the landmark first game in a partnership that would last for eleven seasons, helping cement the bond between the city's sports fans and the new medium.

When the Federal Communications Commission (FCC) allowed commercial telecasting to commence on July 1, 1941—and granted the first licenses to the RCA and Philco stations, followed quickly by WCBS-TV in New York and WRGB-TV in Schenectady, New York—the industry appeared on the verge of taking the country by storm. Sun Oil sponsored the first news broadcast and the Bulova watch company bought the first commercial, paying $4 to show the image of a clock face as the second hand slowly revolved around the dial. But Pearl Harbor changed everything. For the duration of World War II, with set production halted, television remained in a holding pattern. The established stations continued to broadcast to an extremely limited universe and to the vast majority of the country, to the millions who arranged their schedules to catch popular radio programs like *Jack Benny*, *Amos & Andy*, and *The Shadow*, television did not exist.

When the war ended, the powers behind the new medium

quickly refocused their energies and the number of stations and sets exploded. During the last half of the 1940s, more than 100 stations signed on the air in sixty-three different cities—spreading the technology to many corners of the country, especially the largest metropolitan areas of the East Coast, industrial Midwest, and West Coast—and the first regularly scheduled network programming emerged as NBC, CBS, DuMont, and ABC battled for viewers. Between 1947 and 1950, the number of sets soared from 7,000 to 9.2 million, making television a powerful force in most large cities across the country.

Throughout the postwar boom, sports in general, and college football in particular, became a popular vehicle for local stations desperately searching for attractive programming. In 1945, NBC assembled stations in the three trailblazing cities—New York, Philadelphia, and Schenectady—to broadcast the Army–Navy game from Philadelphia, making the Cadets' national championship–clinching victory college football's first network telecast. All across the country in the areas of significant television penetration, college teams eagerly embraced the chance to partner with TV. Oklahoma, Georgia Tech, Southern Cal, and others broadcast their entire home schedules.

Chris Schenkel, a broadcast novice fresh out of college, anchored a three-station Harvard network across New England and, between syllables, helped invent the way the still-developing medium covered the game. "I had nothing to base my role on," he recalled. "Was I supposed to talk as much as a radio announcer or shut up and let the pictures tell the story? Who knew?"

In the emerging world of televised sports, Pennsylvania's longstanding relationship with KYW-TV made it a pioneer without peer. A relatively strong program in an era when the Ivy League still mattered—the Quakers produced three top-20 teams during the late 1940s and routinely averaged 60,000 or more fans at Franklin Field—Penn saw television as a powerful publicity tool and a source of growing revenue. With the television landscape expanding rapidly, university officials expected the investment to pay off to an even greater degree in the years ahead.

In 1950, just as network television began to spread across the country, Penn sold the rights to its home games to the American Broadcasting Company (ABC) for $150,000 and Notre Dame, the sport's biggest name, cut a $185,000 deal with DuMont, slightly larger than ABC at the time and the most aggressive sports programmer of the day.

Television was well on its way to becoming the most powerful medium ever invented. Altering the fabric of American life like no invention since electricity, TV gave consumers a new reason to stay home and advertisers a new place to reach and influence millions of potential consumers. Faced with the competition, the motion picture industry entered a period of wrenching contraction. Newspapers, magazines, and radio found themselves under assault, their dominance as delivery systems for news, entertainment, and advertising forever shattered.

The sports world faced a significant dilemma. In those days, ticket sales provided nearly all of the revenue for every sport, from Major League Baseball to college football. While television represented a wonderful way to spread the various sports to a wider audience, it also created a virtually unlimited supply of free tickets at a time when television rights fees remained relatively modest. Many sports officials believed fans once accustomed to buying tickets were starting to stay home in large numbers and watch for free.

Faced with a decline in Major League attendance of 13.7 percent from 1949 to 1950 and a 19 percent drop for the various minor leagues, baseball executives pinned the blame on competition from television. They started discussing how they could work together to limit the medium's impact on turnstyles. Fred Saigh, the owner of the St. Louis Cardinals, favored the radical step of banning all telecasting—not imagining the day when television's riches would turn .215 hitters into millionaires.

Unrestricted television fostered similar tension between broadcasters and college football. All across the country, colleges in areas of significant television coverage were starting to report sizable declines in football ticket sales in the face of widespread broadcast of college games. The University of Washington blamed a $50,000 athletic deficit on a TV-related ticket shortfall. Over a two-year period when the University of Oklahoma's games were telecast statewide, the Sooners sold 15,000 fewer tickets in the Oklahoma City area, far surpassing the income derived from TV rights fees. UCLA reported a 26 percent attendance decline—even higher than the overall 19 percent drop across the Pacific Coast Conference, which maintained a liberal attitude toward television, broadcasting a total of 30 games in 1950—and an 11 percent reduction in revenue, meaning TV fees were not coming close to bridging the gap.

With no way to generate substantial income to replace declining ticket sales, which subsidized basketball, baseball, lesser sports, and intramurals, college administrators struggled to balance the books. Fearing the possibility of draconian cuts if the trend continued— perhaps an end to football and all the sports it supported—some officials started acting to protect themselves. The members of the Big Ten Conference—home of powerhouses including Michigan and Ohio State—agreed to abstain from live telecasting in 1950. The Southeastern Conference—home of traditional winners including Tennessee, Georgia, and Louisiana State—voted a similar moratorium, but member Georgia Tech defied the ban and telecast its games on an Atlanta station.

Feeling increasingly vulnerable on the subject, the members of the NCAA, a loosely organized union of colleges and universities large and small, commissioned a comprehensive survey on college football attendance patterns by the National Opinion Research Company (NORC) prior to the 1950 football season. The NCAA also appointed a three-member committee—chaired by Admiral Hamilton and including Southern Cal athletic director Bill Hunter and Columbia athletic director Ralph Furey—to study the situation and assess the NORC's findings.

.  .  .

Hamilton infused the effort with unquestioned credibility. A former star halfback at Navy, he had risen through the ranks during World War II to become one of Admiral William F. "Bull" Halsey's most trusted aides. Widely credited with developing the carrier fleet's night raid tactics, which helped win the war in the Pacific, Hamilton eventually became the commanding officer of the legendary *Enterprise*, which gave him tremendous stature among the patriotic men who ran the nation's college sports programs.

"Admiral Hamilton was a giant figure," said Jeff Coleman, the Alabama athletic business manager, who later joined the television committee. "Everyone respected him and valued his leadership."

As he stood before his colleagues and presented his report at the Hotel Adolphus, Hamilton was convinced he was leading the charge against an enemy with the power to destroy college football. The atmosphere was tense. Never before had the sport seemed so imperiled, and the men charged with leading the nation's athletic programs were not worried about overreacting.

"You have to understand that we were dealing with a very dire situation," Hamilton said forty years later. "We were fighting for the future of the sport. There was almost a sense of panic about the whole process."

Between 1949 and 1950, according to the NORC survey, overall college football attendance in areas with some television presence declined by 6 percent. However, more ominously, in the Middle Atlantic region, home to the largest saturation of TV sets, ticket sales plunged by 15.5 percent. Other areas with significant TV penetration produced even bigger declines, including a 28.7 percent drop in New England.

Rather than following tradition and attending a game of their choice, Hamilton argued that many fans were staying home and watching one or more of the many games available on TV.

"Television does have an adverse effect on attendance," Hamilton told his colleagues, "and unless brought under some control, threatens to seriously harm the overall . . . system."

Confronted with the grim statistics, the vast majority of the athletic officials believed they needed to act to tame television. Officials from areas still waiting for widespread telecasting—especially the Southeast and the Great Plains—feared even steeper declines once the medium reached critical mass.

"It is the near-unanimous opinion of the Southeastern Conference," said SEC commissioner Bernie Moore, "that a definite television policy should be established by the NCAA." He added that most of the schools in the league—with the notable exception of Georgia Tech—believed "if direct telecast of Southeastern games is permitted, that such procedure would almost ruin football in that area."

Most troubling to many were the actions of Notre Dame and Penn, who had jumped ahead of their peers by partnering with network TV. Their games could be seen in many parts of the country with access to ABC and DuMont programming, and many officials feared the Fighting Irish and Quakers were on the verge of dominating the medium. "We had to act to keep Penn and Notre Dame from being on every week," said Alabama's Coleman. "That could have been so damaging to college football."

Two years after losing a contentious battle for the Republican presidential nomination, former Minnesota governor Harold Stassen was named president of the University of Pennsylvania in 1950. It did not take him long to cast a critical eye on the Quakers' athletic program. Stassen, a man of big ideas, believed Penn football was not living up to its potential. He thought the Quakers should be able to compete with the major powers like Notre Dame and Michigan, so he started looking around for a dynamic athletic director who could make Penn more of a force on the national college football scene. Francis T. "Franny" Murray came to his attention through a mutual friend.

A member of the Quakers' famed "Destiny Backfield" of the 1930s—which made him a Penn hero when such a distinction carried lifelong implications—Murray was settled into a comfortable job as the director of Inquirer Charities, the philanthropic arm of *The Philadelphia Inquirer*'s publishing empire, where he organized various events, including an early exhibition game between the National Football League's Philadelphia Eagles and the Cleveland Browns of the rival All-America Football Conference. Looking for a new challenge, he immediately hit it off with Stassen, who hired him to take over the Penn sports program starting right after New Year's Day in 1951.

Less than two weeks into his new position, Murray sat in the Dallas hotel listening intently to Hamilton and others talk about the dangers of television. He was stunned. After the committee proposed a nationwide ban on unrestricted television combined with a small number of NCAA-administered "test" broadcasts during the 1951 season, Murray asked for time to address the membership.

He spoke for several minutes about Penn's long tradition of televising its games and expressed the minority view that TV could prove to be a great ally of the sport. "I think we are being a little shortsighted when we look at a crowded stadium and think that is the saturation point," he said. He also raised the specter of such a plan violating the antitrust laws and told the delegates that a decision to abide by such a ban "will not be left just to the athletic director."

But the rest of the NCAA membership was in no mood to listen to Murray. By a vote of 161–7, the NCAA approved the restricted plan. Except for the NCAA-controlled broadcasts, all other telecasting was to cease, meaning Penn, Notre Dame, Georgia Tech, and others were suddenly forbidden by NCAA rules from airing their games.

After more than a decade of telecasting, Penn was being forced off the air by a majority edict in a supposedly voluntary organization—a largely impotent confederation with no precedent for enforcing such sweeping power.

"They were seizing our property rights," Murray said four decades later. "It was un-American what they were trying to do, and I wasn't about to take it lying down."

When he returned to Philadelphia and conferred with his new boss, Murray was gratified to learn that Stassen agreed with him. "He was as angered by the implications as I was," Murray said. "He couldn't understand how a bunch of colleges could tell us what to do with the University of Pennsylvania's property."

Several weeks later, in a routine meeting with members of the Ivy League—still an informal group—Murray raised the possibility of a joint lawsuit challenging the action on antitrust grounds. But Penn's standing within the Ivy League was shaky. For years, some of the prestigious institutions had looked down on Penn because the school played many programs outside the group and appeared to be pursuing more of a "big-time" agenda, especially with regard to athletic scholarships.

"Yale considered Penn part of the great unwashed," remarked future Penn athletic director Jerry Ford. "They thought they were too good for us."

When Murray asked for help, the rest of the league turned a deaf ear and instead voiced support for the NCAA plan.

Unbowed, Murray and Stassen decided to oppose the NCAA alone.

Ignoring the ban, Murray negotiated a $180,000 contract with ABC, granting the network the right to telecast all of the Quakers' home games in 1951. He then sent a telegram to Hugh C. Willett, a member of the University of Southern California faculty, who held the appointed position of NCAA president, the highest-ranking official in the organization. In addition to asking for a special meeting to consider the ramifications of the policy, the telegram said Penn would not be bound by the NCAA rule and would "carry on as an obligation to its alumni, friends, and the public its eleven-year record of television." Murray said Penn would split the television revenue equally with its opponents.

Attempting to seize the high moral ground, Stassen issued a

statement denouncing the NCAA. "Central control is a kind of disease which slips into the minds of men around the world," he said. "But it is not the American approach to problems."

Immediately, the NCAA counterattacked. "By breaking away," Hamilton told reporters, "Pennsylvania is setting itself apart and incidentally taking advantage of the artificial vacuum caused by the willingness of other schools to pass up financial gain this year."

The day after Murray's announcement, the NCAA declared the university a "member not of good standing," painting Penn as a renegade in the eyes of the college sports establishment. This very public censure held the potential of preventing Penn teams from participating in the small number of NCAA-sanctioned events in other sports, including the upcoming International Rowing Association championship, but otherwise had little practical effect on the football team or the rest of the athletic program.

But, pressured by the NCAA membership, four members of the Ivy League—Cornell, Columbia, Dartmouth, and Princeton—announced that they would cancel scheduled 1951 games against Pennsylvania unless the university acquiesced on the television front, a boycott that represented a potentially crippling blow to Penn's entire athletic department. Several other opponents straddled the fence. It was a historic moment. When the four schools came to the defense of the virtually powerless NCAA, they infused it, unwittingly and irrevocably, with new authority.

"I was just stunned by their response," Murray said. "It was like they were holding a gun to our head."

While Murray considered his options, Notre Dame officials, who read about the Ivy schools' actions with a sense of outrage, fired a shot across the NCAA's bow. On June 15, nine days after Murray's telegram, Father John J. Cavanaugh, president of the nation's most prominent Catholic university, issued a statement challenging the NCAA's authority and charging the association's policy makers with using "dictatorial powers." In part, it read:

We have the firm intention of supporting the unity of the NCAA. We certainly wish to cooperate in any program which is for the overall good of athletics, but we do not see this good promoted by blindly acquiescing to very dubious principles and procedures simply because such policies and procedures are forced into practice under threat of a boycott . . .

Cavanaugh stopped short of announcing Notre Dame would defy the ban and continue to televise its home games. But even as the university weighed its options—with DuMont anxious to extend their relationship into 1951—Cavanaugh, top assistant Father Theodore Hesburgh, and others struggled to make sense of the NCAA's actions. The most controversial part of the restricted plan called for the NCAA to receive 60 percent of the rights payments from all 1951 telecasts, which Notre Dame considered an ominous precedent. "If these powers are permitted," Cavanaugh said, "what would prevent some future committee from telling a school how many games it might play or where it might play them or to levy a 60 percent tax on the proceeds from ticket sales?"

Confronted with a major crisis, the athletic officials who led the effort to restrict television wanted only to protect college football. It was quite understandable for these well-intentioned men to look at the statistics and conclude that television was having a negative effect on attendance—even though the correlation could not be proven and no one could yet say whether such declines resulted more from the novelty of television than a long-term trend. It was a world full of unknowns, and the administrators who pushed the panic button certainly were justified in joining forces to try to solve the problem. But the officials failed to consider how they were allowing their fear to trample on the ideals of their organization. No matter how noble their intent, they did not have the right to force dissenting schools to comply. They did not have the right to bully Penn.

By attempting to coerce Penn to surrender its television property, the NCAA and the four Ivy League schools crossed a line. It was a despicable, shameful act of thuggery, a strong-arm tactic worthy of back alley hoodlums and pulp fiction gangsters.

Without offering to compensate Penn for its losses, the association just picked the school's pocket and dared the Quakers to do something about it, hiding behind majority will, allowing the organization to be overtaken by a mob mentality that betrayed the members' honorable history of decency and fair-mindedness. It was the sports equivalent of a third-world dictator nationalizing a foreign corporation's assets, and such socialistic robbery violated the foundations of American justice and economic liberty.

The very public fight caught the attention of the Department of Justice, and Murray came away from a meeting with Attorney General J. Howard McGrath believing the government supported his challenge. "He said the NCAA's legal position was weak," Murray said. "He said to bring a suit because our chances were very good."

When Murray asked the NCAA to join Penn in submitting the plan to the federal government for review, the NCAA quickly refused.

Suddenly, Penn faced a defining choice. It could challenge the ban in court, defy the restriction and risk losing at least four games and possibly others once the college sports leadership started applying pressure, or relent on the television issue and make peace.

The NCAA and the renegade program were playing a high-stakes poker game, and Penn was falling victim to the Big Bluff.

The NCAA was holding a lousy hand. Even though the entire college sports landscape was lined up against Penn, the NCAA plan was built on a shaky legal foundation; the association did not have the legal authority to seize Penn's television rights even with a majority vote of the membership; the body did not have the constitutional power to punish Penn to encourage compliance; and the Ivy boycott looked suspiciously like an antitrust violation.

By raising the stakes to a tremendous level—forcing Murray to choose between gambling the future of the program and folding his hand—the NCAA was bluffing with all attitude and no cards.

But Murray and Stassen were taking a beating in the media, and the combination of the bad press—which painted Penn as selfish, greedy, and unwilling to help college football solve its biggest problem—and the possibility of a decimated schedule motivated them to throw in their cards. Unwilling to risk the potentially dire consequences of standing up for the principle of institutional autonomy, Penn surrendered the point and canceled its deal with ABC on July 19.

"We dropped the ball by not taking the thing to court," Murray said. "But what were we going to do, take on the entire college sports establishment?"

Notre Dame reluctantly agreed to abide by the ban.

The following January, Murray fought the issue on the floor of the annual NCAA Convention in Cincinnati. But he was one lonely voice facing a group motivated by fear and jealousy, by emotion rather than reason.

"No one wanted to stick their neck out to help Penn," said Bud Dudley, Villanova's athletic director in the early 1950s. "Murray was right about the whole thing, but he was all alone."

The findings of a more detailed attendance survey convinced most of the membership that controlling television was the only way to save college football, so, by a 163–8 margin, they voted to empower the television committee to create a full-fledged national TV series for the 1952 season. The membership also enacted a ninth bylaw to the NCAA Constitution granting the association new powers to create and enforce legislation—closing the loophole challenged by Cavanaugh and establishing a framework for compelling institutions to follow NCAA policy.

Although no one fully appreciated it at the time, the television crisis fundamentally altered the relationship between the NCAA and its members, setting the stage for a new age NCAA built on the authority of majority rule. The fear created by television became the catalyst in the transformation of the NCAA into the most dominant force in college athletics.

By bluffing Penn so skillfully, the NCAA emerged more powerful, like a bully with a reputation. To the rest of college athletics, Penn was a reminder, a warning: Don't challenge the majority.

Eventually, someone would call the bluff.

# 2

## IN HIS IMAGE

In the summer of 1951, as Franny Murray waged his futile battle against mob rule, the NCAA consisted of several file cabinets and a few boxes of stationery at the rear of the Big Ten Conference office in downtown Chicago. In those days, the NCAA did not inspire fear, loathing, or contempt. It was not yet the massive, overarching governing body destined to become virtually synonymous with the term "mindless bureaucracy." In fact, it had no full-time employees and in the grand scheme of collegiate athletics at the time, virtually no power. The story of the NCAA up to that point would have been completely unremarkable, except for one little fact: Its creation probably saved college football.

In the early years of the twentieth century, the relatively new game of football was gaining popularity on campuses from coast to coast. But football was still an incredibly violent game tempered by very few rules. According to news accounts at the time, 18 young men were killed and 149 were seriously injured while playing football in 1905, and talk of banning the sport gained momentum. After seeing the picture of a bloodied Swarthmore College player in a newspaper and hearing about the brutal tactics employed by some teams, President Theodore Roosevelt summoned presidents from

Harvard, Yale, and Princeton to the White House and urged these giants of academia to do something about the game, which their Ivy League then dominated. Several weeks later, they formed what would become the NCAA.

In their first order of business, the leaders of the new organization formalized a series of rules intended to civilize the sport. By banning dangerous facets of football such as the flying wedge, hurdling, clipping, and spearing, the delegates succeeding in reducing serious injuries and quelling the call for government intervention. NCAA membership quickly grew from a few colleges in the East to several hundred scattered throughout the country. Over the next forty-five years, the organization existed primarily as a forum for the colleges to agree upon uniform playing rules and eligibility standards. Eventually, the umbrella organization launched championship events in several sports, including basketball, but for many years the NCAA basketball tournament would remain trapped in the shadows of the more prestigious National Invitation Tournament at New York's famed Madison Square Garden. It would be decades before someone coined the term "Final Four," longer still before "March Madness" grew into a national obsession.

Like the federal government during the era of the Articles of Confederation, the NCAA in 1951 was a loosely organized, largely impotent union, created and sustained out of some vague notion of the need for national unity, but rendered mostly irrelevent by the hundreds of member colleges and universities who remained distrustful of each other and, at the very least, ambivalent about the whole concept of centralization. Conferences held most of the power, and they functioned with almost complete autonomy.

The NCAA's one attempt to project strength had actually resulted in a significant weakening of the association.

Concerned by the emergence of organized recruiting and under-the-table financial inducements in big-time football, a small group of college presidents started a movement within the NCAA shortly after World War II to create a national standard governing amateurism. In 1948, the presidents developed a set of guiding principles, to become known as the Sanity Code, which outlawed awarding scholarships on the basis of football ability, banned off-campus recruiting, obligated member institutions to deny admission to athletes who failed to meet the school's normal academic requirements, and prohibited subsidies and inducements to athletes. The resolutions dealing with financial inducements and academic standards garnered wide support, but the membership split over the issue of recruiting and scholarships, and this lack of consensus doomed the Sanity Code.

Two years later the NCAA identified seven members—Boston College, The Citadel, Villanova, Virginia Military Institute, Virginia Tech, Maryland, and Virginia—as flagrant violators of the rules. Known in the press as the "Seven Sinners," the colleges admitted they had provided financial aid outside the parameters of the NCAA regulations, insisting that the scholarship rules were unrealistic and unfair to the athletes. Many other athletic officials shared their viewpoint, particularly those representing major southern colleges who saw the football scholarship as an essential element in their system. During the 1950 NCAA Convention in New York City, when the NCAA leadership asked the membership to expel the "Seven Sinners"—an unprecedented moment in the history of college athletics—the measure failed to receive the necessary two-thirds majority, which dealt a devastating blow to the forces who favored a strong national governing body.

Humiliated, exposed as a paper tiger unable to enforce its own rules, the NCAA returned authority over financial aid and recruiting to the individual conferences. Newspapers proclaimed the death of the NCAA. But the television fight changed everything, establishing the NCAA's authority in a stunning reversal of the Sanity Code failure.

For many years, Kenneth L. "Tug" Wilson, the commissioner of the Big Ten Conference, oversaw the day-to-day activities of the NCAA. As secretary-treasurer of the organization, he worked closely with the president and the ruling NCAA Council, appointed positions consisting of academics and athletic officials around the country. But most of the work fell to Walter Byers, his assistant, a workaholic former United Press reporter who spent his time alternating between Big Ten publicity director and NCAA duties, working out of a cramped office in a small coverted suite on the second floor of the Sherman Hotel. Byers published various annual reports, answered correspondence, dispatched press releases, and managed the annual basketball tournament.

About the time of the Sanity Code fiasco, some athletic officials started talking about the need to create a national NCAA office separate from the Big Ten.

"There was a pretty widespread feeling that the relationship between the Big Ten and the NCAA was too cozy," said longtime University of Alabama athletic business manager Jeff Coleman. "Some folks thought it was a conflict of interest, that we needed to have a totally independent NCAA."

Wilson supported the idea, but for a different reason. Despite the failure of the Sanity Code, Wilson favored a strong national governing body, and he believed creating a central office with a full-time executive was the only way to put teeth into the enforcement process.

Because of the knowledge he had developed at Wilson's side, Byers was the logical choice to head the new age NCAA. He was smart, hardworking, and well respected among the members of the ruling NCAA Council. But he was conflicted about the choice.

Soon, Byers had been told, his job with the Big Ten would be expanded to an assistant commissioner's position, which would allow him to move up the ladder and assume more responsibilities for one of the nation's premiere athletic conferences. His future had Big Ten commissioner written all over it.

Staying with the Big Ten was a sure thing for a man intent on a career in athletic administration. Becoming the face of the NCAA was, by any measure, a gamble. Knowing that his future would be framed by the choice, Byers vacillated for several weeks.

Finally, he placed a call to an old friend named Bill Reed. For several years before becoming an aide to U.S. Senator Homer Ferguson, Reed had worked as the Big Ten's publicity director and, like his successor, handled much of the NCAA's affairs. Byers had heard that Reed was anxious to return to athletics if the right job ever came along.

According to a close friend of both men, Byers offered Reed the choice of a lifetime: the Big Ten or the NCAA? When Reed said he would like to return to the Big Ten, Byers said that was just fine. He wanted to see what he could do with the NCAA. Just like that, the course of college athletics was irrevocably altered.

Several weeks later, the NCAA Council hired Byers as the organization's first executive director at a salary of $11,000 and instructed him to establish an office in Kansas City, Missouri. In addition to being centrally located—and his hometown—Kansas City was chosen because it was a long way from Chicago and the Big Ten.


On the morning of July 1, 1952, Marjorie Fieber walked into the Fairfax Building in downtown Kansas City and took the elevator to the second floor. She walked down the hall, opened the door to the new NCAA headquarters, stepped in, and then stepped back. The floor was covered in glue, and she didn't want to ruin her good shoes.

"It was a gooey mess," Feiber said. "They were waiting to put new tile down on the floor, but the tile hadn't gotten there yet."

When Walter Byers, her new boss, arrived a few minutes later they started sorting through the boxes which had been shipped from Chicago. But there was only so much they could do with the files in the hall and an adjoining vacant office, so about noon they both went home and let the tile masons get on with their work.

"I had seen the job opening in the paper, and the first thing I did was call my father," said Fieber, who would spend eight years as Byers's secretary and more than thirty years in various capacities with the NCAA. "He said it sounded like a good place to be. He said the way things were going, the NCAA had no place to go but up."

Located above a tavern on a street with a slight incline, the first NCAA office was a small, spartan suite with no air-conditioning. In the blistering summers, it could feel like a furnace. When they opened the windows facing Eleventh Street to try to generate a breeze, and the wind was blowing just right, fumes from the city buses would fill the office, turning the place into a chorus of coughing and wheezing. The prevailing breeze sometimes was so swift that it often sucked papers out the window, forcing Fieber or fellow secretary Joan Woodruff or bookkeeper Helen Audett to run down the street in hot pursuit.

"It was a pretty humble beginning," said Wayne Duke, hired as the NCAA's first all-purpose assistant that summer. "But there was a feeling that we were getting in on the ground floor of something big."

Duke, who had met Byers while he was a student assistant in the University of Iowa athletic department, bumped into him on a trip to Chicago during the 1951 football season. Several weeks after this chance encounter, Duke, then the University of Colorado's sports information director, learned from his boss that he was being considered for a job with the NCAA.

Flattered by the interest, he flew to Omaha, Nebraska, to meet Byers for an interview at the College World Series. His wife Martha was six months pregnant with their first child at the time and he planned to fly in and out on the same day, so he would not have to spend the night away from home. He had no change of clothes.

Sitting in the stands at Rosenblatt Stadium, the two men talked for a while about college athletics and the requirements of the job. The interview seemed to be going fine until a pigeon dropped a nasty payload across the front of Duke's nice blue suit, his only clothes east of the Rockies.

"Pooped on the day I was interviewed," Duke said. "It had to get better."

. . .

Starting from scratch as if sculpting a piece of clay, Walter Byers set about methodically transforming the new age NCAA into the most powerful force in collegiate athletics. The opening of the Kansas City office marked a turning point in the history of college sports, tipping the balance of power from the conferences to the NCAA. When the NCAA started moving into certain areas once controlled by the individual leagues and schools, it represented a shift of responsibilities and authority that the governing body would never surrender.

It was inevitable that the NCAA would become a reflection of its first executive director. Byers was an unlikely candidate to become the most powerful man in college athletics. Wiry and standing just five-foot-eight, he won all-city acclaim as a high school center in Kansas City, but saw his dreams of college stardom evaporate when a coach at Rice told him he was too small to play the game. Discouraged, Byers transferred to Iowa, where he majored in journalism. After Pearl Harbor, he dropped out of college to join the U.S. Army but was discharged a short time later because of a condition called wandering eye, which made his left eye appear crossed and impaired his vision.

"I think the eye problem contributed a great deal to Walter's personality," Duke said. "It made him self-conscious and may have given him an inferiority complex."

Blessed with a terrific memory and a brilliant analytical mind, Byers's cold, calculating aloofness suggested arrogance. Meticulous in every facet of his life, Byers expected attention to detail and no excuses. Once in the early days of the football television plan, a forty-eight-page annual report detailing the previous season's results contained a one-letter typographical error:

". . . the general spirit of this revolution . . ."

Noticing that the "s" in resolution had been transposed with a "v," Byers blew his stack and ordered the book reprinted at a substantial cost.

An early riser, Byers arrived at the office by 7 A.M. and expected no less of his employees. A tireless worker, he once collapsed from exhaustion at his desk and was forced to spend several days in the hospital. Secretive and calculating even during rare moments of weakness, he issued one last order as they wheeled him out of the office on a stretcher: Don't tell the membership.

Naturally, no one dared.

Fair in dealings with his employees, Byers nevertheless was not the kind of man to stop by a subordinate's desk to make casual conversation. Despite his background as a publicity man and wire service reporter, he disdained public relations, which colored his empire in many ways. Brick by brick, he built the NCAA into a coldly efficient organization that enforced the rules without exceptions. He was often derided as dictatorial, but he could never be accused of favoritism. A loner, he never developed many close friends in college athletics. In ways both good and bad, Byers's personality would shape the NCAA and its relationship with college football as much as the policies he implemented.

The television plan started taking shape in the months before the Kansas City office opened. After forcing Pennsylvania to abandon its challenge to the new system, the athletic officials charged with developing a plan found themselves negotiating a minefield of legal questions, selfish desires, and network concerns.

"We wanted to make it fair for everybody, but that was easier said than done," said Admiral Tom Hamilton.

On a chilly morning in late April 1952, Alabama's Jeff Coleman walked into a sixth-floor suite inside New York's Biltmore Hotel and unfurled a large U.S. map. It identified which cities were connected to coaxial cable and capable of receiving live network broadcasts, which seemed as mysterious to the members of the committee as the blueprints to a hydrogen bomb.

"Nobody knew anything about television," Coleman said. "It was all so new, and we were just a bunch of people in athletics trying to make sense of the whole mess."

The mandate to create a national television plan left the committee with wide latitude in deciding how to best serve the membership. The overwhelming majority wanted a limited number of games to reduce the effect on attendance. Most wanted to spread the appearances around as much as possible to prevent any one team from dominating the series. Everything else was up for discussion.

Asa Bushnell, the commissioner of the Eastern Collegiate Athletic Conference, who would become the plan's link to the networks as program director, lobbied hard to get a piece of the action for the mostly small schools in his confederation of leagues. An amiable, middle-aged man who was deathly afraid of flying, Bushnell tried to push the committee toward sharing the wealth with all NCAA members.

"The big schools were never going to let that happen," Coleman said.

Robert Hall, the Yale athletic director, wanted to pursue the idea of splitting the package between two networks. Bill Hunter, the Southern Cal athletic director, tried to convince the committee to allow each member two appearances per season, no doubt envisioning the Trojans' big games against Notre Dame and UCLA beamed coast to coast.

"The networks would love to have Notre Dame on every week . . . have it wide open," Bushnell lectured his colleagues. "But we have to draw the line somewhere."

As they argued over where and how to establish the boundaries, the officials leaned heavily on the advice of legal counsel Joseph Rauh, Jr. A small man who always wore a bow tie, Rauh was a powerful force in Democractic Party politics who had gained notoriety representing several artists and writers caught up in Senator Joseph McCarthy's anticommunist hysteria. His fierce defense of Lillian Hellman, Arthur Miller, and others caused several members of the committee to view him with suspicion.

"Some of those people didn't like me at all for my stand against McCarthy," Rauh said nearly forty years later. "They thought I was some sort of communist, which was about the worst thing you could say about someone in those days."

But the officials decided to trust his legal advice. Several members wanted to pursue blackouts, which had been used during the 1951 test period, but Rauh advised against such a strategy, because the National Football League had already proven vulnerable on the issue. Especially pivotal was Rauh's advice to limit each school to one appearance per year, basing a legal argument on the social aim to prevent the rise of a TV aristocracy.

"One is safe," Rauh told the committee. "You don't want someone on more than once because it means too much return for them. This seems unassailable, because it restricts TV without having to say your purpose is restriction."

After meeting with Assistant Attorney General Stanley Barnes, Rauh believed the plan was safe from legal challenge—at least from the Justice Department. "I saw it as a wink," he said. "I came away thinking [the federal government wasn't] going to come after us, because they knew football supported intramurals and all the rest, and pressing the issue would only hurt the colleges."

But he never seriously considered advising the NCAA to seek an antitrust exemption. "I knew we were on the fence legally, and I didn't think we could get an exemption," he said. "Notre Dame and Penn would have fought us."

No man shaped the resulting plan more than Byers. As the NCAA's only full-time executive, he had emersed himself in the television situation and knew more about the medium than anyone else. Those first tentative meetings in 1952 set the tone for the next three decades: Byers dominated the proceedings with a combination of knowledge and personality.

"Walter didn't have an agenda like some of the others," Coleman said. "Everybody naturally listened to what he had to say."

After several sessions running late into the night, the NCAA television committee crafted a plan and put it up for bid. The first NCAA television package would include single games on eleven different Saturdays. No school could appear more than once. Avoiding the controversial sixty-forty split that had so enraged Notre Dame officials during the 1951 test period, the committee spurned Bushnell's share-the-wealth designs and instead placed only a 7.2 percent assessment on the rights fees paid to the colleges, although the small cut immediately became the NCAA's largest source of revenue.

On June 6, the NCAA signed a $1.14 million contract with NBC, consolidating the governing body's control of televised college football and setting in motion a series of events none of the athletic officials could possibly have imagined.

One thought dominated every decision contemplated by the men who shaped the plan: Television was the enemy. In their eyes, the medium represented a threat to college football attendance and the game's balance of power. They wanted to protect the sport. They assumed they could.


In the first four years of his tenure, Byers presided over two other key policy initiatives that would fundamentally alter the relationship between college football and the NCAA. The newfound authority seized in the name of television paved the way for both.

Working with the newly formed extra events committee, Byers moved to create order within the postseason bowl games, establishing the NCAA's role as a regulator of the system. For the first time, bowls were required to meet certain guidelines (such as returning 75 percent of their proceeds to participating schools) to meet NCAA certification, which was essential because the NCAA banned members from playing in uncertified games. The national office asserted its authority to dictate minimum payouts, eligibility of teams, playing dates, and a variety of other decisions once left at the discretion of the individual bowls.

By achieving control over television and the bowls, the NCAA strengthened its hand as an enforcer of the membership's rules. Under the old compliance committee, the association enjoyed no real leverage because its punitive options regarding football were limited to censure and expulsion, two extremes which amounted to a slap on the wrist and a death sentence. In 1952, Byers created a new enforcement division and quickly established the police force's power by suspending the University of Kentucky basketball team for one season following a widely publicized point-shaving and recruiting scandal. Kentucky, a dominant program led by legendary coach Adolph Rupp, declined to fight the punishment. And the NCAA emerged more powerful.

"That made the enforcement division and it was all Walter," said Wayne Duke.

In 1956, when the NCAA placed the Auburn football team on probation for recruiting violations, the punishment included a two-year ban on television and bowl appearances, which established the governing body's ability to inflict significant pain without canceling an entire season.

"Walter knew we had to put teeth into the enforcement process or it would never be effective," said Arthur J. Bergstrom, the NCAA's director of enforcement during that period. "Our relationship with television and the bowls gave us a way to enforce the rules."

Television, bowls, and enforcement became the pillars of the Byers era, setting the stage for a whole new age of college football. In forging this new era, the NCAA established a precedent for national control of many facets of the game, vesting the organization with tremendous authority. No one could have fully comprehended that they had given Walter Byers the power to build an empirial bureaucracy in his own image.

# 3

# THE BIG BANG

**J**. V. Sikes wanted his players to feel like a family. He wanted to turn his University of Kansas Jayhawks into a band of brothers, because he was gunning for Oklahoma.

Sikes, a tall Georgian with a rather thick southern drawl, often told his players they could challenge Bud Wilkinson's Sooners as the dominant program in the Big Eight, filling their heads with a dream that seemed so big it filled up their world. But he told them it would take more than great talent, more than hard work, more than perfect execution. He believed they needed to develop a special bond with each other, like warriors, so in the summer of 1952 the coach moved his team into a makeshift athletic dormitory. The three-story, turn-of-the-century house at 1043 Indiana Street needed a paint job, more bathrooms, and a bigger kitchen, but it would do. It would do just fine.

Many of the Jayhawks were not very happy about their new accommodations, which required them to move out of their apartments, dorms, and fraternity houses so they could cram their stuff into the dusty old house and live like army draftees. A jock dorm meant curfew, bed check, and isolation from the rest of the student body.

But Sikes was right. The proximity to each other gave the

Jayhawks a new sense of unity. His players ate their meals together, slept several men to a room, washed their clothes together and, in the evenings, after another exhausting day of classes and practice many of them piled around the small black-and-white television set in the first floor lounge. In the Kansas football dorm, as in a growing number of American homes, the television set was becoming the focal point of the house, the sociological descendent of the pioneer's stone fireplace.

For young college students like Galen Fiss, a senior fullback from tiny Johnson, Kansas, the invention was a source of amazement. "It was so new to all of us that it was a big deal just to sit down and watch whatever came on," Fiss said. "I'd never seen a television set until I went off to college."

Several weeks after the Jayhawks moved into their new dorm, they helped launch college football's national television era. On September 20, 1952, when Truman lived in the White House, the Dodgers still played in Brooklyn, and Elvis still drove a truck, several million viewers from coast to coast watched Kansas defeat visiting Texas Christian 13–0 in the first game of the NCAA series.

"Coach Sikes made a really big deal of it in his pregame talk," Fiss said. "We felt like we were part of history."

Mel Allen, the celebrated voice of the New York Yankees, hosted the coverage across the NBC network, which utilized three cameras positioned in the stands and the press box. During breaks in the action, Allen narrated live commercials for General Motors, the sole sponsor of the series. He spent much of the afternoon praising the play of Kansas quarterback Gil Reich, who tossed two touchdown passes. The limits of the technology of the day caused the TV people to miss some fast-developing plays and it was a generation before instant replay, crowd shots, sideline cameras, and rifle mikes.

Fewer than half of the country's homes contained a TV set at the time, and many of the young men who played in those first nationally televised games had never seen Lucy tormenting Ricky or

Uncle Miltie covorting in a dress. Like most of his teammates Alabama defensive back and kickoff specialist Cecil "Hootie" Ingram didn't own a set, so he frequently stopped by a Tuscaloosa drugstore and watched the NFL games over a soda. "I noticed how the TV folks always zoomed in on the guy kicking off," he said. When Alabama prepared to kick off to Georgia Tech at Grant Field in Atlanta, Ingram took his time lining up the ball on the tee. He put it down, stepped back like he was going to kick, then reached forward to pick it up, mashed it in his hands, walked around with it, and finally placed it once more on the tee.

"I was a real ham," said Ingram, who later became the athletic director at Florida State and Alabama. "I wanted to make sure that camera stayed on me a while."

Television was sweeping across the nation like a wildfire, and the number of stations on the NBC network increased every week. Forty-eight hours before the final game of the year, KTBC-TV signed on the air in Austin, Texas, giving NBC a 65-station network and 20.4 million potential sets for Navy's 7–0 upset of Army.

What most athletic officials failed to recognize at the start of the game's national television era was the medium's enormous and unprecedented ability to multiply the number of people who cared about the sport. That was the ballgame, and none of the people who crafted the plan got it. They were too busy acting out of fear. Determined to protect the sport from television's ability to create free tickets, they never understood that the only thing they had to fear was television's ability to put money in their pockets.

For most teams, the fan base in the early 1950s was limited to, or at least dominated by, alumni and students. Many prominent programs—especially schools in rural areas of the South and Midwest—played in stadiums with fewer than 30,000 seats. However, the promotional power of television became the most important factor in the tremendous growth in the number of people who followed the sport. The televised game captured the fascination of millions who had been aware of it only through radio and newspapers—or not at all—and the impact on the colleges through the years was unmistakable. As new fans gravitated to a particular team—despite having no academic link to the institution—the colleges soon felt the need to enlarge their stadiums to accomodate the demand for tickets. Over time, the nonalumni, nonstudent fans grew to dominate the audience for most programs, making the teams prosperous but also more beholden to a group who saw college football as separate and distinct from the academic mission.

In the context of history, the first season of the NCAA television package was much more than the start of a popular and profitable series. It was the birth of the modern era of college football, with television installed as an increasingly influential partner. It was the moment in time when the game became a commodity, elevated by television to a whole new level of popularity, seduced by television's charms to accept a whole new set of compromises. It was the dividing line between an era of stubborn amateurism and an age of creeping commercialism. It was the demarcation point between the impotent, ineffective NCAA and the powerful, activist NCAA, emboldened by its ability to lead, tempered only by the limits of majority will. It was college football's Big Bang, an epic event destined to unleash a chain reaction across a half century of drama and intrigue—the first step in the sport's transformation to a billion-dollar industry, the start of an evolution that would one day lead to the TV-driven realignment of conferences and the TV-dominated creation of the lucrative and controverial Bowl Championship Series.

In the early days of radio in the 1920s and 1930s, many colleges felt the need to protect themselves from the new technology. Ticket sales paid all the bills and anyone with a radio could stay home and listen for free, they reasoned. But Knute Rockne, the legendary Notre Dame coach, appreciated radio's immense power to promote his program, which he believed far exceeded any potential decline in ticket sales. His exploitation of the medium played a large role in building the Fighting Irish into the nation's most beloved college football team.

In fact, Rockne's vision was vindicated every time a South Carolina boy named Edmund P. Joyce flipped on his radio and listened to the Irish.

Two decades later, Joyce was a Notre Dame graduate and the university's newly installed executive vice president, which placed him in control of the Irish athletic department and on an unpopular side of an old debate about a new medium.

"We were dealing with some frightened people," Joyce recalled many years later. "But, of course, a lot of them were just afraid of competing with Notre Dame."

Even as Notre Dame grudgingly participated in the NCAA television plan, university officials remained outspoken in their opposition to the manner in which the governing body had nationalized Notre Dame's TV rights.

In a memorable debate with TV committee member Jeff Coleman on the DuMont network's *Keep Posted* program on November 21, 1952, Joyce assailed the NCAA's "dictatorial ways." An eloquent academician who exuded a certain disarming charm, Joyce pulled no punches.

"There is such a thing as minority rights," he said forcefully, the primitive TV lights glaring in his face. "The freedom of the college should be fairly complete to manage its own football team."

Joyce proceeded to attack the TV plan as "socialistic," the ultimate code word in the era of Joseph McCarthy, the Rosenbergs, and Alger Hiss.

Coleman, a courtly southern gentleman with a deep, gravelly accent, clung to the only defense at his disposal: majority rule. He explained that 92 percent of the NCAA membership had sanctioned the television committee's actions.

"We are trying to save the game of football," he said.

Despite joining the TV debate a year after Penn and Notre Dame reluctantly succumbed to majority rule, Joyce became a vocal critic of the NCAA plan. At every opportunity, he railed against the association's shortsightedness and heavy-handed dominance. In 1953, after Harold Stassen left Penn, Franny Murray was forced to resign—"They told me I had become synonymous with big-time football, like that was some kind of disease"—which left Notre Dame alone in opposing the NCAA's television monopoly. In 1955, the Big Ten and Pacific Coast Conference challenged the plan at the convention, which gave Joyce a glimmer of hope. But after being threatened with some of the same tactics the NCAA had employed against Penn, the two leagues agreed to a compromise granting them more regional appearances, leaving Notre Dame alone in opposition to the package.

Challenging the plan in court was not a viable option in those days. "We would have been ostracized as a radical outfit, and that would have been disastrous for Notre Dame," Joyce said.

The only difference between a bunch of radicals and a movement is the size of the crowd. Year after year, Notre Dame continued to vote against the NCAA plan, but after a while, Joyce stopped attacking it in public. He waited for his radical idea to grow into a movement.


While many athletic officials preoccupied themselves with the television issue, the sport faced an equally significant turning point on the subject of scholarships. But the two were actually very closely linked. Resolving the financial aid situation to create a workable national standard could not have been accomplished without the authority the NCAA asserted and enforced regarding the television dilemma.

Through the years, college programs approached the idea of the athletic scholarship in various, sometimes widely contradictory, ways. Some provided room, board, tuition, and fees to recruited players in return for their athletic services. At other schools, the scholarship covered tuition and fees but the players were required to hold down a campus job to earn their room and board. It was common at some schools for a wealthy alumnus to "sponsor" a promising athlete and pay his way through college. Other high-minded institutions spurned the whole concept of the athletic scholarship, which they considered a vulgar reflection of the game's mounting commercialism, and required prospective athletes to qualify for financial aid based on need.

Even during those days when the athletic scholarship was loosely defined and enforced with little vigor by the various conferences, abuses were common. Pay-for-play scandals and incidents of academic fraud grabbed headlines even before World War II, which provided the impetus for the first major attempt by reform-minded presidents to tame the beast. But too many coaches and administrators, particularly at the major schools in the South, considered the Sanity Code unrealistic, because it tied financial aid to need and required players to work for their room and board. Even in those days, it was hard to imagine a football player juggling school, practice, and what amounted to a second job, just to satisfy some arbitrary standard. Opponents of the Sanity Code also believed the regulations encouraged cheating and placed the less prosperous schools at a financial disadvantage against the prestigious universities and their rich alumni, who would find a way to circumvent the rules.

When the Sanity Code collapsed, the compensation issue reverted to home rule. At the dawn of the television age, when the modern game of college football was still struggling for definition, the sport faced a critical decision: Would it follow the lead of the once powerful Ivy League, whose members essentially de-emphasized in 1955 by swearing off the athletic scholarship and all it represented? Would it allow the conferences to maintain their own rules and risk spiraling into an endless series of regional bidding wars for talent? Or would it adopt a workable national standard?

After five years without any national regulations, the membership of the newly activist NCAA decided everyone needed to play by the same rules. In 1956, the NCAA passed legislation codifying what would come to be known as the grant-in-aid, a standard package of benefits to include tuition, fees, room, board, and $15 per month in so-called laundry money. Some giddy advocates boldly predicted the new system would dramatically reduce illicit payments, but they were wrong. There would always be overzealous boosters determined to beat the competition, whatever the standard, especially as the spoils associated with winning multiplied in the years ahead. Opponents of the grant-in-aid, who still pined for the Sanity Code, derided it as pay-for-play.

While some argued that the new age athletic scholarship mocked the principles of amateurism underpinning the college sports establishment, the realities were much more complicated. In one respect, the grant-in-aid made the system much less hypocritical and, at least in theory, turned the recruiting process into an aboveboard quid pro quo. Over the last half century, hundreds of thousands of young men and women have used the grant-in-aid to work their way through college by leveraging their athletic talents. It has proven to be one of the great institutions of the American meritocracy.

But the creation of the grant-in-aid also represented an unmistakable step toward commercialism. How could a student be considered an amateur if he entered into a formal deal to be compensated for his athletic talents? Understandably sensitive on the subject and fearful of what might happen if some legal body interpreted the arrangement as an employment contract, the NCAA coined the term "student-athlete" and started using it as often as possible.


On the night before the 1954 Cotton Bowl, Lindsey Nelson felt a bit nervous. Instead of ringing in the new year on the town, Nelson stayed in his Dallas hotel room and read through the rulebook with Red Grange, the legendary former Illinois running back once known as the Galloping Ghost. He was determined to nail his big break.

Eighteen months after joining NBC as assistant sports director to the influential and highly respected Tom Gallery, Nelson convinced his boss to let him try to develop his talents as a play-by-play announcer. Because the Cotton Bowl between Rice and Alabama represented his first big chance behind the mike, Nelson wanted to make sure he and Grange, his expert analyst, were ready for television.

As he flipped through the rulebook, Grange suddenly stopped and looked at his partner with a quizzical expression.

"Have you ever seen anyone come off the bench and make a tackle?"

Nelson shook his head.

Grange started telling him about a wild day in Canada when he had seen a player dash from the sidelines and lay a thunderous hit on an unsuspecting runner. He told him how the officials awarded the runner a touchdown, as the rules provide.

"That must've been something to see," Nelson said with a laugh.

After discussing a few more rules, the pair decided to call it a night.

The next day marked the second straight year fans from coast to coast could see the Rose, Orange, Cotton, and Sugar bowls with the flip of a switch. The Rose Bowl had been the first to join the television revolution in 1951, and the other three games soon followed the California game's lead. For two decades, the major bowl games had existed primarily as in-person events, tourist lures which cast big shadows only in Dallas, New Orleans, Pasadena, and Miami. But television was destined to transform the big four into national treasures. Soon New Year's Day would seem virtually synonymous with college football.

As Nelson and Grange worked through some early jitters, Southwest Conference (SWC) champion Rice and Southeastern

Conference (SEC) champion Alabama traded touchdowns. Midway through the second quarter, the Owls led the Crimson Tide, 7–6.

On a routine sweep from his own five yard line, Rice halfback Dicky Maegle found a seam in the Alabama defense and started racing upfield. A tough back who could really take a lick, Maegle possessed a deceptive burst of speed in the open field. By the time he approached the Alabama forty yard line, Crimson Tide defenders William Oliver and Vincent DeLaurentis were fast on his heels. It looked like a footrace to the goal line.

On the Alabama sideline, halfback Tommy Lewis watched with a sense of frustration as Maegle ran toward him. Then something inside him snapped. The football player's most primal instinct took over and Lewis, with his helmet strapped on and his mind thinking only of his ability to prevent a touchdown, ran onto the field and hammered Maegle.

The crowd at the jam-packed Cotton Bowl was stunned. After a few seconds, many fans started to boo. The chorus of disapproval and disbelief grew louder and louder as Maegle, shaken by the hit, lay motionless on the grass. When he finally got up and staggered off the field, Lewis walked to the Alabama bench, slumped over, and pushed his head into his hands.

In the press box, Nelson tried, in his understated tone and East Tennessee twang, to convey what had happened to the national television audience. But he could hardly believe it himself.

"It was strange enough to see that happen, but it was stranger because Red and I had been talking about the same thing the night before," Nelson recalled many years later. "I can't describe how eerie that felt."

As the officials conferred, Nelson turned to Grange off camera and flipped the palms of his hands toward his partner, who took the opening and ran with it. By the time the officials awarded Maegle a ninety-five-yard touchdown, Grange had already explained the rules to millions of stunned viewers.

A few days after Rice's 28–6 victory, a remorseful Lewis appeared with Maegle and Rice head coach Jess Neely on Ed Sullivan's

*Toast of the Town* program on CBS, which cemented his unlikely and unwanted celebrity. He apologized and lamented that he had been "too full of Alabama."

"I couldn't believe the number of people who came up to me on the street after that game talking about that incident," Nelson said. "It demonstrated to me the potential impact of the medium."

In the years after Princeton and Rutgers played the first intercollegiate football game in 1869, the sport spread quickly throughout the East and eventually across the rest of the country. Of course, the game barely resembled the modern sport of football. It was more like a brawl, with twenty-five players to a side and very few rules. The evolution to the contemporary game, with innovations such as the forward pass, would take several decades.

Most colleges fell into predictable scheduling patterns. It was quite logical for Princeton to play Harvard and Yale, because those esteemed universities already cooperated in a multitude of academic endeavors. When the Alabama Polytechnic Institute, located in the village of Auburn, started a team in 1982, it made perfect sense for the college to play a game against the new football squad across the state at the University of Alabama. It was just that simple.

By the turn of the twentieth century, most of the nation's football-playing colleges gravitated to more formal groups of like-minded institutions. These came to be known as conferences.

Most leagues were formed according to one overriding factor: geography. Since football teams of that era enjoyed neither the luxury of big budgets nor unlimited time off from their studies, they created relatively small groups, usually a dozen or fewer schools, that were located within 200 to 300 miles of each other. In those days, most teams traveled by train, making proximity to rail lines important. The Ivy League, Western Conference (which became the Big Ten), Southern Conference (which spawned both the Southeastern Conference and Atlantic Coast Conference),

Southwest Conference, Big Eight, and Pacific Coast Conference emerged as the most important circuits in their respective regions.

The high cost of travel prevented most teams from scheduling games outside their region of the country, which tended to make the individual conferences extremely insular, provincial institutions. But this sense of geographic isolation also gave rise to the concept of the bowl game, a postseason event featuring two strong teams from different parts of the country, which played an important role in transforming college football into a truly national sport.

Although they started out primarily as a mechanism to simplify the scheduling process, the conferences eventually assumed greater responsibilities, especially as schools added other sports such as basketball and baseball. When colleges started recruiting players and compensating them for their athletic talents, it was the conferences who first attempted to bring order to the process.

At the dawn of the television age, the conferences dominated college football. But that was about to change. Even as the NCAA assumed the mantle of leadership, one man devised a bold plan that could have dramatically altered the college landscape.

After a bitter fight over sanctions imposed on several members as punishment for rules violations, the nine-member Pacific Coast Conference disbanded following the 1958 football season. It was an ugly divorce. They even destroyed the files in the conference office.

When the five schools still talking to each other decided to form a new conference several months later, Admiral Tom Hamilton interceded and told the officials from Southern Cal, UCLA, Washington, Stanford, and California they needed to think big. He wanted to use the five Pacific Coast schools as the base for a super-conference including Army, Navy, Air Force, Notre Dame, Penn, Penn State, Duke, Georgia Tech, and several others.

"We called it the 'airplane conference,'" Admiral Hamilton said many years later. "My idea was to bring together some of the top institutions in the country and establish the most prominent conference in the nation. Air travel was becoming a common thing, which would have made travel among those distant schools practical."

"It was going to be a monster football league," said Penn athletic director Jerry Ford, who participated in the discussions.

Meeting discretely with athletic officials in cities throughout the country in 1959 and 1960, Hamilton pushed the idea of creating the most important, most popular, and inevitably most powerful football league in the country, a conference with the clout to challenge the NCAA's burgeoning influence and cut its own deals with television and bowl games.

Using his connections with the military, Hamilton thought he had secured the participation of Army, Navy, and Air Force. But someone in the Pentagon vetoed the idea. When the service academies backed out, the movement collapsed. Within a few months, the Pacific Coast teams reorganized as the Pac-5, under the leadership of Hamilton, their new commisssioner, and grew into the Pac-8 over the next five years.

"That conference could have changed the face of college football," said Tom Hansen, Hamilton's former assistant, who eventually became the commisssioner of the Pac-10. "Tom had this vision of creating something that could have been a real dominant force."

To most athletic officials of the day, the notion of a nationwide conference undeterred by great geographic distances seemed farfetched. But Hamilton was just ahead of his time.

One day, ambitious athletic officials would compete with each other to create geographically sweeping superconferences—and television would be the glue that made such alliances possible.

When Paul "Bear" Bryant left Texas A&M to take over the struggling Alabama program in 1958, his contract included an unusual provision: ownership of the Crimson Tide's game films.

Forbidden from televising their games on Saturday outside the strict confines of the NCAA plan, coaches like Bryant adapted and used their game films as the basis for popular and lucrative Sunday highlight shows, usually seen on small statewide networks of three to six stations. The Saturday ban stoked demand for such programs, turning them into must-see TV for fans with no other weekly access to their favorite team, giving them a precious look at the great touchdown run or the controversial fumble described by their local radio announcer. Coaches exploited the intense interest by selling sponsorships to national or regional advertisers, using the power of their positions to generate tremendous revenue above their salary and achieving a measure of financial indepedence from their employers. Through the years, this trend continued in other areas as the colleges willingly traded a certain amount of influence to sponsors and boosters who were able to significantly increase the coaches' earnings potential—keeping them happy and preventing the schools from needing to meet the true financial demand for their services.

Football fans all across the state of Alabama arranged their Sunday afternoons around watching *The Bear Bryant Show* presented by Coca-Cola and Golden Flake snack foods ("Great pair says the Bear!"), making it a much bigger ratings winner than the competing NFL games. But it was more than a highlights show. The program quickly became the most powerful link between Bryant and his fans, fostering a kind of intimacy, making the fans feel closer to the man and more invested in his team. Capturing and distilling his unique combination of rugged dominance and down-home humility, the show connected the coach to the football-crazed state in a profound way, helping to create and sustain the legend of Bear Bryant.

In contrast to the previous era, when big-name coaches like Tennessee's Robert Neyland, Army's Red Blaik, and Notre Dame's Frank Leahy existed, despite their enormous success, in the shadows of the public consciousness, their faces largely unknown to the general public, television transformed men like Alabama's Paul "Bear" Bryant, Ohio State's Woody Hayes, Texas's Darrell Royal, and Notre Dame's Ara Parseghian into recognizable personalities. Coverage on the NCAA package and in bowl games elevated such coaches to iconic status, making many as well known as movie stars and politicians.

No one sold college football and the giants of the sidelines like ABC Sports.

# 4

## TWO ENVELOPES

Leonard Goldenson knew television was the future, and he desperately wanted a stake in the future.

Goldenson, the Harvard-educated chief executive of the Paramount Theaters chain, had been fascinated with TV ever since he watched a primitive demonstration of the new invention at the 1939 World's Fair in New York City. As Goldenson and thousands of others looked on in disbelief, President Franklin D. Roosevelt appeared on a tiny black-and-white set, the flickering image conveyed via telephone lines from the White House more than two hundred miles away. At a time when radio and electricity were still new advancements in many parts of the country, the grainy picture struck a surreal chord, as if transmitted from a distant future of infinite possibilities.

By the time commercial telecasting finally started to take hold nearly a decade later, Goldenson was preoccupied with trying to save his company. After a long and costly battle, Paramount—which owned a major studio as well as a large chain of theaters—was forced to split into two corporations by the federal government, which saw the combination of production and distribution as a threat to competition. After the divestiture, which took effect on January 1, 1950, Goldenson wound up as president of the theater company at a time when the industry was imperiled by the growing popularity of television.

All across the country, TV was prompting millions of people who once flocked to the movies several nights a week to instead stay home and flip on the tube. Hundreds of theaters, unable to sustain the drop in business, closed their doors forever. The studios looked upon television as a menace. Jack Warner, the Warner Brothers chief who personified the image of the all-powerful movie mogul, prohibited any of his pictures from so much as mentioning the word television. Warner and his colleagues had no intention of coexisting with the phenomenon; they were desperately trying to devise ways to thwart the miserable beast that was ruining their business.

But in the midst of this war, Goldenson staked a contrarian position. He was determined to get his company into the television business.

In the early 1950s, the medium was growing rapidly but faced two significant technological speed bumps. In 1948, the Federal Communications Commission (FCC) had placed a moratorium on the granting of licenses while it reorganized its system of channel allocation, so even as demand for sets and licenses soared, no new stations were permitted to hit the airwaves for four years. In an era before satellites, the only means of transmitting live network programming to television stations for rebroadcast was through coaxial cable, and connecting cities throughout the country to this heavy wiring was an expensive, time-consuming process. It was just a matter of time before both problems would be solved, allowing network television to spread from a small group of East Coast cities to every corner of the country.

When Goldenson started looking for a way to make his company a player, four networks were battling for viewers. The National Broadcasting Company (NBC), headed by General David Sarnoff, and the Columbia Broadcasting System (CBS), led by William Paley, had exploited their dominant positions in radio to pioneer the new medium. At the beginning of 1953, CBS counted seventy-four affiliates. NBC had seventy-one. Together they collected about 75 percent of all advertising dollars spent on television.

The American Broadcasting Company (ABC) and the DuMont Network lurked far behind, with fourteen and twenty-two affiliates, respectively. These struggling enterprises were more concerned with their own survival than trying to compete with their more established rivals. Both were deep in debt and sinking fast.

Allen B. DuMont, an engineer who invented the first practical cathode-ray tube, the medium's core technology, earned millions from the sales of sets manufactured by DuMont Labs. He spent much of his fortune trying to make a go of his network, which hit the air in 1946. It introduced the world to several future stars, including Jackie Gleason and Mike Wallace, featured the sci-fi cult favorite *Captain Video*, and aggressively pursued sports programming, becoming the first network to broadcast National Football League games. But cash-strapped DuMont was never able to grow beyond a small base of stations, especially after CBS and NBC attracted most of the choice frequencies—stations broadcasting on the more powerful VHF band—before the license freeze was lifted in 1952. CBS and NBC were more attractive to station owners because they aired a stronger lineup of shows. The more people who watched, the greater advertising revenue a station could generate.

ABC, like Paramount Theaters, was a creation of the federal government. In 1941, the FCC ruled that no single company could control more than one radio network, which was a bullet fired directly at NBC's Sarnoff, an imperious figure who cast a large shadow over the burgeoning industry. After two years of haggling, Sarnoff sold the lesser of his two operations, the Blue Network, to a conglomerate headed by candy titan Ed Noble for $8 million. When the war ended, the new company, which Noble christened ABC, ventured tentatively into television.

If broadcast television had been a horse race, ABC would have been the longest of long shots in those days. But it was a network, and Goldenson wanted a network.

Convinced that the industry would eventually attract enough advertising to sustain a third profitable network, Goldenson approached Noble, who was anxious to bail out, and somehow convinced his board to pay the staggering sum of $25 million for ABC, which was on the brink of bankruptcy. The deal, which closed in 1953, launched one of the great underdog success stories in the history of American industry.

As they started looking around for attractive programming, ABC executives recognized the immense power of televised sports. Two years after the NCAA launched its unified plan, ABC outbid NBC for a two-year deal covering 1954 and 1955, which represented a major coup for the fledgling network. As part of its $2.5 million rights fee for 1954—nearly 50 percent more than NBC had paid the previous season—ABC agreed to televise a 26-week series of lesser NCAA events, including the postseason basketball and baseball tournaments. At the time, the struggling third network consisted of just forty affiliates, which left much of the country unable to see college football. But the larger contract and the minor sports coverage were too attractive for the NCAA to ignore.

Then ABC blew its big chance. Due to the problems associated with their smaller universe and some internal politics, the sales department turned a potential landmark series into an unmitigated disaster. After failing to land any major sponsors for the package, ABC was forced to market much less lucrative commercial spots on a weekly basis. Half of the inventory went unsold. After losing more than $1 million on the 1954 season, ABC, embarrassed by the debacle, paid the NCAA a $350,000 penalty and allowed the contract to revert to NBC in 1955.

For quite a while, no one at ABC had the nerve to mention the word "sports" around Leonard Goldenson.

About the time Goldenson started pursuing ABC, Edgar Scherick moved to New York and landed a low-level job in advertising. He knew nothing about advertising, but that didn't stop him. He was a quick study. Within a few years, Scherick emerged as a fast-rising star at the Dancer Fitzgerald Sample agency, where he controlled the lucrative Falstaff Beer account in the early days of television. But Scherick, a stocky, high-strung man whose mind seemed to race as fast as his mouth, which rarely stopped talking, and his feet, which rarely stopped pacing, was as susceptible to boredom as brilliance. After achieving success on Madison Avenue, he abruptly left to start his own television-production company.

Exploiting some contacts he had made during his advertising days, Scherick cut a deal to syndicate Big Ten Conference basketball games. The sport was growing in popularity, and television stations all across the Midwest were hungry for programming. His strategy of creating a Big Ten game-of-the-week and selling it directly to stations across the region quickly became a profitable venture for the league and the wily deal-maker. Local stations, who paid a rights fee to Scherick and the Big Ten, turned a profit by selling local advertising on the telecasts.

A short time later, Scherick set up shop in New York and started looking around for other properties under the unpretentious banner of Sports Programs, Inc. His small headquarters at 11 West Forty-second Street was cluttered with strewn papers and overflowing trash cans. The place offered no hint of a budding broadcasting empire. A crime scene, maybe. But not a place of network legend. The office and the company reflected Scherick, whose hyper personality and lack of outward organization concealed his significant talents as an entrepreneur and master strategist.

His original staff included technical director Jack Lubell and assistant Chet Simmons. Simmons, hired away from an advertising agency as an all-purpose aide for $75 per week, often found himself playing the referee in shouting matches between Scherick and Lubell, which sometimes turned physical.

"One time, Jack literally lifted Ed off the floor with his hands around Ed's neck," said Simmons, the future president of the ESPN cable channel and the onetime commissioner of the doomed United States Football League. "I thought Jack was going to kill him, because Ed was turning blue and making these gurgling noises with his throat. Then the phone rang, Jack let him down and told him they'd settle it later."

"Ed was one of the most dynamic, original people I've ever met," Simmons added. "But he could be a bit manic at times."

On the afternoon of January 29, 1959, Harriett Simmons rushed into her husband's office. She was in labor. They needed to get to the hospital right away, but Scherick would not hear of it.

"No, you can't have that baby right now," he insisted. "We're too busy. You'll just have to do it some other time."

Floored by his boss's completely serious response to the impending birth of their first child, Simmons proceeded to argue with him about the inevitability of some acts of nature. Finally, he gave up and hurried out the door with his wife, wondering if he would have a job when he returned. Several hours later, after Harriett gave birth to a beautiful, healthy girl, Scherick sent the proud parents a large display of flowers surrounding a big blue bunny—the kind of gift customarily presented to new mothers of baby boys.

When Simmons arrived for work the next day, he thanked his boss for his generosity. "But, by the way, Ed," Simmons pointed out, "we had a girl."

"No, you had a boy," Scherick insisted.

Simmons rolled his eyes and went back to work.

Nine months later, the Milwaukee Braves and the Los Angeles Dodgers were locked in a furious duel for the National League (NL) pennant, making the third divisional playoff in NL history a distinct possibility. At some point during the last few weeks of the season, Scherick discovered that NBC's World Series contract didn't include rights to a possible playoff, which represented a huge loophole and a marvelous opportunity for a broadcast entrepreneur looking for a big score.

Scherick had become aquainted with Tom Moore, the head of programming for the ABC network, so he arranged a meeting with the gregarious Mississippian, who was a huge sports fan. NBC and

CBS televised all of the major sporting events in that era, just as they dominated prime time, daytime, late night, and the news. Underdog ABC, still reeling from the fiasco of 1954, had no sports division, which Scherick was determined to exploit in a big way. He pitched Moore on the idea of televising the playoff, if there was a playoff, and subsequently went off to work his magic on Major League Baseball, which awarded Sports Programs the rights to a playoff, if there was a playoff. Then fate smiled on the enterprising former ad man. The Braves and Dodgers finished tied, and when they met in a three-game playoff for a berth in the World Series—won in two games by Los Angeles—Sports Programs began a historic production relationship with ABC, which celebrated a rare victory against its more established rivals.

After that, Tom Moore always took Ed Scherick's calls.

Several months later, Scherick learned that NBC was planning to cancel *Friday Night Fights*, the long-running boxing series. He also heard that Gillette, the sponsor of the program, was not happy about the network's decision. Always thinking, like every good salesman, of his next score, Scherick made a deal with Gillette to move the boxing show and its entire television advertising budget to ABC. After securing a contract as the network's exclusive sports producer, Scherick started developing a strategy to use the resulting $8 million bankroll from Gillette to obtain other sports programming.

Naturally, as a big thinker, a dreamer, Scherick wanted college football. Like most of the top properties on television, the NCAA package was controlled by NBC Sports, headed by Tom Gallery, a balding, cigar-chomping former actor.

Stealing the college games away from NBC would require cunning, not salesmanship, so Scherick devised a scheme fit for a James Bond novel. After collecting a significant amount of intelligence about Gallery's business tactics, Scherick believed his rival would arrive at the Manhattan Hotel, where the NCAA was scheduled to accept sealed bids in March 1960, with two envelopes: one containing a relatively modest number, probably about 10 percent above the current contract, if NBC faced no competition; one containing a much higher bid, if CBS decided to compete for the package.

No one expected ABC to bid. In those days, CBS and NBC were the Coke and Pepsi of network television. ABC was more like RC Cola. At both 30 Rock and Black Rock, the formidable Midtown Manhattan headquarters of NBC and CBS, respectively, ABC was derided as the "Almost Broadcasting Company." In the chest-thumping world of network television, ABC was the punch line of a thousand jokes.

Scherick understood how important the popular and profitable NCAA package was to Gallery. He believed that Gallery would dig far into his much deeper corporate pockets to protect the property if he thought it was vulnerable, and he knew ABC could never afford to top the figure most likely contained in Gallery's more generous envelope. In the days leading up to the bid submission, Scherick prepared his offer under a cloak of secrecy, because he understood surprise was his only advantage against Gallery.

Jim Colligan, who worked for Scherick, was well known for his shorthand and typing skills, which he had developed during his days as an assistant to Broadway producer Billy Rose. On frequent trips to Atlantic City, Colligan liked to hang out on the Boardwalk and challenge strangers to, of all things, shorthand contests. On the night before bid day, Scherick dictated the deal memo to Colligan, hovering over his shoulder while he typed. Paranoid that someone would see the critical figure, he waited until the very last moment the next morning to fill in the amount—with his own pen.

After weeks of plotting, Scherick dispatched an obscure ABC accountant to the Manhattan Hotel at the appointed time. Tall and thin, Stan Frankle wore thick glasses and looked like a thousand middle-aged men who rode the subway every day. He did not look like a hotshot network executive, which was the point. "Ed picked him because he was Joe Average," Chet Simmons said. "He wanted someone to go unnoticed, and Stan was the perfect guy."

Just as scripted, when the network and NCAA officials gathered at the hotel, Frankle blended into the wallpaper. No one noticed him. He followed Scherick's instructions perfectly. When Asa Bushnell, the NCAA's television program director, asked all interested parties to submit their bids, Gallery looked around and, seeing no evidence of competition, reached into his breast pocket, retrieved his low envelope and placed it on the table. At that moment, Frankle stepped forward, announced himself as a representative of ABC and dropped his envelope on the table.

Gallery was dumbfounded. Scherick had caught him completely by surprise.

As the NCAA officials went off to a nearby room to open and inspect the envelopes, Scherick and several members of his staff waited in Tom Moore's office inside the ABC headquarters on West Sixty-sixth Street, a onetime horse stable adjacent to Central Park. "The phone seemed to ring every twenty seconds, but it was always some other call for Tom," Simmons said. "We felt like we were waiting for word about Lindbergh landing in Paris."

After a while, the NCAA officials returned to the hotel suite and announced that ABC had captured the rights to the NCAA football series. The network's bid of $6,251,114 for 1960 and 1961 exceeded NBC's offer by less than $200,000.

"We went nuts when the call came in," Simmons said. "We knew we were in business when we got college football."


In the months leading up to the 1960 football season, Sports Programs grew into a full-fledged production arm for ABC. Scherick bought the rights to the fledgling, renegade American Football League and started a bowling show called *Make That Spare*. But college football was the franchise. If the college football package worked, Scherick figured he could write his own ticket with his network partner.

The NCAA, however, remained leery of ABC under any name. The events of 1954, which made ABC look like a bunch of bumbling incompetents, were still fresh in the minds of some college officials. They considered their football package one of the crown jewels of televised sports and it was hard for them to shake the feeling that they were trusting their precious asset to a bush-league operation.

Wayne Duke, the NCAA official who served as the liaison to the networks, arrived at the Sports Programs offices several weeks before the season to meet his new associates. He was mortified. "It was an absolute maze of clutter," Duke said. "I didn't say anything, but I thought to myself: 'These are the people we're involved with?'"

Over dinner and drinks at the New York Athletic Club, Duke was incredulous while producer Roone Arledge outlined his plans for the telecasts. "He started talking about how he was going to have lots of crowd shots and put mikes on the coaches and use sideline cameras," Duke recalled. "And I looked at him and told him he was crazier than hell. I told him it would never work, that college football needed dignity."

Duke was not alone. Arledge made some very important people nervous.

When he came to the attention of Scherick, Arledge was a twenty-nine-year-old producer spending his days watching Shari Lewis and her hand puppet, Lambchop, explore the boundaries of the puppetry arts on *Hi, Mom!*, a kid's show on NBC's New York station. He was an ambitious, talented young man quickly becoming bored with his job. Scherick hired him after seeing a pilot he had created called *For Men Only*, impressed less by the concept of the show than by the way it was produced. The chance to produce college football and other sports programming for $10,000 a year seemed like a step up for Arledge, even though it meant leaving the security and prestige of NBC.

After a trade paper reported that the unknown producer of a puppet show with no sports experience would be responsible for the look and feel of college football, executives at ABC, Gillette, and the NCAA felt blindsided. Some wanted him fired. Both ABC and Gillette had plenty riding on the success of the football package, especially the network, which saw the series as a tool to grow its lagging affiliate base. Between winning the contract and the first kickoff that fall, ABC attracted nearly two dozen new affiliates, stations who would not have considered making the switch without the lure of college football. Neither the network nor the sponsor were in any mood to gamble, but Scherick was one hell of a salesman, and he convinced the key players to give Arledge a chance.

Without any experience producing sports, Arledge brought a whole new sensibility to the task. In dramatic contrast to the tightly constrained productions of the day, which utilized a small number of static cameras positioned high above the field and rarely strayed beyond the action on the playing surface, Arledge was driven by one thought: He wanted to turn televised college football into showbiz.

Convinced that NBC's reverential, distant coverage had ignored many of the essential elements which made the game such an obsession for fans, the whiz kid was determined to translate as much of that excitement as possible to the small screen. Exploiting new technologies such as handheld cameras and rifle mikes, he planned more lively coverage from the field and also a new concentration on other aspects of the game-day experience: hopeful cheerleaders, anguished fans, frustrated benchwarmers.

After Scherick finally green-lighted Arledge's bold plans, he started assembling a team to implement his vision. Upset that some freckle-faced kid had been hired for a job he had wanted, Jack Lubell, the fiery technical director who frequently clashed with Scherick, refused to work with Arledge. So Arledge hired NBC veteran Bill Bennington as his primary director. The NCAA series included several weeks in which the network would cover several different games for simultaneous presentation—one game would be beamed to areas of the Midwest, another to the South, and so on. This required several different technical crews, so Arledge spent much of the summer furiously hiring the personnel to produce at least three games at once.

Just past seven o'clock on a Sunday morning in Los Angeles, a telephone rang. Andy Sidaris was sound asleep. Startled by the noise, Sidaris fumbled for the receiver on his bedside table. He had been partying until the wee hours, and was in no mood to talk. Still groggy and a bit hungover, Sidaris tried to concentrate as Arledge introduced himself. The name Roone Arledge meant absolutely nothing to him. The voice on the other end of the line said he was looking for directors for ABC's upcoming college football coverage, and he started quizzing the barely conscious, twenty-seven-year-old Sidaris about how he would direct a game.

"At first, I thought it was some sort of gag," Sidaris said.

After a few moments, Arledge realized Sidaris was in no condition to discuss the philosophy of televised college football. "Jot your thoughts down in a letter and send it to me," he said before hanging up.

When Sidaris finally rubbed the sleep from his eyes, the importance of the telephone call started to sink in. At the time, the transplanted Texan was directing the kids' show *Magic Land of Alacazam* for CBS but like Arledge, he was a bright young man looking for a bigger stage. He decided to make sure Arledge and the Sports Programs brass were sufficiently impressed. Enlisting the help of an artist from the kids' show, he assembled an elaborate ten-page storyboard showing how he would place rolling cameras and handheld cameras at field level and how he would emphasize the peripheral parts of the game, such as gorgeous cheerleaders and outrageous fans.

"I said I wanted to show lots of beautiful women in the stands and whatever made that game or that campus special," Sidaris recalled.

The proposal blew Arledge away. He hired Sidaris as a freelance director for $300 per game.

On the night before Alabama's 21–6 season-opening upset of Georgia, the ABC crew dined as the guests of Crimson Tide head coach Paul "Bear" Bryant at The Club, a posh establishment overlooking Birmingham's Red Mountain. At one point during the evening Chuck Howard, the lowest man on the ABC team, got into an argument with Bryant, a towering figure unaccustomed to being challenged, especially by some glorified gofer. Heads turned throughout the dining room as they shouted at each other.

"Eventually, someone told Chuck to get the hell out of there," said Chet Simmons. "Those Alabama and Georgia people were wondering who these aggressive young guys thought they were, coming in to televise college football."

For ABC and college football, it was a whole new ballgame. Unimpressed by the conservative broadcast philosophy established by NBC, unintimidated by the sport's dominant personalities, the brash young mavericks led by Scherick and Arledge were determined to create a new standard for a new age. They were sure of themselves and often full of themselves, and because they worked for a fledgling outfit without a bureaucracy or an institutional history, they were fearless and sometimes reckless.

"We were the rebel outfit," said Jim Spence, who joined the Sports Programs staff as a production assistant in 1960 and worked his way up to senior vice president. "We were not part of the network establishment, and that made it easier for us to push the envelope."

Several weeks into the season, Sidaris directed his first game for the network, a showdown between rivals Arkansas and Texas at Memorial Stadium in Austin. Coach Darrell Royal's Longhorns were heavily favored, but late in the game, Arkansas trailed by only two points when the Razorbacks moved the ball into Texas territory.

When the Razorbacks started marching toward the Texas red zone, one of the ABC cameramen caught a shot of Royal's wife clutching her two children. Sidaris loved it. Sitting in the truck, he told the cameraman to stay on the wife, whose pained expression told the unfolding story much better than words. Another Hogs first down, another cut to the wife, who clutched her children and prayed for a turnover. After Mickey Cissell kicked a twenty-nine-yard field goal to secure a 24–23 Arkansas victory, millions of viewers saw the coach's wife fighting back tears.

"Roone went crazy over that image," said Sidaris, who spent nearly two decades as the lead director on the NCAA series. "That's what he was looking for: a single person to capture the emotion of a stadium full of people."

Arledge saw the drama in every game, and he knew how to tell a story through bold sights and sounds. He recognized the value of the perfectly timed close-up of the quarterback who just tossed an interception. He appreciated the importance of seeing the face of a delighted young fan. He understood the dramatic impact of showing fast-developing plays from several different angles. He recognized the significance of campus scenes, cheerleaders, and miked referees. He sensed the power of capturing the pageantry of the sport: cadets gathered around the bonfire at Texas A&M, Tommy Trojan galloping along the sidelines at Southern Cal, Touchdown Jesus looming over the end zone at Notre Dame, Mike the Tiger growling behind bars at LSU, the marching band dotting the *i* at Ohio State. Strung together, these elements brought the viewer closer to the game, reducing the distance between the stadium and the living room.

For nearly a decade, television had succeeded in taking the game to the fans at home. But Arledge took the viewers to the game, giving them the best seat in the house. He made them feel it, hear it, smell it, love it. In the process, he reinvented televised college football and enhanced the sport's connection to the American public. Over the years, millions of fans gravitated to college football through the portal of the televised experience, and no man shaped the game's on-air presence more dramatically than Roone Arledge.

In time, resistance from the more cautious officials melted away in the glow of Arledge's growing mystique. "Shows you what I knew," Wayne Duke said many years later. "Roone was a genius who transformed sports television, and it all started with the way he personalized college football."

Bolstered by his company's success with the NCAA series, Scherick soon started an anthology show called *Wide World of*

*Sports* and began a weekly series following the Pro Bowlers Tour, landmark programs that would still be on the air more than forty years later. No one quite understood it at the time, but he was creating the foundation of the most innovative and emulated sports division in television history. Within a few years, the once ridiculed and mocked ABC would be the gold standard in sports television.

One Monday morning in early 1963, Simmons started getting worried when his boss failed to show up for work, because Ed Scherick was an early riser who always beat his employees to the office. After lunch, with no word from the boss, Simmons called the network to ask if anyone had seen him.

He waited on the line while the receptionist asked around. Then he was stunned when a woman answered: "Mr. Scherick's office . . . "

When Simmons finally got Scherick on the phone, he learned that the opportunistic deal-maker had sold his company to ABC over the weekend, for $1 million in stock, and had accepted a job as vice president of sales. Just like that, the short but influential era of Sports Programs, Inc., was over. Within a few weeks, the company would be moved into the network's headquarters and officially become ABC Sports, headed by vice president Roone Arledge.

"I was just dumbfounded," Simmons said. "I said, 'Ed, isn't this kind of sudden? What about all the personal belongings in your office?' He said to throw it all away. He'd moved on. He never even came back to the office."

It would take a long time for ABC to reach overall parity with NBC and CBS, and when it finally achieved Leonard Goldenson's holy grail in the 1970s, Scherick was long gone. By the time he died in 2002, Scherick was known primarily for his subsequent career as one of the most successful producers of television movies. Hardly anyone knew he was the father of ABC Sports and, therefore, an important man in the evolution of college football.

. . .

As the exclusive home of the NCAA series for nineteen of the next twenty-three years starting in 1960, ABC set the standard for the televised game. In fact, ABC's initial success with college football created a whole new level of interest among the other two networks, driving up ratings and rights fees and causing ABC to lose the franchise for a four-year period. CBS won the rights for 1962 and 1963 and NBC bought the package for 1964 and 1965.

Both networks were influenced by the Arledge philosophy, which could be seen in their coverage of college football and other events, though their executives were reluctant to admit it. But the single greatest innovation in the history of televised sports premiered during a college football game on CBS.

Tony Verna spent much of the 1963 season preparing for his shot at history. Verna, the director of the NCAA series, borrowed a specially designed, high-powered lens from the CBS News crew which covered the space shots at Cape Canaveral. He carried the lens in his suitcase as he traveled from campus to campus, buried between his underwear and socks. For several weeks, he tinkered with the technology as he traversed the country, determined to make his gimmick work on air. He planned to unveil his invention during the Army–Navy game at the end of the season, and he did not want to look like a fool on national television.

On the morning of December 7, 1963, Verna piled into the back seat of a cab between play-by-play man Lindsey Nelson and analyst Terry Brennan. Jim Simpson, the host of the halftime show, sat up front. As they left the Bellview Statford Hotel and headed for Philadelphia's Municipal Stadium, Verna started telling his announcers about his plan.

Before he could finish explaining his idea, Nelson interrupted. "You're going to do what?"

Then Verna told Nelson to listen carefully, because he would have to explain the new invention to viewers. The instant replay was about to be born.

Although ABC Sports had first used a video tape machine to replay a crucial moment at halftime of a 1961 college game—more than an hour after the play occurred—Verna would go down in the history books as the man who created the instant replay.

"I wanted to add the dimension of cause-and-effect to the broadcasts," said Verna, who was twenty-nine years old at the time. "If you could see a crucial play again, you could dissect it and see what went right or wrong. Plus, the replay could energize the look of the telecast. We were wasting so much time between plays just showing the huddle or whatever."

After selecting the Army–Navy game as his premiere, Verna spent the better part of a day customizing a large studio tape machine and connecting it to a camera in the south end zone. He knew it would be foolish to waste more than one camera on the idea, so he played the percentages, anticipating a dramatic play near the goal line by Roger Staubach, Navy's Heisman Trophy–winning quarterback.

With no score in the second quarter, Army quarterback Rollie Stichweh marched the Cadets into scoring position. On a second down call from the Navy two yard line, Stichweh rolled right and lunged into the south end zone to give Army the lead.

Sitting in the truck beneath the stadium, Verna told Nelson to get ready. His replay was on the way. A few seconds later, the image of Stichweh scoring reappeared on the screen, and Nelson tried to describe the play and the innovation as his heart raced.

"Ladies and Gentlemen," Nelson said, aware that his voice was rising with excitement, "what you are seeing is a tape of Army's touchdown. This is not live, but is something new . . . "

Roger the Dodger led second-ranked Navy to a dramatic 21–16 victory, but Stickweh's name would go down in the history books.

"I was just glad to get one in," Verna said years later. "I was really worried about confusion to the viewer, so I had Lindsey explain what we were doing several times."

ABC's "up close and personal" strategy changed the televised game in a fundamental way, but no single advancement affected the medium's coverage of college football as profoundly as instant replay, which gave the viewer an edge over the fan in the stands: a second look. Within a short period of time, instant replay, slow-motion re-play, and other permutations of the original idea enhanced the so-phistication of televised college football, making the broadcasts from the 1950s look like home movies from the dark ages.


Even before ABC recovered its fumble of the NCAA package, Arledge wrestled with one last missing piece of the puzzle. His network needed a star.

In those days, ABC hired on-air talent on a freelance basis, but as Arledge started plotting to regain the college football series in 1965, he felt the network needed a recognizable voice, someone who could energize the broadcasts and provide ABC with an in-stant jolt of credibility. He decided ABC needed Chris Schenkel.

Schenkel, under contract to CBS as the voice of the New York Giants and several major sporting events including The Masters and the Kentucky Derby, was one of television's biggest personal-ities. The man who called the action in the Colts' landmark sudden-death victory over the Giants to win the 1958 NFL championship—the game widely credited for launching the mod-ern era of pro football—was a huge star in New York, which was important because he was beloved by the small group of men who bought time for the major advertising agencies.

After pursuing Schenkel for several months by repeatedly tak-ing him to lunch and telling him how important he could be in the development of ABC, Arledge finally called him at home on a Sat-urday morning. He offered Schenkel the then-staggering sum of $125,000 per year to switch networks. Schenkel, a man who ad-libbed for a living, was virtually speechless. He was already the highest paid talent at CBS, where he earned $75,000. He thanked Arledge for the offer and asked if he could think about it and talk to him in a few days.

"I need an answer today," Arledge said.

Schenkel struggled for a response. "I'll call you back," he said.

Schenkel, a gentle man who was widely admired and liked by

his colleagues, felt obligated to give CBS an opportunity to match the offer. But when he reached CBS Sports president Bill MacPhail on the phone, MacPhail was equally stunned. He understood Schenkel's value to his network, but the only man who could authorize him to meet the competition for the announcer's services was Jim Aubrey, the president of the network. They tried to reach Aubrey, but he was out of town for the weekend. As he struggled to make a decision, Schenkel called some of his close friends, including Giants owner Jack Mara, who advised him to take the money.

"I decided to make the move mostly for the money," Schenkel said many years later. "I thought about how many things I could do for my family. Plus, Roone promised me I'd be back doing football within a year."

Throughout the first fourteen years of the NCAA series, as the package bounced among the three networks, the telecasts were hosted by a series of very competent announcers, including three of the best in the history of the medium: Mel Allen, Curt Gowdy, and Lindsey Nelson. But Chris Schnekel was the first real voice of college football. As the lead announcer on the NCAA telecasts from 1966 to 1973, his understated midwestern eloquence became synonymous with the sport. He wasn't just a play-by-play man; he was the narrator of an entire era—the charming, low-key presence who welcomed fans to ABC for "a wonderful way to spend an autumn afternoon."

"When we got Chris, we had a guy out front who everybody knew and who, by coming over to ABC, seemed to be saying we had arrived as a sports divison," said longtime network executive Jim Spence.

The decision to pair Schenkel with Bud Wilkinson enhanced ABC's credibility with viewers. Wilkinson, architect of the Oklahoma dynasty of the 1950s, was a giant figure in the sport. He brought new insight to the expert analyst's position. By the time he walked away from the broadcast booth, millions of fans would know him not as the firebrand who won a record 47 straight games, but as the grandfatherly figure who taught them to understand the trap play.

. . .

For a generation of fans who came of age as the country transitioned to living color, college football was not just a sport showcased by television. It was a sport that existed most vividly in the realm of television, which provided it not only with a home but also with definition, attitude, and context.

Despite the NCAA's determination to spread the appearances among as many schools as possible, an elite group including Notre Dame, Alabama, Texas, Ohio State, Michigan, Southern Cal, Oklahoma, and Nebraska always appeared as often as the regulations allowed. In contrast, lesser teams from the same conferences rarely appeared on the series at all.

"When we sat down to make out the schedule, we started with what I called the power elite," said former ABC director of college sports Donn Bernstein. "It was like a superconference of the airwaves. Those teams dominated the package. They drove the ratings and the ratings drove the advertising money, which dictated our ability to pay large rights fees. As part of the cycle, television elevated a small number of teams to an exalted status."

In the process of showcasing the elite programs, television turned the spotlight on several important rivalries and enhanced their national stature. These games included Notre Dame–Southern Cal, Oklahoma–Nebraka, Alabama–Auburn, Ohio State–Michigan, and Texas–Oklahoma.

"Television didn't create any of those rivalries, but it brought them a tremendous amount of national attention," said Bernstein. "They became our national treasures. In a way, it gave us national symbolism, as if to say to the viewers: This is college football."

As the spoils associated with the game started to increase and the game slowly began to take on elements of a high-stakes business, the TV powers enjoyed significant advantages over lesser teams. They could count on generating large checks from appearing on television, even after splitting their cut with conference partners. Even before television's profits were factored in, championship programs like Texas and Nebraska enjoyed tremendous financial advantages over conference also-rans like Rice and Iowa State. Throwing TV money into the mix exacerbated their dominance, allowing the more prosperous schools to spend larger amounts of money on providing more scholarships, hiring more coaches, and building larger stadiums and more modern administrative and training facilities. But it was not just a matter of money. Television became the most important publicity tool for the members of the TV aristocracy.

In the first two decades after World War II, the recruiting process grew much more sophisticated. In 1944, Clem Gryska won a scholarship to the University of Alabama after being spotted by a local booster in Stuebenville, Ohio, who recommended him to 'Bama head coach Frank Thomas. He had never seen the campus. In fact, he had never seen a college football game. The Crimson Tide offered him a free ride without watching him play a down of high school ball. Gryska, tempered by the Great Depression, saw the handshake deal as a way to earn a college education.

"(Thomas) told my folks he'd watch after me, and that was all they needed to hear," Gryska said.

Twenty years after his athletic career ended, Gryska played a much different game. As the recruiting coordinator for the Alabama powerhouse, he worked at the center of an intense evaluation process. The Crimson Tide's coaches spent a large percentage of their time watching high school players on film and traveling to see the best prospects in action. All of the recruits deemed worthy of an athletic scholarship were brought to the campus for an all-expenses-paid weekend.

The biggest change was the presence of television. Before a prospective student-athlete shook hands with his first college recruiter, he knew all about the major powers through television, which made a much stronger impression than newspapers or radio. Being part of the TV aristocracy gave a program unmistakable cachet.

"Every young man wanted to play on TV, and we were always

on TV as many times as you could be on," said Gryska, whose program posted the sport's winningest record of both the 1960s and 1970s. "That wasn't something our rivals could say, so it represented a real edge for us."

Recruiting became a nationwide proposition for some programs thanks to the power of television. Nebraska coaches could walk into a recruit's home in Cincinnati secure in the knowledge that the player knew all about the Cornhuskers. "Being on TV with some regularity gave us an identity," said former Nebraska head coach Bob Devaney, who built the Cornhuskers into the dominant team in the Big Eight, culminating with consecutive national championships in 1970 and 1971.

Most athletes of the era still saw the college scholarship primarily as a way to earn an education, but as salaries in the NFL, driven by television money, started to increase and more prospects began to view the college game as a proving ground for the NFL, the TV powers wielded even greater leverage in the recruiting process. Playing for a member of the TV aristocracy represented the opportunity of national exposure and the security of being seen by the pros. Given the choice between Nebraska and Big Eight rival Iowa State, which rarely appeared on televison or played in bowl games, the talented kid from the industrial Midwest almost always chose the Cornhuskers.

"Television exposure made schools like Nebraska and Oklahoma known quantities nationwide," said Jackie Sherrill, who worked as an assistant at Iowa State in the late 1960s. "It was very difficult for us to compete."

In some cases, television's mounting influence over college football proved much more overt.

Frustrated by being passed over for the top job at ABC Sports, Chet Simmons moved to NBC Sports as vice president in early 1964. He quickly set his sights on picking the Orange Bowl out of ABC's pocket.

After several years of mediocre ratings for the Miami game, which annually matched the Big Eight champion against the best available opponent, ABC wanted to reduce the rights fee from $275,000 to $250,000. This idea did not sit well with Ernie Siler, the Orange Bowl's executive director, who wanted to break the contract with the Big Eight and turn the game into a totally open bowl able to match the best two available teams.

"Ernie was full of big ideas," said Wayne Duke, who became the Big Eight commissioner in 1963. "He thought he could make the Orange Bowl the king of the mountain, and I think a lot of that was the influence of NBC."

After learning about ABC's negotiating posture, Simmons and his boss, Carl Lindeman, Jr., flew to Miami and offered the Orange Bowl $350,000—but only if they moved the game to New Year's night. All of the bowl games were played during the day in that era, but NBC was willing to gamble that it could retain the huge Rose Bowl audience for a prime time Orange Bowl.

The Orange Bowl had been played in the afternoon for nearly thirty years, carving out a cherished place in the sporting tradition of Miami. But Siler was a savvy operator who understood what NBC was offering him, and the deal they signed was the best thing that ever happened to the Orange Bowl. The switch allowed the game to stake out a distinct and prestigious prime-time window and placed the bowl in a very strong position to generate increasingly generous television rights fees, giving it a competitive advantage against the Cotton and Sugar Bowls.

But it also represented a turning point in college football history. Television had been a key player in the bowl games for more than a decade—transforming the Big Four into some of the most watched sporting events in America—but now NBC was no longer just a rights holder. It was a partner, dictating terms. The deal set the stage for the networks to assume greater control over the college bowl system in the years ahead.

Despite the restrictive guidelines crafted by the NCAA, ABC gradually exerted similar influence over the regular-season package.

With the network kicking in a few hundred thousand dollars and all the accordant national publicity, most schools were happy to shift their kickoff times to meet television demands.

"They loved to get that phone call," said ABC's Chuck Howard, who directed the network's scheduling process. "That call from ABC represented money and exposure."

For many years, the NCAA forced ABC to create its entire schedule in the summer, which required a tremendous amount of guesswork on the part of the network. Eventually, ABC convinced the governing body to allow a small number of "wildcard" opportunities, giving the network the ability to showcase hot teams and key games which might not have been on the radar screen months before.

In the summer of 1969, as Arledge and his staff began assembling the NCAA lineup for the upcoming fall—which marked the 100th anniversary of the first college football game—they noticed that Southwest Conference rivals Arkansas and Texas were scheduled to meet in Fayetteville toward the middle of the season. Both teams were loaded. The winner of the game was expected to compete for the national championship.

As he pondered the schedule, Arledge had a thought. He picked up the telephone and called Arkansas head coach Frank Broyles, then Texas head coach Darrell Royal. Believing that both teams were good enough to run the table, he convinced them to move their game to the end of the season so he could turn it into a made-for-television spectacular. He envisioned a monster rating, as long as the Razorbacks and Longhorns lived up to their end of the bargain by entering the clash undefeated. And they did.

More than 30 million people watched in late November when unbeaten Texas rallied for two fourth-quarter touchdowns to knock off unbeaten Arkansas, 15–14, in one of the decade's most thrilling games. After witnessing the game from the press box, President Richard Nixon walked into the Texas locker room and presented a plaque to Royal and his players, proclaiming the Longhorns the national champions on national television.

Joe Paterno—whose Penn State Nittany Lions finished undefeated, untied, and uncrowned for a second consecutive season—
was not amused.

The AP and UPI polls subsequently agreed with Nixon in
annointing Texas as the number-one team in the land, but the
president's validation suggested something powerful about college football at 100: It happened on television, so it had to be
true.

# 5

# POWER AND INFLUENCE

I t is impossible to understand the evolution of televised college
football without knowing the leaders who built the NCAA and
the influence cultivated by the man who shaped the governing
body.

In the decade after Walter Byers packed his bags and set out for
Kansas City with little more than a letterhead, the NCAA carved
out an increasingly powerful place at the center of college athletics. The television plan, launched amid so much public acrimony,
grew more popular and lucrative with each passing year. After two
decades in the shadow of the rival National Invitation Tournament, the NCAA's postseason basketball playoff was poised to
leave the NIT in the dust. The association also became an instru-
ment of cohesion and mounting legislative activism. Spurred to
action by the ever thickening rulebook and some schools' willingness to ignore it, the enforcement division developed into a full-
fledged police force with the authority to deny various privileges
of membership.

Even the national headquarters reflected the NCAA's growing
importance. In 1955, the association stopped paying rent and built a
spacious, air-conditioned home—using the penalty fee paid by ABC
when the struggling network defaulted on its contract to televise

college football. Majorie Fieber was grateful. She no longer had to run down the street chasing the occasional airborne file.

While growing in scope to meet the demands of the membership, the national office remained a small, thrifty operation. Three administrators—Walter Byers, Wayne Duke, and Arthur Bergstrom—managed everything from tournaments to eligibility questions. But they needed help. When the NCAA Council authorized Byers to hire an extra man in 1961, Ivan Williamson pulled the executive director aside and told him about Chuck Neinas, the producer and play-by-play man for the University of Wisconsin's football and basketball radio network. At first, the earnest young broadcaster with perfect diction knew nothing of the job or Williamson's lobbying on his behalf. But some weeks later, after impressing the only person who counted, Neinas abandoned his radio career and moved to Kansas City as an assistant to the executive director. Stripped of pretense, this meant he was another trumpet player in Byers's band.

Cocky but likeable, Neinas arrived at the governing body with no experience in athletic administration. He quickly earned Byers's confidence and the respect of his peers with his adept handling of a variety of chores. He served as a liaison to various committees, represented the association in its sometimes stormy relationship with the Amateur Athletic Union and the Olympic movement, and worked as Byers's administrative aide, which placed him at the center of virtually every major policy decision.

"Walter Byers gave me a terrific education because the place was expanding and he kept throwing me out on different projects," Neinas said.

A basketball guy who loved to talk hoops and play ferocious games of one-on-one on the weekends, Neinas scored many points at the NCAA with his favorite sport. First with Duke and then on his own, he supervised the growth of what would later come to be known as the Final Four. He also nurtured the college division basketball tournament from its infancy and became an ardent champion of the small college cause.

No yes-man, Neinas frequently clashed with his boss.

"We argued a lot," Neinas said. "He always told me I should tell him what I thought, and I did. Sometimes he didn't like what I told him and he'd finally have to look me in the eye and say, 'Stow it, Neinas.' But I never held back."

During Nienas's first year on the NCAA payroll, when the National Football League (NFL) started lobbying for an antitrust exemption that would allow the league's members to pool their television rights, some college officials became concerned by the possibile ramifications for their sport. Byers dispatched Neinas to Washington to lobby on the colleges' behalf, arguing that any new law should prevent the pros from infringing on the colleges' Saturday "territory," a problem they had experienced in the early 1950s. He did his job well. Thanks largely to Neinas's efforts, the resulting law protected the high schools and colleges from competition on Fridays and Saturdays, but otherwise gave the pro leagues carte blanche in marketing their television rights.

A watershed moment in NFL history, the exemption paved the way for pro football's dramatic rise to become the nation's most popular spectator sport. The NCAA never considered lobbying for inclusion in the legislation. "No one thought we needed it," Neinas said.

In the 1960s, the NCAA mistakenly believed the television plan was safe for all the reasons Joseph Rauh, Jr., had asserted a decade before. They presumed the series was legal because its stated intentions were to protect football attendance and prevent the rise of a small group of dominant powers. Byers had no way of knowing that the man he sent to Washington would one day lead an uprising against him and the incredibly vulnerable television plan.


In the years after he started developing the modern NCAA, Byers gradually emerged as the industry's predominant figure.

"You couldn't do much without his blessing," said longtime Liberty Bowl executive director Bud Dudley.

The structure of the organization allowed Byers tremendous latitude in cultivating power. The NCAA Council and the NCAA Executive Committee, the two bodies charged with running the association and approving all important recommendations of the various lower-level committees, consisted of athletic officials appointed through an insular cycle. It was perfectly understandable for the volunteers who held these important posts to defer a tremendous amount of discretionary authority to their full-time chief executive.

In his capacity as Byers's administrative assistant, Neinas took notes on all meetings of the Council and Executive Committee, many of them consisting of conference calls among the members. Neinas saw the most subtle form of Byers's clout take shape during such meetings:

> If you were the faculty rep somewhere and you had only a limited amount of time to make a decision about an issue which you may not have known very well, it was only natural to say: "Walter, what do you think?" And Walter would have an answer that most of the time would make perfect sense. It was perfectly natural for the committee members to trust Walter's judgement, because he knew more about the issue than they did. But of course, this gave one man a tremendous amount of power.

With a nominating committee consisting largely of members of the council and executive committee that filled most of the vacancies, the executive director, who sat on both, exuded tremendous influence in naming replacements.

"Walter's power was vested to a great degree in the people on the top committees, and he watched them very closely," said Alabama's Jeff Coleman, who served terms on the television committee in the

1950s and 1960s and the executive committee in the 1970s. "You couldn't get appointed to a position if he didn't like you."

Because the small colleges dominated the membership in a numerical sense, most members of the two powerful bodies sprang from their ranks.

The officials who created the national office wanted a strong executive and Byers filled the role with enthusiasm, exploiting the structure and the membership's increasingly activist mind-set on television, enforcement, and other matters.

Shrewd in cultivating his shadowy presence, Byers always faded into the woodwork at the annual conventions. He rarely gave speeches or interviews and remained a very private person.

"Walter never displayed any raw power but there was never any doubt about his authority," said Wiles Hallock, the former Pac-10 commissioner who served under Byers in the 1960s. "He always worked through channels to get his ideas approved, which was part of his genius."

Several days after Chuck Neinas joined the NCAA, Wayne Duke returned from a trip and stopped by to meet his new colleague.

"Hey, Chuck. Would you say you were better as a football announcer or a basketball announcer?" Duke asked with a sincere look.

While Neinas considered the question, Duke moved in for the kill: "Well, from what I hear, the basketball folks think you're a better football announcer . . . and the football folks think you're better at basketball!"

A smile rose across Neinas's face. Thus began a terrific friendship.

Over the next several years, Duke and Neinas worked closely together on many matters at the burgeoning NCAA. The basketball tournament was growing rapidly in those days, and it occupied much of their time. After hustling to get everything ready for the 1963 championship between Loyola and Cincinnati, they sat down for a pregame breather in the stands at Louisville's Freedom Hall.

"All of the sudden, we discovered we had everything except a ball," Duke said. "So here we were, minutes before the final, scrambling to find a ball."

During off hours, Neinas and Duke often opened and closed bars around Kansas City and elsewhere discussing the problems of college athletics over a few belts. Their two families frequently grilled out together, a ritual which often ended with a game of pickup basketball in the driveway of Neinas's lakefront home. Both Duke (an Iowa graduate) and Neinas (a Wisconsin graduate) were proud and loyal Big Ten men, but after Duke moved across town to become commissioner of the Big Eight, Neinas and his son Toby frequently challenged Duke and his son Dan to a "Big Ten vs. Big Eight" showdown.

"The mighty Big Ten always prevailed," Neinas recalled with a measure of pride.

"They usually killed us," Duke said.

On Duke's fortieth birthday, his wife Martha planned a surprise party at their home and invited all of their close friends. His parents made the trip from Iowa. Martha instructed Chuck to keep Wayne busy for a while after work until all the guests could arrive, so Neinas concocted a ruse about meeting some Orange Bowl people at the airport. They never showed, of course. But Neinas just kept loading his buddy with martinis.

When they finally walked through the front door and the house full of guests yelled "surprise!," the birthday boy was so smashed that he could hardly stand up.

"My dad's a teetotaler and he didn't like that at all," Duke said with a laugh. "Chuck did such a good job, Martha's still mad at me."

The two titans of athletics thought they would be friends forever. They didn't know television would drive a wedge between them.


By multiplying the number of people who empowered the sport with their collective passion and increasing the financial stakes in both direct and indirect ways, TV gave rise to a new level of competition for talent, which led, inevitably, to more widespread cheating.

As the pressure to win intensified, the rogue booster determined to help his favorite team and the ethically challenged coach willing to look the other way became undeniable facts of life. The grant-in-aid, intended to streamline the acquisition of talent while ending the widespread practice of providing "subsidies" to players, eventually gave the best athletes greater leverage in the new age recruiting process, allowing them to demand a little something extra. Some programs maintained a high moral ground and refused to play the under-the-table game. Others surreptitiously bought players with cash and cars. When one school offered something above the value of the scholarship, even honest rivals faced a difficult choice: meet the competition or lose the prospect. With championships, bowl games, television revenue, and jobs on the line, some coaches and boosters found the temptation too powerful to resist.

By the 1960s, as national recruiting started to emerge when commercial air travel became common, the NCAA's Enforcement Division struggled to keep pace with the illicit activity.

"There have always been people willing to break the rules," remarked David Berst, the NCAA's longtime director of enforcement. "But we definitely saw [cheating] increase through the years as the sport took on a greater importance in the lives of some people."

Gradually, the nature of the relationship between the NCAA and many of its members grew more adversarial because of the power exerted by the enforcement division.

By leading many of the early investigations himself, Byers set the precedent for the way the college police force conducted business. Through the years, it was frequently criticized by some for selective enforcement and by others for failing to provide due process. The NCAA cops often projected an image of arrogance and mind-boggling inflexibility, which reflected Byers's personality and his rigid sense of duty. But he could say in all candor that he was merely interpreting the will of the membership, which gave him wide latitude to decide how to enforce the rules.

"Even when I was working for Walter Byers, I saw things that disturbed me about the process," Neinas said. "There were times when the NCAA was more interested in projecting an image of evenhandedness than actually being evenhanded."

Because television and the television-dominated bowl games represented such a tremendous source of revenue and promotion, the possibility of losing access to these perks of the system represented a significant deterrent. With so much riding in the balance, indicted institutions started fighting charges more vigorously, the NCAA started investigating more aggressively, and eventually, it became yet another American institution dominated by teams of lawyers.

The man who was judged too small to play college football was like a coach to many of the people who worked for him. He pushed his employees, demanding long hours and absolute commitment to the cause. No one wanted to disappoint him. Everyone respected him, but he did not allow anyone to get too close.

"Walter's makeup did not create what you'd call close personal friendships," said Chuck Neinas.

"Walter got the reputation for being tough because he was tough," said Lew Spry, who joined the national office in 1966. "Unfortunately, I think his combination of shyness and aloofness left a lot of people with respect for what he did but not a warm feeling about him as a person. He always said, 'If you don't like what we're doing around here, don't let the doorknob hit you on the ass on the way out.' "

Byers engendered tremendous loyalty because he was fair and he rewarded those who were loyal to him by helping to advance their careers. When his subordinates were ready to move on, he helped them land more powerful jobs, like a father pulling strings for his sons. Experience with the NCAA and a good recommendation from Byers was invaluable for aspiring athletic administrators of the day.

Four men who spent time under Byers's tutelage would play important roles in the next generation of college athletics. Their success represented an unmistakable expansion of his influence. Wayne Duke left to become commissioner of the Big Eight in 1963. Wiles Hallock, who joined the NCAA after Duke's departure, was hired as the commissioner of the Western Athletic Conference in 1967 and moved to the Pac-8 in 1971. Chuck Neinas replaced Duke as commissioner of the Big Eight in 1971, when his buddy took over the Big Ten. Tom Hansen, who joined the NCAA after Neinas left, was named commissioner of the Pac-10 when Hallock retired in 1982.

When Big Ten commissioner Bill Reed died suddenly in the spring of 1971, Duke and Neinas emerged as the top contenders for the job. Both men had been close friends of Reed's. Duke was happy at the Big Eight and really didn't want to leave Kansas City, but the search committee kept calling. Neinas was ready to move out of the NCAA, and he wanted the job.

During a break between sessions of a television committee meeting at a North Carolina resort, Byers pulled Duke aside and told him he was supporting Neinas for the Big Ten post. "He said I already had a good job and he wanted to see Chuck do well," Duke said. Several days later, Byers started making calls on Neinas's behalf and wrote him a glowing letter of recommendation.

But the Big Ten wanted Duke.

When Duke finally accepted the Big Ten's generous offer, Neinas became the prime candidate to replace him at the Big Eight. Once again, Byers supported Neinas, and this time his lobbying worked. In the autumn of 1971, Neinas, the ultimate basketball nut, became the commissioner of a league that produced the top three teams—Nebraska, Oklahoma, and Colorado—in the final Associated Press football poll. He was well on his way to becoming a big-time football guy, and Byers's fingerprints in his metamorphosis were clearly visible.

The men who left the NCAA to head some of the nation's most prestigious conferences were not simply administrators who owed Walter Byers. They were not just professionals who had learned the business from him. They shared his philosophy about college athletics, and this was the true measure of his expanding clout.

But in the revolution to come, longtime friends and colleagues would be forced to choose sides.

# 6

# ASSETS AND LIABILITIES

All of the usual superlatives seemed so inadequate. Toward the end of the 1966 football season, the whole country was talking about the impending showdown between unbeaten, first-ranked Notre Dame and unbeaten, second-ranked Michigan State. The Spartans, coached by the colorful Duffy Daugherty, featured a bruising defense led by Bubba Smith. The Fighting Irish, coached by the intense Ara Parseghian, featured a potent offense led by quarterback Terry Hanratty. It was billed as the climactic battle for the national championship, but, if possible, the game seemed even more important than that, which is to say, it was hyped beyond any reasonable sense of proportion. Tickets were so tight and in such demand, one man offered to trade his liquor store for two on the 50.

But the most incredible, historic, and ultimately frustrating aspect of the classic game was set in motion several days before kickoff.

Prior to the late-season matchup, both teams had appeared once on ABC's NCAA television package: Notre Dame nationally against Purdue and Michigan State regionally against the Boilermakers. This presented a problem for the NCAA. According to the rules written and enforced by the all-powerful television committee, no school could appear more than once nationally or twice regionally in a given year, so the NCAA initially planned to show the game to a regional audience which amounted to slightly more than half of the country. As anticipation for the game mounted across the country and word of the NCAA's plans appeared in the media, the governing body was flooded with irate telegrams and telephone calls. One southern fan filed suit against the NCAA, enraged that he would be denied access to one of the most hyped clashes in college history and instead be subjected to a rather meaningless game between Tennessee and Kentucky.

Faced with a dilemma, the NCAA television committee crafted what it tried to sell as a compromise. Rather than showing the game live to the entire country—which the members feared would risk opening the floodgates to other exceptions down the line—the NCAA decided to air it live to the Northeast and Midwest while the rest of the country watched Tennessee–Kentucky. Only after the Vols–Wildcats game ended would the rest of the country be allowed to see Notre Dame and Michigan State battle to their infamous and controversial 10–10 tie on tape, which made about as much sense as preparing a juicy prime cut of steak and waiting three hours so it could be served cold. The videotape solution accomplished nothing except to reinforce the growing perception of the NCAA as an unyielding bureaucracy holding college athletics captive to a series of arbitrary regulations.

Instead of being gratified by the overwhelming interest in the game, the NCAA seemed mortified by the implications. Fourteen years after developing the unified plan for television, the governing body continued to act less out of reason than fear. Years before, the organizers of the NCAA had bought into the foolhardy notion that they could market a popular series while preventing some teams from benefiting more than others. Even within the tightly controlled system, the medium was already magnifying the advantages of the teams who appeared with regularity.

Because the major schools who supplied the viable product exercised so little influence in the administration of the plan, the

NCAA often appeared more interested in acquiesing to the desires of the larger membership than accomodating the TV powers, who wanted to please the fans. The commercialization of college football was mounting, driven in many ways by televison, and to try to pretend that the TV plan was not a commodity was both foolish and hypocritical. The bureaucracy was beginning to strangle the logic right out of the plan.

While the NCAA's strict adherence to the appearance rule loomed as a significant liability for the television plan, the man who administered it represented an equally formidable asset. Through the years, Walter Byers proved incredibly skilled in crafting the plan to maximum advantage and manipulating the networks to win increasingly large contracts for his constituents.

"Walter had a tremendous understanding of the market and the medium," said former NCAA assistant executive director Dave Cawood. "When he went into a negotiation, he knew as much—or more—about the market and the network's financial situation as the network people."

For fourteen years, the NCAA had awarded the rights to the series through sealed bids. When the number and strength of the bidding networks varied from year to year, the system generally favored the colleges. It kept the networks guessing and probably prompted some to pad their bids.

After the 1965 season, however, Byers convinced his fellow committee members to change tactics—because he was mad at NBC. The Peacock Network had bought the rights to the NCAA package for a combined $11.7 million for 1964 to 1965, and NBC was determined to keep the series under contract. But Carl Lindeman, Jr., the president of NBC Sports, failed to realize how much Byers hated pro football.

"Walter thought pro football was the enemy," said former ABC Sports executive Jim Spence. "He thought the pros were stealing the colleges' thunder."

With the established National Football League locked in a bitter war with the upstart American Football League, Lindeman scored a major coup by signing a deal with the AFL. At the news, Byers blew his stack. Infuriated that NBC would taint "the college network" with pro games, he convinced his fellow committee members that they, too, should be enraged.

"To Walter, the AFL deal was the ultimate betrayal," said Wiles Hallock, the NCAA's television liaison at the time. "Walter was dead set against NBC getting the package again."

Under Byers's leadership, the committee abandoned the sealed bid process and pursued direct negotiations with ABC. During the secret talks, Byers made clear his disdain for the NFL. Roone Arledge, the brash young head of ABC Sports, understood that NBC's decision to play ball with the AFL was the only reason ABC had been given a chance to bid on the college package.

"Are you really going to abandon the pros if we come with you?" Byers demanded.

"Scout's honor," Arledge responded.

"Are you ready to put that in writing?"

"Of course we are. The way the colleges have to look at it, Walter, it'll be like having their own television network."

A few weeks later, the NCAA agreed to a four-year, $32.2 million contract in what amounted to a preemptive strike against NBC.

Lindeman, who had never been given a chance to renew the package, read the news in his morning paper. He was livid. He quickly fired off an obscenity-laced, 76-page telegram to Byers.


By jettisoning sealed bids for direct negotiation, the NCAA unleashed Byers's foremost talent.

"There has never been a better negotiator in sports," said Kevin O'Malley, a former executive with CBS and Turner Sports. "Walter could be dictatorial and eccentric, but he played the networks like a piano."

To Byers, negotiation was like a fist fight. During a rare moment of self-expression, he once explained to Lew Spry, the NCAA's longtime comptroller, his philosophy on the subject:

> He told me to imagine I was in the middle of a room and the guy standing next to me hit me in the mouth. He said you could do one of two things: step back so he wouldn't hit you again or step forward and hit him. If you step back, you're eventually going to be standing against the wall and the other guy is going to have the advantage. So the only thing to do is hit back.

Byers was no wallflower.

In the negotiating process, Byers turned his abrasive personality traits in his favor. "A negotiation was like Walter's bowl game," said former television committee member and Atlantic Coast Conference (ACC) commissioner Gene Corrigan. "You could almost see the adrenaline pumping."

He saw the network officials as the enemy. He could dine with them, drink with them, do business with them. But he didn't believe a word they said. He was convinced they thought they could put one over on him, just because he hailed from the Midwest, just because he liked to wear cowboy boots.

"Walter didn't trust anyone from New York—and that went double for television people from New York," said former ABC Sports executive Chuck Howard. "He saw us as people to be dealt with, nothing more."

The combination of keen intellect, superior knowledge, lengthy experience, and take-no-prisoners negotiating philosophy made Byers a powerful advocate for college football. He knew how to push the networks' buttons and he used his skill to win increasing millions for the rights to the NCAA football package.

. . .

The negotiating battles between Walter Byers and Roone Arledge became legendary among college and network circles. Even their casual conversations sometimes deteriorated into extemporaneous speeches.

"They would just scream at each other," said former ABC Sports executive Jim Spence. "It was usually started by Walter, but Roone would have to respond. I once asked Roone why he let Byers talk to him that way, and he said that's just the way Walter worked. If you showed any weakness, he buried you."

But Byers was not intimidated by Arledge's press clippings or his multiple Emmys. He saw him as just another slick operator from New York who needed to be cut down to size.

Instead of allowing Byers to steamroll him, Arledge played the game. If the cowboy from Kansas City fired the first shot, the gentleman from Manhattan fired right back. Both understood that their random conversations on the telephone, their dinners at the 21 Club, and their booze-drenched arguments at the end of some hotel bar were, in fact, one endless negotiation.

"I'd have dinner with them and it would be like Ali–Frazier," said former ABC play-by-play man Chris Schenkel. "They'd argue about the specifics of the series . . . and then they'd argue about whatever else came to mind. Here were two men who had great respect for each other, but two men who were immensely competitive who wanted to beat the other guy, whether they were arguing over the appearance rule or the quality of the soup."

Especially after the era of sealed bids came to a close, the existence of a negotiating committee was mostly pretense. Byers and Arledge made the deals, each man deciding which demands to pursue and which concessions to accept.

One night before a negotiating session at New York's Park Lane Hotel in the mid-1970s, the members of the committee and various ABC officials gathered for dinner in the restaurant. While the mortals waited half the night to be served, Byers and Arledge moved to the end of the bar, where they proceeded to drink scotch and argue. And drink scotch. And argue.

The next morning, the members of the negotiating teams were waiting in the hotel suite, ready to do battle. "After we'd been in there a while," recalled former NCAA official Tom Hansen, "Roone and Walter finally walked in all hungover and bleary-eyed. One of them said, 'We made a deal last night.' And that was it. Away we went."

For ABC, winning the rights to broadcast college football was like an exercise in political patronage. When it won the franchise away from NBC in 1966, ABC agreed to broadcast a series of small college games, such as the Grantland Rice Bowl between Tennessee State and Muskingum and the Pecan Bowl, which featured North Dakota and Parsons. In subsequent contracts, the deal included coverage of NCAA championship events in sports such as baseball, swimming, and track and field. All of these represented money losing propositions, but Arledge swallowed and accepted the reality of the situation. To get Notre Dame, Nebraska, and Texas, he had to televise the Camelia Bowl and the College World Series.

As the leader of a diverse organization, Byers wanted to promote small college football and other NCAA championships, so he incorporated his desires into his list of objectives. Like any good negotiator, he simply leveraged ABC's intense interest in the major football schools for the benefit of the larger organization.

ABC wanted to experiment with night games, be allowed to sell alcohol advertising, increase the number of commercial minutes during a telecast, and be permitted to liberalize the appearance rules. All of these issues produced heated discussions during the late 1960s. Byers eventually consented on every one, skillfully using ABC's wish list to fatten the NCAA's check. In allowing some of these changes during the late 1960s, the NCAA was able to convince ABC to renegotiate the final two years of the pact, but not before the issue wound up in court. The parties agreed to terms only after Byers squeezed the network for another $5.2

million. Even when he granted Arledge's requests, Byers seized the advantage.

Then Arledge crossed a line.

In 1970, ABC launched *Monday Night Football*, which would prove to be one of the most important events in the history of television. But at the time, it was simply a huge gamble for the network and the NFL. No one knew if football would work in prime time, and even with their low-rated entertainment lineup—which consistently ranked a distant third behind CBS and NBC—ABC executives approved the program only after Arledge convinced them that Pete Rozelle was prepared to sell it directly to their underperforming affiliates.

None of this mattered to Byers, who felt personally betrayed. He always knew he couldn't trust those TV folks, and now he had the proof.

Even after consummating the original NCAA deal, ABC officials persisted in insisting they had no intention of "tainting" the network with a pro game. Minutes of a television committee meeting on October 11, 1967, at the Manhattan Hotel in New York implied as much:

> . . . (ABC President Tom) Moore suggested that the two parties work together in making the college football program more attractive and hence more lucrative for the colleges. He pointed out that the air is being flooded with professional football, but emphasized that there is no pro football in ABC's future . . .

"Walter got up at a committee meeting and said Roone had promised him [ABC would not become involved with pro football], and how ABC had breached its agreement," said former ABC executive Chuck Howard, who watched in amazement. "He went on and on about not being able to trust those TV people. It was ugly. And he was just plain wrong. He didn't have anything in writing."

For once, Byers found himself with very little leverage. He raised hell about ABC's reversal but what was the NCAA to do? When ABC launched *Monday Night Football*, there were no more networks "untainted" by the pro game. He was painted into a corner, and he knew it.

Eventually, cooler heads prevailed and ABC remained the network of college football. But Byers never forgot. Even before they negotiated the next contract, he demanded and was granted a strict separation between the college and pro games, including a promise from Arledge (in writing) that no *Monday Night Football* promos would appear on the NCAA series and that the network would not raid the college broadcast team for the NFL package.

Byers and the NCAA were locked in an inevitable competition with Rozelle and the NFL, but the two rivals were heading in opposite directions. At a time when the NFL was creating made-for-television events to strengthen its television franchise, the NCAA was diluting the value of its package by forcing ABC to carry unprofitable events while limiting the network's ability to showcase the top teams.

In 1960, the NCAA and NFL television packages generated $3.125 million and $3.1 million, respectively. But a decade later, the year of the NFL-AFL merger, the pro game's $45.6 million combined television revenue dwarfed the NCAA's $12 million contract with ABC. On a per game basis, the NCAA still earned more, which was a credit to Byers's skill and the power of exclusivity. But while the NCAA zealously horded access to Notre Dame, Alabama, Michigan, Southern Cal, and the other marquee teams, the NFL became the envy of the entire sports community by establishing a presence on all three networks without overexposing the game.

The NFL surpassed the NCAA because they were playing vastly different games. Rozelle saw television as a tool to sell his sport. Byers, for all his vast knowledge and negotiating acumen, viewed the medium primarily as a danger from which the colleges needed protection.

It was only a matter of time before the major football powers grew tired of this game.

# 7

## BOWLING FOR DOLLARS

On the morning before the 1973 Sugar Bowl, Roone Arledge walked into the ABC production trailer outside Tulane Stadium, dropped his rain-soaked umbrella on the floor and approached Andy Sidaris with an agonized expression.

"I wonder if we can postpone this thing?" he said frantically.

Sidaris looked at his boss like he had lost his mind. "Postpone it? What do you mean, postpone it? You really think we could do that?"

For weeks, Sidaris and his crew had been preparing for the national championship showdown between unbeaten, first-ranked Alabama and unbeaten, fourth-ranked Notre Dame. The historic first meeting between the tradition-rich programs loomed as a landmark event, a clash of enormous talent, will, and ghosts lurking in the shadows.

But with only a few hours remaining before the New Year's Eve kickoff, the area around the ancient bowl was a dark, dank mass of puddles, umbrellas, and drenched television people. The field was soaked. "It was coming down in buckets," recalled Sidaris, the veteran college football director. "I was just glad I had a dry place to sit." Weather forecasters offered little hope, casting a dark cloud over the most anticipated bowl game ever, a confrontation some folks had been waiting for since the early days of radio.

For Arledge, the near mythic figure who had rewritten all the rules of sports television, the obvious solution was to put the game off for a day or two.

"I couldn't believe it," said Sidaris, a laid-back California dude with a gold chain dangling from his neck. "Roone was dead serious. He starting talking about how this huge game between these giant programs should not be played in such bad weather. He said he thought (the teams) would go for it—if ABC thought it was a good idea."

Did ABC really have that kind of influence? To postpone the Game of the Century? No way. Not even ABC could pull that kind of string, especially given the tens of thousands of fans whose attendance was complicated by jobs, lives, and hotel considerations, to say nothing of the impact on the teams. Can you imagine that conversation with Bear Bryant and Ara Parseghian?

But Arledge thought, if only for a few crazed moments, that his network could sell the game's organizers on the unthinkable, which reflected the increasingly symbiotic relationship between television and the bowls.

Arledge didn't act on his brainstorm, the weather slowly improved and the Sugar Bowl went on as planned. Even though the field was wet and slippery, Notre Dame's 24–23 victory over the Crimson Tide, which vaulted the Fighting Irish to the AP national championship, would go down as one of the most memorable games in college football history.

Unlike the regular season NCAA plan, whose appearance rules continued to cause tremendous friction between the governing body and the major powers, the bowl system operated in a free market environment. The bowls controlled their own television rights and selected the participating teams in cooperation with the major conferences.

In the years after the Big Four first allowed their events to be televised in the early 1950s, the medium completely redefined the bowl system. Launched by community leaders in Pasadena, Miami, New Orleans, and Dallas to promote tourism and sell tickets, the games gradually became less important for their original purpose and more valuable for their worth as popular television programming. In any given year, fewer than 400,000 fans jammed into the four stadiums to watch the Rose, Orange, Sugar, and Cotton Bowls, but in time, the networks transformed the games into blockbuster events anticipated and enjoyed by millions of fans from coast to coast. Baby boomers and subsequent generations grew up automatically associating New Year's Day with the Big Four, a cultural link that became every bit as traditional as resolutions and black-eyed peas.

The Rose Bowl towered over the others, before and after television. First played in 1902, contested every year since 1916, the Pasadena event invented the concept of the bowl game. For many years, the organizers invited a host team from the West Coast to play a powerful team from the East, Midwest, or South.

In the era before the advent of wire service rankings, the winner of the Rose Bowl was usually considered the national champion. In 1946, the game signed a contract with the Big Ten and the Pacific Coast Conference, reserving the two slots for the champions of the powerful leagues, an arrangement which enhanced its security and stability. When television came onto the scene and NBC started beaming the game coast to coast, the Big Ten/Pacific Coast deal increased the game's clout by making it a powerful afternoon attraction for sports fans in two regions with high concentrations of TV homes.

Launched in the midst of the Great Depression, the other three major bowl games caught on quickly but remained in the shadow of the pioneering Rose Bowl.

The Orange Bowl, played in Miami for the first time in 1933, maintained a deal with the Big Eight at various times in the 1950s and 1960s before switching to prime time and becoming a totally open bowl from 1965 to 1975. The independence paid off, allowing the bowl to attract several high-profile matchups during the period, including four games with national-championship implications. But the Orange Bowl coveted the predictability of a host team, and with the encouragement of NBC, locked up the Big Eight champion starting in 1976, a deal that would last for nearly twenty years.

The Sugar Bowl, which brought the party to New Orleans in 1935, featured at least one Southeastern Conference team thirty-six times in its first forty years—not always to the game's advantage. For several years in the 1950s and 1960s, segregationist sentiment prohibited the game from scheduling non-southern teams, which prevented it from competing effectively. With ABC's blessing, the Sugar Bowl moved to New Year's Eve in 1973. Despite the success of the Notre Dame–Alabama clash, the game returned to New Year's Day after consummating a deal to take the SEC champion starting in 1977. The two events set the stage for an era of significant growth and stability.

The Cotton Bowl, launched in Dallas in 1937, became the postseason destination of the Southwest Conference (SWC) champion for more than a half century. Through the years, this arrangement imbued the bowl with significant clout, especially during the days when SWC powerhouses Texas and Arkansas frequently arrived in Dallas with national-championship aspirations. For more than three decades, the Cotton Bowl occupied the early afternoon window on CBS, sometimes competing against the Sugar Bowl.

Nearly two dozen other lesser bowls were born in the 1930s, 1940s, and 1950s but most died quickly, including the Salad Bowl in Phoenix, which lasted four years; the Dixie Bowl in Birmingham, which played two games; and the Bluegrass Bowl in Louisville, which sank after one game. It was not uncommon for fledgling bowl games of that era to fold without living up to their obligations to the participating teams.

The Gator Bowl in Jacksonville, launched in 1946, staked out a position as the most important second-tier bowl, especially after becoming a staple of the holiday season on ABC. The Sun Bowl in

El Paso, which played its first game in 1936, struggled for years to attract teams from the major conferences but grew steadily after linking with CBS.

With television crafting a new paradigm and the NCAA holding the bowl organizers to increasingly rigid standards, the system entered the 1970s riding a powerful wave. The postseason landscape grew from six games in 1958 to 11 in 1971, with the addition of the Liberty Bowl in Memphis (1959), the Bluebonnet Bowl in Houston (1960), the Peach Bowl in Atlanta (1968), the Tangerine Bowl in Orlando (1968), and the Fiesta Bowl in Tempe (1971).

For decades, ticket sales provided nearly 100 percent of the revenue generated by the bowl games. Then television entered the picture. Through the years, as the universe of sets expanded, ratings soared, and advertisers recognized the value of those large, demographically desirable audiences, the networks started paying increasingly generous rights fees to retain their valuable college football programming. In the 1970s, television money surpassed ticket sales as the primary source of revenue for many bowl games. The Rose Bowl, watched in an average of 21.8 million homes in the late 1970s, saw its rights fee soar from $2 million in 1974 to $4.3 million in 1981. The prime-time Orange Bowl's TV revenue jumped from $1.2 million to $2.8 million over the same period.

"In the '70s, something happened that I'm not sure any of us understands even today," said Mickey Holmes, the longtime executive director of the Sugar Bowl, who saw his game's television contract quadruple in the decade. "The networks and syndicators began an escalation of TV rights fees that lacked any kind of rationality. The downside to that, although we didn't know it then, was that we were evolving from an era when ticket sales, which we maintained a measure of control over, were giving way as the dominant revenue source to TV rights fees, where our control was considerably less."

In the early days of the bowl system, organizers sold the experience primarily as a treat for the players, a bonus trip to an exotic locale on the heels of a successful season. It was. Still is.

But from the start, the bowls also lured participating teams with the promise of a substantial payday, a factor which grew steadily through the years as the nation's football programs began to morph into increasingly sophisticated business operations. Starting in the 1960s, the conferences developed revenue sharing plans for bowl and television money, and the members of the most powerful leagues grew to depend on the source of funding, pumping the dollars back into their football programs and supporting more competitive nonrevenue sports for both men and women.

When television rights fees exploded in the 1970s, the major games became huge cash cows for the participating teams and their conferences. The Sugar Bowl, which paid Tulane and Temple $22,759 each in 1935, was able to raise the payday from $236,000 in 1967 to $900,000 in 1977. Over the same period, the Orange Bowl's payout jumped from $259,324 to $1.05 million.

"The money was pivotal in our relationship with the Big Eight," said Nick Crane, a longtime member of the Orange Bowl board. "It was very important that we be able to pay more than our competition to get the Big Eight under contract."


For many years, the Southeastern Conference, Big Eight, and Southwest Conference dominated the bowl selections—and not just because they produced outstanding teams. While those three leagues maintained liberal bowl participation policies—embracing the system as a source of revenue and promotion—the Big Ten and the forerunner of the present-day Pac-10 prevented their members from playing in games other than the Rose Bowl. During the same period, Notre Dame spurned all postseason invitations, citing conflicts with the academic calendar.

But change was in the air.

Four years after Notre Dame returned to the bowl scene after an absence of 45 years, Big Ten commissioner Wayne Duke campaigned to bring his league into the real world. He could see how the rule was handicapping the Big Ten. Wiles Hallock, commissioner of what was then the Pac-8, joined Duke in pushing for a change. In 1971, six SEC teams went bowling—nearly one-third of all available berths at the time. The Big Eight placed four teams into the postseason.

The advantages for the conferences were impossible to deny. Each team enjoyed a rewarding trip to a fun location, played before a national television audience, generated a generous payday for the school, and reaped the benefits of practicing for an additional month.

The policy imposed by the Big Ten and Pac-8 punished some of their most successful teams. In 1973, after tying Ohio State to finish 10–0–1, Bo Schembechler's sixth-ranked Michigan Wolverines were forced to stay home when the Buckeyes received the Rose Bowl bid. The same year, ninth-ranked UCLA went nowhere after losing to Pasadena-bound archrival Southern Cal.

"Not competing in other games represented a real recruiting disadvantage," Hallock said. "The other conferences were loading up on appearances and it was hurting our teams not to be on national television. The money was also significant, because the payouts were just starting to take off."

After intense lobbying by Duke and Hallock—and with the approval of Rose Bowl partner NBC—the Big Ten and Pac-8 voted to end the ban in 1974. This decision automatically introduced an additional four to six quality teams worthy of bowl invitations, an explosion of qualifiers that would force the system to expand in the years ahead.

In preparation for the new era, Duke paid what amounted to sales calls on the various bowls during the offseason in 1974. He carried a map highlighting the number of television households in Big Ten country because he understood the influence the networks were exerting in the process.

"Going to other bowls was a real turning point for the Big Ten," Duke said. "It helped us move from the Big Two (Michigan and Ohio State) and the Little Eight (everyone else) to a conference with a number of strong teams. The bowl experience helped in recruiting and it certainly generated a lot of revenue."

Soon, the burgeoning Rose Bowl guarantee—which reached a combined $5.2 million in 1979—and the addition of other bowl money would give the two conferences a virtual lock on nearly half of all postseason dollars.

The new bowl attitude set the stage for a much less isolated sport. On the heels of the widespread intregration of the southern colleges—who had previously been unwilling or unable to schedule non-southern teams with African-American players—the policy shift by Notre Dame and the Big Ten and Pac-8 promoted a much greater level of intersectional play.

The Fighting Irish, who returned to the postseason in a loss to Texas at the 1970 Cotton Bowl, soon wound up in bowl games against Alabama, Penn State, Georgia, and Houston. Teams from the Big Ten and Pac-8, who had only occasionally ventured out of their own group—the Notre Dame–Southern Cal rivalry was a fifty-year-old exception—started showing up in New Orleans, Miami, Jacksonville, and Memphis. Bowl matchups like Ohio State–Colorado, Arkansas–UCLA, Ohio State–Alabama, and Michigan–Auburn infused the system with a jolt of excitement and helped usher in a new era of college football.


Although many of the bowl organizers talked a good game about maintaining their independence, the networks started demanding more influence as they lavished the events with increasingly generous wads of cash. In the age of disco and gas lines, television was a significant factor in every key decision, from playing dates to team selection. Officials who once based every move on how it would affect ticket sales found themselves forced to negotiate a delicate balancing act between television's desire to generate a high rating and the traditional need to fill seats. Because a competitive Nielsen number gave them greater leverage with the networks in the next round of negotiations, many organizers were willing to make sacrifices to ensure television success.

"When I first started the Liberty Bowl, and for years after, we would set a date that was good for us and the network would automatically agree," said Bud Dudley, the Memphis game's founder and longtime executive director. "But it got to where television called all the shots."

The system exploded to fifteen games by 1978, with the addition of the Independence Bowl in Shreveport (1976), the Hall of Fame Classic in Birmingham (1977), the Holiday Bowl in San Diego (1978), and the Garden State Bowl in East Rutherford (1978). Several of the new age games would not have been viable without television. The Peach, Hall of Fame, Tangerine, and Independence Bowls struggled to sell tickets but survived because demand among viewers and advertisers for televised college football was surging, and the various networks and syndicators were willing to pay inflated fees even for mediocre matchups with limited national appeal.

During this period, the nature of bowling started to change. For decades, playing in a bowl game had been considered a reward for an outstanding season. The invitations to the Big Four were reserved for conference champions or teams who came very close to capturing a ring. The limited number of minor bowls, including the Gator and Liberty, had their pick of a long list of good one-, two-, or three-loss teams. But when the universe began to expand, it was common for the holiday landscape to be littered with 7–4 and 6–5 also-rans celebrating the dubious achievement of a winning season. Competition among the bowls for the best available teams intensified, and as much as the loud blazer crowd enjoyed schmoozing college officials during visits to campus, the bottom line of the new era was the bottom line.

The tradition-rich Big Four dominated the system, battling each other for teams and TV ratings. Everyone else was a second-class citizen. The bowls fell into a pecking order, their worth defined by how much they could pay participating teams, a figure which was directly proportional to the size of their television contract.

"All the schools were mindful of generating revenue, and that payout figure became very important," said the Pac-10's Hallock.

By the end of the 1970s, the bowl system was returning more than $15 million per year to participating teams, almost of it all funneled through the five most prominent conferences.

In the days leading up to a nationally televised game between Purdue and Ohio State in 1967, Woody Hayes reluctantly provided ABC announcer Chris Schenkel with a playbook. All the coaches did it. Schenkel liked to familiarize himself with the various offenses so he could more intelligently describe the action during the telecasts.

But Hayes had second thoughts.

Around dinner time on the night before the game, Schenkel answered a knock on his hotel door. He was surprised to the see the scowling Ohio State coach.

"Give me the playbook," Woody grunted. "I don't trust you."

Hayes, one of the greatest coaches in college football history, could be incredibly abrasive. Most of his coaching contemporaries understood the importance of courting the television people, but not Woody. He treated Schenkel dismissively and made no attempt to woo any of the TV announcers of the day.

"Woody Hayes was a very difficult man for televison people to work with," said ABC announcer Keith Jackson. "There was absolutely no relationship between Woody and me. None. The man wouldn't cooperate, wouldn't let you get close to him."

On the night of December 29, 1978, Hayes's violent world imploded. Television, which he viewed with a combination of contempt and indifference, became a coconspirator in his self-destruction.

With Clemson clinging to a 17–15 lead over Ohio State in the closing minutes of the Gator Bowl, the Buckeyes were marching toward a game-winning score. But Clemson defensive back Charley Bauman saved the victory for Charley Pell's Tigers by intercepting an Ohio State pass near the Buckeyes' sideline. Then, in a matter of seconds, a brilliant twenty-seven year head coaching career highlighted by 238 victories, twelve Big Ten titles, and three national championships ended in a thoughtless, instinctive, unforgivable act.

As Bauman ran off the field, Hayes grabbed him and punched him several times while millions of stunned fans watched in disbelief.

In the ABC production truck, producer Bob Goodrich, college sports director Donn Bernstein, and the rest of the crew could not believe their eyes.

"Holy shit!" Bernstein yelled. "He hit him! Did you see that?"

Sitting in the booth high atop the Jacksonville stadium, Keith Jackson and color man Ara Parseghian somehow missed the blows. They were preoccupied with the action on the field, and due to a monumental blunder on the part of the network, the announcers would not get a second look.

With the final moments ticking off the clock and the network feeling pressure to be off the air as soon as possible to avoid running into the affiliates' late news, Goodrich encouraged Jackson to say something about the shocking event. But Jackson refused.

"I hadn't seen it and they couldn't show it to me and I wasn't about to comment on something I hadn't seen with my own eyes," Jackson said.

Sitting in his hotel room in New Orleans, where he was preparing for the upcoming Sugar Bowl, executive vice president Jim Spence saw the slugging, phoned the truck and instructed Goodrich to order his play-by-play man to say something. But Jackson refused.

Several minutes later, ABC signed off without remarking on the incident. About the same time, the image of the geriatric Hayes using Bauman's body for a punching bag started popping up on local newscasts all over the country, including many ABC affiliates, who had taped it off the air.

The jarring moment careened off the sports pages and exploded into a blockbuster news story. Some writers even suggested that Jackson's silence on the subject was an attempt to cover up for Hayes, which was ludicrous, especially considering their disdain for each other.

The controversy raised an important question, however: Was television a partner with the bowls or a credentialed journalist? It was trying desperately to be both. Even as the networks gained tremendous influence over the operation of the various games, they were walking a fine line between the clout purchased with rights fees and national exposure and their determination to maintain credibility with viewers. ABC Sports had proven its commitment to journalism through the years, and Jackson's reputation as a straight-shooter was well established. No one asked him to pull his punches.

But the network blew it that night.

Placed in an impossible situation, Jackson became a victim of ABC's cost-cutting fervor. He took the public fall for the network management's decision to save perhaps $5,000 by not purchasing a so-called "net return" feed of the outgoing broadcast routed back to the Gator Bowl. Without such a connection, the producers on-site couldn't replay the shot, which meant they couldn't show it to Jackson. How was he to comment on something he had not seen?

"You could argue that Keith should have come back on the air and said something had happened that he didn't see or whatever," said Bernstein. "But Keith was just being conservative. The culprit was the decision not to have the feed, which was an economic decision, and a bad one."

If the event had occured away from the national spotlight, especially in an era when only a limited number of games were televised, Hayes might have been able to salvage his job. Like longtime Indiana basketball coach Bobby Knight, Hayes was well known for his volatility. Hearing about such an act would not have had the same impact, especially if only a small number of people had witnessed it close-up. But when millions saw it live and then the whole country was subjected to it over and over again on the news, elevating the meltdown of the coaching icon to a national outrage, Ohio State had no choice. Hayes was fired, and he deserved to be fired.

Frustrated by the consequences of his network's penny-pinching, Jackson saw the replay for the first time the next morning on the local NBC affiliate, which had taped it off the air. "The whole thing still pisses me off," Jackson said. "Too many people ducked and ran for cover."

The incident proved to be one of the most embarrassing gaffes in the history of ABC Sports. Many years after the network infused the televised experience with new elements of storytelling, the goalposts were shifting. The viewing public, conditioned by the growing sophistication of sports reporting in both print and broadcast, was starting to hold television to a higher standard. Fans expected a little journalism with their football, and even as the Gator Bowl demonstrated the enormous visceral impact of one chilling moment, it also showed what can happen when a network lets the technology get in the way of telling the story.

In the late 1960s, Frank Kush built the Arizona State program into a dominant force in the Western Athletic Conference, capturing five straight league championships. While the program caused quite a stir in the desert, the rest of the country barely noticed. In those days the WAC existed on the outer edge of the big-time game, branded as inferior by the sport's establishment including the bowl games, who mostly ignored the Sun Devils.

In 1971, a year after an undefeated Arizona State team knocked off North Carolina in the Peach Bowl, some enterprising community leaders in Tempe launched the Fiesta Bowl. The organizers made a deal to provide a postseason home for the WAC champion, which didn't have very far to travel since the game was played in Sun Devil Stadium. To the surprise of nobody, Arizona State played in the first three Fiesta Bowls, beating three unranked teams just glad to get out of town for the holidays.

With the addition of four newly unshackled Big Ten and Pac-8 teams fighting for the limited number of bowl invitations, the fledgling game and the frustrated powerhouse caught a break in 1975, when unbeaten Arizona State secured the bid with one of Kush's strongest teams. Chuck Neinas, the Big Eight commissioner, called Fiesta Bowl executive director Bruce Skinner and brokered a deal to send the loser of the Oklahoma–Nebraska game to Tempe. The winner was headed to the Orange Bowl.

Nebraska played hard to get because the Cornhuskers thought they were bound for the Sugar Bowl to play SEC champion Alabama. At the last minute, however, Paul "Bear" Bryant, who carried tremendous clout in the selection process, vetoed Nebraska. He wanted Penn State.

Given the choice between playing in the lowly regarded Fiesta Bowl or staying home for the holidays, Nebraska officials struggled with the decision for several days before finally accepting the bid. Then something unexpected happened: Arizona State pulled off a stunning 17–14 upset of the seventh-ranked Cornhuskers, which brought the league, the bowl, and the Sun Devils a new level of respectability.

Several months later, CBS convinced the Fiesta Bowl to move from its late December date to Christmas Day.

"From the standpoint of local support the move was a nightmare," Skinner said. "But the move was done purely for television. We thought it could give us national exposure on a good day for football because of all the people at home."

They were right. Attendance suffered, but as the only game on Christmas Day, the Fiesta garnered a strong rating. Penn State's 42–30 victory over Arizona State in 1977 attracted the fourth-highest TV audience of the bowl season, surpassing even the venerable Sugar Bowl.

When Arizona State and archrival Arizona joined what became the Pac-10 in 1978—a move that would not have been possible without the prestige generated by the Fiesta Bowl—the Tempe game dropped its affiliation with the WAC. They planned to try independence for a while. About the same time NBC, impressed by the game's steady growth as a TV property, stole the Fiesta Bowl away from CBS by nearly quadrupling the rights fee to $400,000, making the seven-year-old game the most profitable of the second-tier bowls.

Armed with a willingness to use television as the ultimate tradition-smasher, the organizers of the Fiesta Bowl set their sights on the big time.

"We wanted to be more than a good bowl," Skinner said. "We wanted to be one of *the* bowls."

# 8

# MAJOR FRUSTRATIONS

Even as the bowl games presented a picture of big-time college football to the world and generated increasingly generous fees for the most important conferences, the sport was engaged in a contentious struggle for self-definition. Twenty years into the national television age, major college football was like a large and unwieldy extended family. The sport consisted of some obvious members, some distant relatives, and some desperate wannabes who kept trying to crash the family reunions, undeterred by the fact that no one wanted to have anything to do with them.

A disparate group of more than 150 colleges and universities with a wide range of ambitions and commitments, major college football existed on four distinct levels: the Headliners, the Spoilers, the Pretenders, and the Ivys.

The Headliners dominated the sport—on the field and in the nation's consciousness. This group of about 60 schools included the members of the Big Eight, Big Ten, Pac-8, Southeastern Conference, Southwest Conference, and the most important independents, including Notre Dame and Penn State. In most of the ways that mattered, the Headliners *were* college football. These schools played the game at the highest level and attracted the most intense fan interest. The vast majority of the NCAA television games involved Headliner teams. During the first two decades of the TV era, these programs captured all but one of the mythical national championships, routinely occupied the top ten positions in the wire service rankings, produced seventeen of twenty Heisman Trophy winners, and grabbed more than three-quarters of all of postseason bowl bids, maintaining a virtual lock on the New Year's Day games. Even within this level, resources and competitive strength varied widely, from the powerful members of the TV Aristocracy—like Oklahoma, Alabama, and Southern Cal—to the also-rans of their respective conferences—like Kansas State, Vanderbilt, and Washington State. But they all shared the same goals. Kansas State was a poor relative, but nonetheless, it was a recognized member of the family, legitimized by its association with Oklahoma, Nebraska, and the rest of the Big Eight.

The Spoilers occupied a less secure place in the hiearchy of college football. They had one foot in the big-time game, the other in no-man's-land. This group included teams from the Atlantic Coast Conference and Western Athletic Conference and lesser independents including Florida State, Miami (Fla.), and Southern Mississippi. They tended to have much smaller budgets than most of the Headliner schools. They never contended for the national championship—at least not since Maryland won the big prize in 1953—and rarely played in New Year's Day bowl games. The best of the bunch earned invitations to second-tier bowls such as the Peach, Tangerine, and Fiesta and finished in the latter half of the top twenty. They often played Headliners, and sometimes even won. But such victories were always considered upsets.

The Pretenders were major college teams in name only. These schools, who belonged to leagues including the Mid-American Conference, the Pacific Coast Athletic Association, the Southern Conference, and the Southland Conference, were kidding themselves. They wanted to be considered major for a variety of reasons, not least of which was the perceived negative connotation of playing football in anything other than the top division. But Pretenders like Long Beach State, Kent State, and Tennessee-Chattanooga competed at a level which more closely resembled small college football. Compared to the truly major schools, they operated on modest budgets and played before tiny crowds. They rarely played in bowl games. The only way contests between these schools made it on television was under the NCAA's patronage game.

The Ivys wanted to have it both ways. Two decades after the eight elite eastern institutions known collectively as the Ivy League essentially de-emphasized football and insulated themselves from the modern game, they remained part of the major college establishment, at least within the legislative framework of the NCAA. Even as they managed to live without athletic scholarships and bowl games, the Ivy League schools still expected their appearances on the television series and to be able to exert influence on a game that they no longer played. The Ivys existed on an island of antiquity but still carried as much weight within the NCAA as the Pac-8 schools.

Despite the many advantages wielded by the truly major schools in the early 1970s, the conferences that dominated the rankings, bowl games, and television appearances were outnumbered by the party crashers. No one seemed to notice or care—until it was too late.


As the spoils associated with the game started to multiply in the 1960s—driven directly and indirectly by television—the financial gulf between college football's haves and have-nots grew ever wider. The schools that generated large amounts of revenue could afford to spend more on scholarships, coaches, recruiting, and facilities, which perpetuated their cycle of dominance. The price of admission to the elite club of major college football kept climbing every year, and many programs struggled to keep up.

The members of the TV aristocracy enjoyed tremendous advantages, especially in recruiting. Because of their strength in terms of finance and promotion, teams like Nebraska, Alabama, Texas, and Oklahoma routinely signed more than sixty players per year, which represented recruiting less than gathering. By signing so many players, such programs gave their dominance over less successful teams a certain mathematical probability.

"We felt there was a lot of sense in signing a large number of players," explained longtime Nebraska head coach Bob Devaney. "If you only sign a small number and you're wrong on a few prospects, you're in trouble. But the size afforded us a certain amount of safety."

In addition to filling their specific needs, the powers could diminish the recruiting efforts of their less prosperous rivals by signing up all the best talent. Some derisively referred to this as "stockpiling."

"If we weren't sure about a kid but thought he might sign with someone else, we'd take him to make sure he didn't end up playing against us," said former Alabama recruiting coordinator Clem Gryska.

For many years, the various conferences operated without any restrictions on scholarships. In the early 1960s, the Big Ten passed a rule limiting teams to signing no more than thirty prospects per year, legislation that placed the conference at a distinct disadvantage. By the early 1970s, the Big Eight, SEC, and SWC adopted standards of forty-five grants per year, but all provided provisions for "banking" and "borrowing," which allowed the financially strong to sign sixty or more in a given year. Without overall limits, some prosperous teams continued to keep 150 or more players on scholarship. Many others could not afford to pay the freight for so many student-athletes, which exacerbated their competitive disadvantage.

Rather than some monolithic, homogenous group, major college football was in reality a majority of minorities within the structure of the NCAA: Headliners, Spoilers, Pretenders, Ivys. To make matters worse, the university division and its successor, Division I, also consisted of many other schools who played major basketball but not football and others who played major basketball but football at a lower level. Thus, not only did Harvard wield as much influence over major football related legislation as Georgia, but so did Hofstra, which played football at the nonscholarship Division III level.

For the better part of two decades, the major football schools looked upon the organizational flaw as a minor irritant. The smaller schools never tried to use their numerical advantage as a weapon, and the NCAA continued to legislate mostly on issues in which there was a strong national consensus, like uniform academic standards. But in 1973, everything changed.

Amid reports of a widespread financial crisis in college athletics, the NCAA moved aggressively into micromanagement of the sport. At so-called "cost-cutting" conventions in 1973 and 1975, the mostly small schools who dominated the ranks forced the major powers to accept national limits on scholarships, coaches, recruiting visits, and other matters once routinely controlled by conferences and the institutions themselves.

The legislative flurry—especially the rule that limited programs to signing no more than thirty players per year, and carrying no more than ninety-five on scholarship—incensed many coaches of big-time schools, who resented the NCAA's meddling in their affairs.

"I don't know anything about hockey in Minnesota, lacrosse at Navy, rugby at Cal-Tech, or fencing at Cornell, but I know that football at Auburn, football in the Southeastern Conference, has just been kicked in the pants," said Auburn head coach Ralph "Shug" Jordan, who routinely kept about 150 players on scholarship.

For others, the problem wasn't the concept of national limits so much as the makeup of the schools allowed to decide the legislation. "I don't want Hofstra telling Texas how to play football," said Longhorns head coach Darrell Royal.

No small number of coaches and administrators believed the cost-cutting talk was a sham—although Walter Byers estimated that the changes would immediately save the colleges about $15 million per year. "[The legislation] was more of an attempt to level competition than it was to save money," said Southeastern Conference Commissioner Boyd McWhorter. "[It was being voted on] by people who didn't have to employ such restrictions."

Most troubling to some was the NCAA's decision to limit the number of players a school could dress to sixty for home games and forty-eight for away games. "That was a symbolic piece of legislation because it could mean an end to conference autonomy," Big Eight commissioner Chuck Neinas told reporters. "It means the NCAA is going to control everything."

Most Division I members who voted for severe limits on the most prosperous programs awarded only a fraction of the scholarships, employed only a fraction of the coaches, and made only a fraction of the recruiting visits of the major powers, so they were legislating the powerful down closer to their level of affordability.

Suddenly, the powers felt absolutely powerless within the structure of the NCAA. Frustrated by their inability to control their own sport, coaches and administrators began to see the NCAA as a tyrannical bureaucracy holding them captive to the majority whim of institutions who did not share their ambitions, commitments, or pressures.

But the parity legislation was not simply a skirmish between the haves and the have-nots.

Longtime friends Chuck Neinas and Wayne Duke wound up on opposite sides of a huge philosophical divide. Neinas, the commissioner of the Big Eight, opposed the newly activist NCAA's legislative ambitions. Duke, the commissioner of the Big Ten, supported the smaller schools. He believed in greater national control of the game and saw the limits as a way to create a more level playing field and "place [the Big Ten] in a competitive situation through legislation."

"We may have felt somewhat elitist," Duke said many years later. "We looked at football differently than Chuck and a lot of those people."

This amicable disagreement between two old drinking buddies was more than an isolated event. It symbolized a growing fissure in the seeming solidarity of big-time college football. No one knew it at the time, but the break over scholarships was the precursor to a civil war destined to be fought over control of football television.

The scholarship limitations, which took effect in 1975, forever altered college football, creating a measure of unparalleled parity. With the powerful teams no longer able to sign a virtually unlimited number of players, lesser programs suddenly found themselves able to compete more effectively in the recruiting wars—and on the field.

Many players who might have automatically signed with their first choice during the unrestricted days were forced to look elsewhere. Talent spread more evenly throughout the game, narrowing the gap between the best and worst teams. Conferences once dominated by one or two oustanding teams began to grow stronger from top to bottom.

"The scholarship limits gave everybody a fighting chance," said Florida State head coach Bobby Bowden, who built the Seminoles into one of the most powerful dynasties of the new era.

With the most dominant powers no longer able to rotate three complete units in and out of games, the competitive gap between conference rivals at opposite ends of the spectrum—like Alabama and Vanderbilt, or Texas and Rice—narrowed significantly.

Once lowly programs like Florida State, Miami (Fla.), Clemson, and Kansas State exploited the rules to overturn the established order and become new age powerhouses.

"The limitation on grants was the single most important piece of legislation I saw in my forty years of college athletics," said Wayne Duke. "You can't legislate equality, but you can legislate an opportunity for kids to line up across from each other knowing they have a chance. As far as achieving quality, sanity, and economy, the grants legislation is unmatched."

The limits—eventually pared to twenty-five grants per year—conspired to place even more pressure on coaches to chose wisely. In the old days, a few bad choices could be forgiven amid a sea of riches. But in the new era, a small number of misses could devastate a program and cost a coach his job.

During the battles over the parity legislation, the NCAA bowed to pressure from the major schools and reorganized into three divisions in 1973: Division I for major institutions, Division II for small colleges which offered scholarships and Division III for small colleges that did not offer scholarships.

"No longer will the little guys be telling the big guys what to do," NCAA president Alan Chapman, a professor of astrophysics at Rice, told reporters. "I don't think you will hear any more stories about the superconferences."

But the new structure left too much fat in the top division. Long Beach State and Nebraska remained in the same group with equal votes, which was not reorganization so much as reshuffling. The establishment of three distinct divisions failed to alleviate the legislative logjam. Of the 250-plus members of Divison I who were allowed to vote on major college rules, the sixty-five to eighty-five major football schools constituted a small minority captive and vulnerable to majority will. In addition to the four levels of supposedly major football schools, Divison I also consisted of large numbers of institutions that played big-time basketball and other sports but not football on any level (such as St. Louis and North Carolina-Charlotte) and members that played big-time basketball and other sports but football at a lower level (such as St. John's). Schools that played football at the nonscholarship level or not at all carried as much weight in determining major football rules as Michigan and Notre Dame. In an increasingly activist organization, democracy stripped of commonality was not democracy so much as mob rule.

As the truly major schools struggled for autonomy among the

NCAA's majority of minorities, they experienced increasing difficulty in separating their legitimate quest for self-determination from the mounting number of scandals that gave the whole sport a bad name.

To many among the major powers, Walter Byers became a symbol of the NCAA's unchecked power and apparent unaccountability. He publicly supported further realignment, but failed to push it through the bureaucracy. At the annual conventions, he continued to maintain a low profile, but his support of the parity legislation was a matter of public record. When Neinas found much to criticize at the 1975 Convention and voiced his concerns to the press, Byers wasted no time in responding. "The issue of whether institutions wish to give up their authority to a national body was never stated more clearly than when the convention itself voted to control the number of scholarships," he said.

Just as Byers deserved credit for the strength of the television plan and all of the other major achievements of his administration, the failure of the NCAA to meet the needs of the major football institutions rested chiefly on his shoulders. At a time when the NCAA needed a dynamic leader who could unite the major powers to create a workable autonomy, Byers failed to use his clout to make it happen.

"I think Walter was scared of the major schools," said Notre Dame's Father Edmund P. Joyce. "He derived his power from the great number of small programs. To have given us more say in our own affairs would have diminished his power."


Like scholarships and an increasing array of other matters, the football television plan was yet another source of friction between the major powers and the NCAA. After the 1973 reorganization, the governing body created championship playoffs for Division II and Division III, and convinced ABC to televise the events. The majors saw this as another example of their product being watered down, which cost them money and exposure.

But times were fat, and no one wanted to push the issue.

With ratings soaring, the NCAA package generated $16 million for the colleges in 1974, which translated to $487,856 for a national game and $355,000 for a regional appearance.

ABC had taken college football to a whole new level of acceptance and popularity. But as ABC kept raising the bar on itself, audiences were becoming more sophisticated. Football fans were starting to expect more from the broadcasts, and Roone Arledge knew he had to make a difficult decision.

Despite Chris Schenkel's obvious talents and his unquestioned role in the development of ABC Sports, the play-by-play man was widely criticized at the NCAA and throughout the college sports establishment for his low-key style. Schenkel may have been the perfect choice to lead the telecasts in 1966, but by 1974, his soft-spoken eloquence seemed as anachronistic as a buzz cut. Not many people had noticed in 1966 when he failed to question Ara Parseghian's decision not to try to win in the closing moments against Michigan State, but such verbal reserve was widely mocked in the more cynical age of Watergate.

"Chris's style of communication was attacked for not having enough bite, and there was a certain amount of truth in that," said ABC executive Jim Spence.

Some of his closest associates suggest his style was a reflection of a lack of enthusiasm for the sport. "On the plane going to a site, I'd try to engage him about the game," recalled former ABC producer Chuck Howard. "But he wouldn't show much interest. He was far more interested in horse racing or something else, and the viewers could see that."

The frustration mounted over several years. In a confidential memo to Walter Byers dated April 23, 1969, NCAA staffer Tom Hansen addressed the issue:

> It is disappointing to study the minutes of the TV Committee in which provisions of the new plan

were discussed and not find any reference to our sad announcer situation. I hope the reason is that I'm in the minority of one in disliking Schenkel rather than that the Committee again forgot to consider the problem. It's criminal to have this guy ho hum our best teams, our best games. Isn't anyone concerned?

In the spring of 1974, Arledge arrived at Schenkel's apartment on Central Park South in New York and broke the news before they went off to dinner with Chuck Howard and Jim Spence.

"It was a colossal blow, right between my legs," Schenkel said. "But I've always respected Roone for one thing relating to that episode. At least he had the balls to come and tell me face to face."

When Arledge replaced Schenkel with longtime backup college announcer—and former *Monday Night Football* play-by-play man—Keith Jackson, the impact on the broadcasts was immediate and profound. It was like the difference between classical and rock 'n' roll. It was as if someone had flipped a switch and ABC Sports had joined the 1970s in progress.

Jackson—eventually paired with the insightful, articulate former Arkansas coach Frank Broyles—infused the sport with unmistakable passion. He combined an intimate knowledge of college football with an unrestrained, exuberant style, which connected him with the viewers in a powerful way.

To the generation of fans who came of age over the next two decades, Jackson was not just the voice of the game. He was a big part of the game—a colorful character who helped make the televised experience special and memorable. With his distinctive, often imitated southern drawl and his predeliction for colloquial phrases, Jackson tapped into the electricity of college football like no announcer before or since, making all other play-by-play men seem bland and uninspired.

. . .

Even as the NCAA appeared intent on nationalizing many facets of college football in the mid-1970s, the association effectively abdicated its authority over academic standards. Many big-time football schools were horrified when the NCAA recinded the so-called 1.6 predictor rule—a relatively tough standard—and replaced it with a much less stringent national requirement built around a 2.0 high school average. Suddenly, all a talented high school running back needed for admission to most colleges was a high school diploma which, in many cases, required little more than a pulse.

Rather than feeling the need to prepare student-athletes for the rigors of college life, many high schools became much more likely to pass marginal student-athletes at all costs, which conspired with other factors to create a generation of student-athletes who were less prepared for college and, in many cases, took the experience less seriously. Although the various colleges retained the right to raise their noses and apply a higher standard, doing so placed them at a competitive disadvantage in the recruiting wars. Very few programs were willing to cede the star running back—who just happened to be an academic underachiever—to their less-choosy rival.

"The move to the 2.0 standard was extremely regressive," said former University of Georgia president Fred Davison. "It took all the pressure off the high schools to make sure that the athlete was reasonably prepared for college."

During the same period, the lure of professional football riches started to become a significant factor in the college game. As the NFL was flooded with television dollars, superstars suddenly found themselves able to command million-dollar salaries. Even mediocre offensive linemen and defensive backs could earn enough in a few seasons to be set for life, which gradually devalued the college experience for many student-athletes who started to view the campus game as a pipeline to the pros.

. . .

Although the NCAA tossed some bones to the marginal leagues—
too many in the view of the major powers—the vast majority of the
rapidly growing revenue from the ABC contract—up almost three-
fold in fifteen years—was paid to the major football schools who
supplied the games that drove the deal. Nearly all of the rights fees
were funneled through the Big Ten, Big Eight, Pac-8, SEC, and
SWC.

But with the costs of running athletic departments rising rapidly, some have-nots started lusting after the television money. In
1975, Dr. Stephen Horn, the president of Long Beach State,
floated a proposal that called for 50 percent of the TV revenue to
be split evenly among the Divison I schools and 50 percent among
the Divisions II and III institutions. He also suggested distributing
postseason revenue in a similar fashion.

A few years before, the radical idea probably would have elicited
little more than a hearty laugh from the major powers. But no one
was laughing in 1975. After having been forced to surrender many
once-sacred elements of their institutional autonomy to an increasingly powerful bureaucracy, the big-time football schools saw
Horn as a dangerous man. The NCAA was one majority edict from
a share-the-wealth socialist revolution, and the big schools knew
they didn't have the votes.

The ruling NCAA Council, no doubt fearing a revolt of the
major schools, rejected Horn's proposal, widely derided as "the
Robin Hood plan." The Council said it opposed the proposal "in
the strongest terms," warning that it would mean the end of the
NCAA "as we know it."

Even though they had been divided over the general drift of
the NCAA into national control of the sport, the leaders of the
major schools were united in opposition to the Robin Hood plan.

"It was a major stimulus for unity," Neinas said.

Unnerved by Horn's proposal and frustrated by their inability to
achieve any workable autonomy to decide the various issues facing

their high-profile, big-budget schools, Neinas, Duke, and other leaders among the major establishment started discussing other avenues of empowerment. The Robin Hood proposal represented yet another symbol of their vulnerability. About the same time, the NCAA Council recommended further restructuring to create a top level of seventy-eight major football schools, but the membership voted it down.

"We needed to get together and find common ground among ourselves," Neinas said.

Like all revolutions, theirs began with an idea, not a weapon.

More than two decades after the major schools stood idly by as the NCAA seized Pennsylvania's television rights in the name of the greater good, they felt trapped and made impotent by the monster they had created. They never understood until it was too late that by enlarging the association's powers, they had diminished their own. They never imagined that the authority they voluntarily ceded to the governing body to tame television would be expanded to assume such sweeping control of their athletic affairs.

In addition to the obvious friction caused by the disparity of commitments among the vast Division I membership, the majors felt constricted by two fundamental facets of the NCAA's anti-quated system of governance.

Coaches enjoyed no role in the legislative process. "It was like the NCAA thought we were either not smart enough or couldn't be trusted to have input into the game we knew better than any-body else," said longtime Nebraska head coach Tom Osborne. "Coaches had no voice. We were in a situation where we had to obey rules made by people who knew less about the game."

This isolation led to the passage of sometimes flawed, unwork-able legislation and created an understandable amount of bitter-ness toward the governing body. "The frustration level was very high," said former Georgia head coach Vince Dooley.

Equally troubling was the process under which university

officials named to the various NCAA committees felt no pressure or obligation to vote on behalf of constituent groups. Appointed through the NCAA's insular nominating process and not as part of the membership rotated among the various conferences, committee members were free to vote their own consciences or whims, which often made a mockery of the NCAA's supposed democracy. At one point in the mid-1970s, a faculty member of a Big Eight school serving on the NCAA Council actually voted in favor of abolishing the athletic scholarship, which was like a Baptist preacher opposing Sunday school.

Given such organizational flaws, leaders among the major powers believed that their best chance of affecting NCAA legislation—short of NCAA sanctioned autonomy, which they continued to seek—was to create a separate, noncompeting organization and attempt to reach consensus on the various issues affecting the sport. No man shaped the new group more than Father Edmund P. Joyce, Notre Dame's eloquent, erudite executive vice president, who infused the alliance with credibility as more than a bunch of rebel football coaches. A quarter-century after the Big Bluff, Joyce found philosophical allies among some of the same schools who had once mocked his television stand as a product of greed. The NCAA's micromanagement of the game united schools like Notre Dame and Georgia as strongly as television had once divided them.

"It was not some conspiracy to take over college athletics, like some people thought," Joyce said. "We just needed to be able to talk among ourselves to see what we could accomplish."

In a Denver hotel ballroom in December 1976, representatives of the major powers hammered out rough objectives for their new union and planned a full-scale meeting of prospective members for the next spring. The group included Chuck Neinas, Boyd McWhorter, Father Joyce, and several dozen athletic directors and coaches. Wayne Duke chaired a committee on membership, played a leading role in the planning and discussion, and, at the appropriate point, stood up and made the motion that launched the College Football Association (CFA) into existence.

But at some point over the next few months, Duke soured on the idea of the CFA. After playing a significant role in the development of the new organization, the leaders of the Big Ten and the Pac-8 failed to show up for the first regular meeting in Atlanta in the spring of 1977.

Duke and Pac-8 commissioner Wiles Hallock became convinced that the CFA represented a threat to the NCAA. Some college leaders believed they were pressured by Walter Byers to avoid any involvement with the rebel group. "[Duke and Hallock] were always in bed with Walter on all kinds of matters," Joyce said. "And Byers was deathly afraid of the CFA."

"There's no doubt in my mind that Walter was instrumental in keeping [the Big Ten and Pac-8] out of the CFA," Neinas said.

Duke and Hallock downplayed Byers's influence but said they saw the CFA going too far. "It wasn't my intention to form a different organization," Duke said. "Mine was to provide greater input for NCAA reorganization, to [help us] control our own destinies. But when our presidents heard about my involvement, they got mad as hell at me, 'cause they didn't want to see another structure."

According to several college sources, Don Canham, Michigan's powerful and well-respected athletic director, pushed his Big Ten peers to join the CFA. Like his counterparts at big-time schools like Oklahoma and Texas, he was angered by the NCAA's newfound power and saw the CFA as a way to exert greater collective strength. But after one rather contentious meeting, they agreed to abide by unit rule—all would join the CFA or none. Soon after the vote failed, the Pac-8 schools—partners with the Big Ten in the Rose Bowl—joined their colleagues in spurning the new organization.

Despite the presence of sixty-three major schools—including the members of the Big Eight, SEC, SWC, ACC, and WAC and independents including Notre Dame, Penn State, and 1976 national champion Pittsburgh—the CFA was immediately devalued by the absence of the Big Ten and Pac-8. Without two of the most important conferences, the CFA would never be able to achieve its foremost goal: to become a unifying force for schools playing football at the highest level.

Instead, the CFA schools and the unofficial coalition of the Big Ten and Pac-8 (which became the Pac-10 with the addition of Arizona and Arizona State in 1978) spiraled into an athletic cold war. The two rival camps grew increasingly distrustful of each other. Some CFA members painted their counterparts as arrogant, hypocritical elitists who were determined to use the cumbersome NCAA structure against them, uniting with smaller schools against their own kind to thwart the CFA's big-time agenda. Some Big Ten and Pac-10 members considered the CFA a radical outfit intent on seceding from the NCAA and destroying college athletics.

"From the beginning, they pointed to us like we were a bunch of troublemakers, and I resented that," Penn State head coach Joe Paterno once said.

"I always thought if we could get all the big schools together, we could run things," Joyce said. "But I blame the Big Ten and Pac-10. They were the dogs in the manger."

Television was rarely mentioned in the early meetings of the CFA. Most talk centered on how the big-time schools could achieve some restructuring of the NCAA, which would allow them greater control of their own affairs. They also spent significant time talking about academics. Perhaps most important, the CFA gave the coaches—long ignored—a voice in the legislative process.

Eventually, the CFA schools started talking about their problems with the television plan. Many were disturbed by the new wrinkle known as the "super regional," which they believed was adversely affecting ratings and unfairly siphoning revenue from the major schools. Under the system, which began in the late 1970s, super regionals were used to televise one important game— such as Oklahoma versus Southern Cal—to as much as 98 percent of the country while beaming one lesser game involving marginal teams—such as Appalachian State versus the Citadel—to as few as two or three markets.

The way the NCAA distributed income based on these games represented a source of mounting friction. The teams that appeared on the huge network of perhaps 200 stations received the same amount as the teams that appeared on the small loop of stations sometimes numbering in single digits. Combined with the NCAA's policy of forcing ABC to carry other unattractive events, the super regional concept bred resentment among the major powers.

The overall system of allotting appearances became a frequent topic of heated discussion. The NCAA annually guaranteed the Ivy League, Southern, Mid-American, and other second-tier conferences a small number of appearances, and the majors believed ratings were suffering from this patronage game, which they saw as an assault on their valuable asset. After trending up for two decades, the average weekly rating (the percentage of television homes in use) and share (percentage of total TV homes) declined from 14.1/37 in 1976 to 13.2/37 in 1977, 12.0/35 in 1978, and 11.4/33 in 1979. Over the four-year period, the average audience for the Saturday games slipped from 10.04 million households to 8.7 million.

"It seemed to a lot of us," Neinas said, "that the NCAA was trying to appease the Stephen Horns of the world by showing so many of those schools. We saw it as a threat to us and a drain on the plan."

With college football divided against itself, Neinas and Duke grew apart. If they had been able to maintain their friendship, perhaps the split could have been repaired, perhaps college athletics could have been spared a long and bitter fight. But the two men who once worked side by side at the NCAA and opened and closed many bars together had been driven apart by their relationship to their mentor, Walter Byers. Duke saw Neinas and his fledgling organization as a threat to the NCAA, and he was determined to support the national organization and its newly asserted authority. Neinas saw Duke and his allies as puppets for the NCAA, and he was determined to fight for greater autonomy—with or without the Big Ten and Pac-10, which he considered out-of-touch elements of an unreasonable establishment.

"When Chuck went off to the Big Eight, he got wound up in the importance of football," Duke said. "The CFA was a product of that. Over time, he and I started seeing college football from two different perspectives."

With each passing year, Neinas, who owed his career to Byers, looked more like an insurgent competitor to the NCAA boss.

"I think Walter felt betrayed by Chuck," Hallock said.

Neinas believes the animosity between the two men can be traced to two specific events. During the late 1970s, Neinas served a two-year term on the football television committee and led a fight to liberalize the appearance rule, which prevailed over Byers's opposition. As the members of the committee walked out of the room on the day of the heated battle, Michigan's Don Canham whispered to his friend Neinas: "This is the last damned committee you'll ever be appointed to." He was right. Byers felt personally betrayed by his former subordinate, and made sure he never held another NCAA post.

The following year, Neinas was subpoenaed to appear before Congress on the issue of the NCAA's controversial enforcement tactics. He testified reluctantly, because he knew his appearance would brand him as a troublemaker at the ever sensitive NCAA headquarters. Neinas was hardly alone in criticizing the NCAA's heavy-handed procedures. Federal Judge Paul Goldman once said, in a moment of judicial hyperbole, "These . . . practices might be considered efficient, but so was Adolf Eichmann and so is the Ayatollah."

After University of Nevada-Las Vegas (UNLV) head basketball coach Jerry Tarkanian—a renegade figure who frequently clashed with the governing body—spent half the day lambasting the NCAA, Neinas took his seat and tried to present a much more reasonable assessment. He offered a well-founded, rational critique of the legislative process, suggesting that the NCAA should work more closely with the conferences and institutions and end some of the confrontational methods employed by the enforcement staff. Like many administrators, Neinas believed the makeup of the enforcement division and the Committee on Infractions constituted too close of an association between jury and executioner, and he was right. By sitting before Congress and challenging the linkage that Byers had himself created, Neinas appeared to be firing a shot across the NCAA's bow:

> ... It is important that the NCAA Committee on Infractions be divorced from the enforcement staff ... The impression of the close relationship between the Committee on Infractions and the enforcement staff leads the accused institution to conclude that the hearing procedure may be less than fair ...

Sitting near the rear of the hearing chamber, Dave Cawood and Tom Hansen, two of Byers's closest aides, carefully took notes. They did not look pleased.

"I knew I was on the shit list after that day," Neinas said. "Part of it was the timing, coming on after Tarkanian. It probably made some think I was an advocate of his, which I wasn't."

It did not matter that Neinas and Byers had actually discussed some of the same ideas over a meal a few months earlier. It did not matter that Byers had actually seemed receptive to his former subordinate's thoughts. In the hallowed halls of Congress, the same former aide who was playing an increasingly large role in the rebel CFA had publicly slapped Byers in the face.

The days of business lunches and rational discussions were over. Just like that. From that point on, Byers and Neinas essentially had no relationship, and the consequences of their feud would prove devastating to college athletics.

. . .

In the wake of the NCAA's power grab, many big-time coaches and administrators complained. Like most of his SEC colleagues, Alabama's Paul "Bear" Bryant saw the new national restrictions as an assault on his authority. "I'm upset about things and the players are shaken," he said. "They've done things at Chicago which would make a liar out of me."

When he filed suit against the NCAA in an attempt to overturn the travel squad limits—which would force him to leave about a third of his team at home—even his archrival, Auburn's Ralph "Shug" Jordan, joined the cause.

"We support Coach Bryant fully," said Mississippi State head coach Bob Tyler, who routinely suited up more than seventy players for road games. "We don't think there should be a limit whatsoever. We can't see a need for a limit."

The NCAA eventually prevailed in the courts. But the most significant challenge to the NCAA's new age regulations came from one of Bryant's assistant coaches.

When the NCAA imposed a national limit of eight assistant coaches for Division I schools, Bryant, who employed a total of fifteen, faced a dilemma. He was forced to cut his staff nearly in half.

Dude Hennessey, who had played for Bryant at Kentucky and coached under the Bear for sixteen years at Alabama, suddenly found himself without a whistle. Bryant arranged a job for him in the alumni office, but Hennessey was a football coach.

"I just wanted to keep on being a coach," Hennessey said. "I didn't want any money. I just wanted my job, which didn't seem like a real big thing to ask for."

Retaining large numbers of assistant coaches gave schools such as Alabama, Oklahoma, Texas, and Georgia advantages in recruiting and instruction. The fact that some smaller schools could not afford such a huge payroll was not their problem. Hennessey, who filed suit in federal court against the NCAA, struggled to understand how the governing body could pass a rule that eliminated his job.

"As far as I was concerned, the only person who could fire me was Coach Bryant, and he didn't want to," Hennessey said. "He was forced to cut his staff because a bunch of smaller schools told him to. That wasn't right. I thought we could reverse the whole trend if we stopped 'em on the coaching limits."

After months of delay, the federal court's Fifth Circuit ruled the NCAA's limits "reasonable" and "consistent" with its objectives. Hennessey lost his job, and the NCAA gained strength.

As the major powers started to oppose some aspects of the television plan, Byers kept a keen eye on all legal challenges to NCAA authority. In a February 8, 1979 letter to television committee chairman William J. Flynn, athletic director at Boston College, and NCAA president James Frank, president of Lincoln University, Byers summarized the association's legal footing:

> The Hennessey Court found that the limitations on the number of coaches were reasonable because they were consistent with the objective of curtailing . . . monopolistic practices of the big schools. . . . There are valid reasons to believe the television plan would stand the test of "reasonableness" . . .

Despite the legal about-face represented by the *Goldfarb* decision—which applied a tougher test to nonprofit organizations regarding the antitrust laws—and the growing unrest among some of the TV powers, on the surface at least, the *Hennessey* decision appeared to vindicate the NCAA's methods. It was a message to the disgruntled majors: Stop bitching, learn to live within the long arm of the NCAA, and hope that the small schools don't decide to ban football altogether.

But ABC was not so sure about the NCAA's legal standing,

especially after Ohio State made a deal with Warner Amex's fledgling Qube pay cable service to telecast several Buckeyes games in the Columbus, Ohio, market in 1978. During the early days of cable, Qube was like a local version of Home Box Office, and the service saw tremendous potential in using Ohio State games to lure subscribers. Anxious to avoid a protracted legal battle, the network agreed to a settlement, which the NCAA reluctantly joined at the last minute. The NCAA faced significant pressure from others to extend the exception to all, which represented a tremendous threat to ABC's exclusivity.

Several weeks later, ABC executive Jim Spence, all too aware of the growing resentment many CFA members harbored about the television plan, urged the NCAA Council to seek an antitrust exemption. But they ignored him. Undeterred, he drafted a letter to Byers, dated January 18,1979, in which he addressed the issue: " . . . We have not made congressional protection a prerequisite for our approval of revisions of the Plan; however, we have and do strongly urge the NCAA to entertain such a course of action . . . "

Tucked into a terse four-paragraph rebuke of the NCAA's cable policy, Spence's suggestion landed with a thud on Byers's desk. He was not the kind of man who liked to be told what to do—especially by some TV person from New York!

Writing back to Spence, Byers was blunt: "Whether the NCAA needs an exemption from the antitrust laws, via action of the United States Congress, is a question for the NCAA to determine."

"We would have loved to have had an antitrust exemption," said Tom Hansen, who served as the TV program director. "But we weren't sure we could get one. It would have meant going before Senator Ted Kennedy [who was chairman of the Senate Judiciary Committee] and a bunch of other liberals, so we didn't have a lock on an exemption by any means."

Nearly two decades after the NCAA blundered by not riding the NFL's coattails to an antitrust exemption, ABC clearly believed the package was vulnerable. The NCAA's decision not to seek protection suggested an unwillingness to deal with the situation. However, if the NCAA had taken its plan before Congress and failed, its posture with the membership would have been significantly weakened, and the likelihood of a challenge would have been greatly enhanced.

But a more fundamental question begged asking: From whom did the colleges require protection?

Spence and his colleagues were not worried about the government. They feared rebel colleges who knew the NCAA was holding a weak hand. In addition to protecting the NCAA from government and television entities, such legislation would have shielded the governing body from its own members, effectively codifying the Big Bluff. Just because the government had the power to pass such a law did not mean it had the right to do so.


After years of pushing for the creation of a super division of truly major football schools, the members of the CFA arrived at a special convention in 1978 with a sense of cautious optimism. The NCAA planned to split the large and diverse top group into Divisions 1-A and 1-AA.

The CFA schools supported a separate division including themselves and the Big Ten and Pac-10, which represented all of the schools who played football at the highest level. But the Big Ten and Pac-10, for reasons that they later struggled to explain, backed legislation that allowed members of the Ivy League—who played at the nonscholarship level—as well as several Pretender conferences—who offered scholarships but played something closer to Division II football—to remain in the highest division. The so-called Ivy League Amendment, which allowed members to be classified Division 1-A if they sponsored at least twelve sports, passed by only three votes. It made a joke of the whole process.

Many CFA members saw the Ivy League Amendment as a desperate attempt by the Big Ten and Pac-10 to prevent meaningful realignment, which would have reduced the two leagues' legislative clout against the numerically superior CFA. But leaders of the Big Ten and Pac-10 say they simply brokered a compromise that allowed the creation of a more sensible—if not perfect—division.

With frustrations mounting toward the NCAA and their rival camp, the CFA schools kept pushing for further realignment. But the cold war cast a menacing shadow. Big-time football was on an inevitable collision course. With itself.

# 9

# CALLING THE BLUFF

For the first three years of its existence, the College Football Association consisted of an idea and precious little else. Without any full-time employees or a headquarters to call its own, the CFA was nothing more than a fledgling group of presidents, athletic directors, coaches, and conference commissioners united by the notion—passed around like sacramental wine—that the nation's major football schools deserved the right to determine their own rules, preferably within the framework of the NCAA. Some of the officials certainly entertained the notion of leaving the NCAA to launch their own umbrella organization—Byers's worst nightmare—but without the Big Ten and Pac-10 such a structure could not possibly work, so it was never a serious option.

Except for the lack of autonomy for football, the CFA schools mostly benefited from their association with the NCAA, which offered them the chance to play in more than twenty national championships, including the annual basketball bonanza culminated by the increasingly popular and profitable Final Four. As they kept fighting for their own NCAA sanctioned super division, the holy grail of their existence, the CFA members huddled at their annual conventions and the various NCAA meetings to discuss the problems of the day and attempted to create a unified front on a variety of issues, such as the movement by a group of smaller schools to abolish the athletic scholarship, a threat to the very core of big-time college football.

In increasingly forceful terms, they complained about the NCAA's television policies. The nation wanted to see Notre Dame, Texas, Penn State, Oklahoma, and the other powers as often as possible and, to many within the CFA, the NCAA's appearance rule—which limited the majors to five exposures over two years—seemed arbitrarily and unrealistically severe. The CFA schools thought four appearances in a single year was a much better number. They resented the NCAA's patronage game, which used their strength as television draws to place a mounting number of small-college contests and extra events on the air. The 1977 to 1981 contract with ABC called for the network to telecast the Division 1-AA, II, and III playoffs; four regular season games in Division II and three in Division III; in addition to the national championships of wrestling, swimming, gymnastics, volleyball, and outdoor track.

The CFA talked a good game on the television issue, but as late as 1980, the organization remained little more than a bitch-and-moan society.

If the CFA was to exist as anything more than a figurative psychiatrist's couch for its members' frustrations, the organization needed a full-time executive director who could provide direction and continuity on their wide range of concerns. Chuck Neinas was the obivous choice. Well-liked among the presidents, coaches, and administrators, Neinas understood the problems of the NCAA from the inside and from the outside—both as a protege and nemesis of Byers. When he walked away from the Big Eight to accept the CFA appointment on April 1, 1980, Neinas set up shop in the Kansas City suburb of Leawood, Kansas, with administrative assistant Betty Keating, a rolodex, and an extremely limited mandate.

He was determined to do something about the television problem.

Several months later, out of the ongoing discussions about television, the CFA formed a TV study committee. Composed of Neinas, Oklahoma law professor Dan Gibbens, Penn State head coach Joe Paterno, Big Eight commissioner Carl James, and Clemson athletic director Bill McClellan, the group secretely created the framework for a possible CFA television plan and marked time until the June 1981 convention in Dallas. ABC's exclusive contract with the NCAA expired after the 1981 season, and many CFA schools thought they could do better for themselves after satisfying their obligations under that deal.

At the same time, the NCAA's television committee proceeded in finalizing the association's 1982 to 1985 plan, presuming the participation of the CFA schools. After all, no school or group of schools had ever declined to participate—not since the NCAA's scare tactics had coerced Pennsylvania and Notre Dame into surrenduring their rights in 1951, which created the framework not only for the television plan but for the entire power structure of the modern NCAA.

For several years, the NCAA had discussed pursuing a two-network strategy, which would generate more money and allow the possibility for more appearances by the major powers. In the spring of 1981, Byers and his associates decided the time was right. The two-network approach was a central part of the NCAA's principles of negotiation for the 1982 to 1985 period, which were circulated among the membership and subject to a majority vote.

The CFA's board of directors advised their members to abstain from voting on the principles of negotiation, which, given the overwhelming majority of smaller schools who benefited from the patronage game, had always represented a rubber stamp for the NCAA leadership. Neinas and his associates believed they could extricate themselves from the NCAA television plan—and seize their TV rights once and for all—by abstaining from the vote. It would not be so easy.

Jerry McConnell, a reporter for *The Daily Oklahoman* in Oklahoma City, learned of the CFA's strategy and reported it on May 3, five days before the voting deadline. The plan was a secret the CFA schools wanted to protect, but when it leaked, McConnell emerged as a conduit between the central figures of the NCAA and CFA, who were no longer speaking to each other but all too willing to make their case in print.

"A vote for the principles," Neinas told McConnell, "would indicate a commitment to the program. A vote in the negative might be interpreted as a willingness to acquiesce to the vote of the majority. Abstention with notice indicates you have not voted and are reserving your options."

Tom Hansen, Neinas's former colleague and current NCAA TV program director, spoke for Byers: "The NCAA legal counsel's position is that abstaining from voting does not give the CFA members the right to negotiate their own contract."

Five days later, at the deadline for submitting votes, Hansen ratcheted up the pressure on the CFA by hinting at possible sanctions against schools that participated in a separate TV deal: "The NCAA would consider that to be a very serious matter . . . that would be referred to the Committee on Infractions."

Regardless of the merits of the NCAA plan, the CFA schools deserved the right to choose to participate or not. The CFA schools owned their television rights as surely as they owned their radio rights and the tickets they sold for admission to their stadiums. The individual schools and conferences controlled their own television rights for basketball, and the NCAA had never attempted to seize authority over TV coverage of the colleges' second most important sport. The contrast between the two positions was difficult even for the NCAA to reconcile. But as the NCAA struggled to maintain its franchise, Byers and his officials could not, would not, concede the most fundamental of points. Acquiescence on television matters should not have been required as a condition of membership, and raising the specter of probationary sanctions for dissenting on the issue diminished the enforcement process and the ideals of the NCAA itself.

For several weeks, the two sides traded jabs in the press.

"The drift of the NCAA plan," Neinas told *The Daily Okla-homan*, "has been to provide more and more money for a social welfare system."

"When you belong to a democratic organization," Hansen countered, "when the vote is counted, you are ... subject to the provisions of the membership."

In a memorandum to chief executive officers of member institutions after the CFA urged its members to abstain, NCAA president James Frank dismissed the CFA's property rights claims. "These arguments demonstrate a lack of understanding of the legislation of the NCAA and the law of voluntary associations," he wrote.

But Frank, the president of tiny Lincoln University, was the one with the comprehension problem. Just because the NCAA had assumed a right for thirty years did not mean that it had been legally or justly conferred. The CFA schools were not talking about randomly choosing which NCAA rules to obey, as Frank and others suggested. In no way was their property rights dispute equivalent to a bunch of schools announcing they would start paying players or engaging in some other illicit activity.

Responding to Frank's memo—which many believed had been dictated by Byers—Georgia president Fred Davison, chairman of the CFA board of directors, seemed equally determined when he wrote a confidential letter to CFA member presidents:

> ... I have some difficulty reconciling the tone of President Frank's memo with membership in a voluntary organization. The current situation involving football television is a characterization of what is wrong with the NCAA. There has been no concern about the NCAA's inability to accommodate the diverse interests of its membership. The football television issue is an example of folks not on our level determining what we can do ... (Also) ... it is unreasonable to assign shady motives to [the CFA]. I

find it hard to accept that the CFA's activities in the area of television would be compared with illegal payments to student-athletes . . . . If the NCAA believes that threat and coercion are necessary to obtain adherance to a questionable television policy, it would appear to be operating from a fundamentally weak position . . . .

The number of abstentions by the CFA schools became a matter of some controversy, but no one was surprised when the principles of negotiation were overwhelmingly approved by the vast NCAA membership. As the NCAA moved forward with its own two-network plan, Wiles Hallock, chairman of the NCAA television commitee, flew to Dallas to try to defuse the situation at the CFA Convention. Hallock, the commissioner of the Pac-10, urged the members of the CFA to reconsider their course.

"The principles are no longer principles . . . but have been adopted as association requirements," he told the CFA leadership, "and member institutions of the NCAA are obligated to observe these policies."

Many CFA members did not appreciate the lecture, which had the ring of a threat. Instead of spooking them into compliance, Hallock's terse speech hardened their resolve. The CFA leaders were determined not to tip their hand, but they started preparing to test the waters with the networks.

During the early stages of the increasingly tense impasse, Jerry McConnell predicted in print and in his conversations with the various parties that the issue would eventually end up in court.

"I all but laughed at him," said Dan Gibbens, the Oklahoma law professor who helped devise the abstention strategy. "I kept saying there was no way such an astute manager like Walter Byers would let it go that far. There were too many reasons for Walter to work it out, to compromise."

. . .

While the CFA considered its options, the NCAA television committee started negotiating with all three networks.

When the NCAA started pursuing the deals with two networks, ABC executives swallowed and accepted the parameters of the new era. But they didn't have to like it. "It was like someone telling us we had to share our toys," recalled longtime director of college sports Donn Bernstein.

Despite the unmistakable drag on ratings caused by all those marginal games, the college football package remained one of the hottest properties in all of televised sports. Advertisers clamored to reach one of the best demographics in television, which drove the price of a 30-second spot from $25,000 to $48,000 between 1975 and 1980—smaller than the NFL's meteoric jump during the period but still huge by any reasonable measure.

The two-network approach—probably first advanced by Beano Cook, then the public relations director for CBS Sports—would allow the NCAA to put more games on the air and presumably generate more revenue. Byers and the NCAA carefully crafted the plan so that the two networks would not be competing directly for viewers, which they believed would allow them to maximize the advantages of the series without overexposing the product.

The new strategy also exploited Byers's skills as a negotiator in a profoundly different way. With three networks interested in college football but only two packages available, he could play the networks against each other and presumably drive up the price.

Negotiating first with ABC, which owned a thirty-day exclusive window, and then with all three, he used ABC's desire to keep the sport at all costs and the competition between CBS and NBC to his advantage.

After four sessions with ABC, Byers and Jim Spence, the network's senior vice president, met at a coastal hotel in Newport, Rhode Island, for what both anticipated as the final negotiation. Arthur Watson, the president of NBC Sports, and Van Gordon

Sauter, the president of CBS Sports, waited in other parts of the hotel for their first negotiating sessions. Sauter stood in his room and watched the sailboats drift by, wishing he could be out on the water instead of awaiting his first sit-down with Byers, the stubborn man from Kansas City whose disdain for television executives was well known.

As Byers and Spence took their seats, Spence said he was ready to make a deal—for $131.5 million over five years.

Byers never flinched. "No, you know what the number is," he said forcefully.

Spence sat in his chair for a moment or two without saying a word. He was not going to lose college football. He could not lose college football. College football was a significant part of ABC Sports, nearly as important as *Monday Night Football* and the Olympic Games. But he needed to be able to go back to his bosses and tell them he had shaved something—anything!—off Byers's asking price, which was a mere $250,000 more than he had offered.

He gave Byers a stern look. "You mean you're not willing to bend a little?"

"You know the number," Byers said cooly.

Determined to keep the package, Spence faced a dilemma Roone Arledge had confronted on numerous occasions. Should he walk away and risk losing the game over such a small amount of money or simply give in and admit he was beaten?

"Walter, if ABC commits $131,750,000—just so we're clear on this—do we have a deal?" Spence said.

"Yes," Byers responded with the hint of a smile.

After several more meetings with NBC and CBS, Byers and CBS's Sauter agreed to the exact same figure, churning even more mileage out of Spence's determination to keep the package. By skillfully manipulating all three networks, Byers managed to double the NCAA's network television revenue from the last season of the 1977 to 1981 contract to the first season of the 1982 to 1985 pact, an amazing feat under any circumstances.

Byers was a master negotiator who knew how to get what he

wanted when he sat down with television executives, because he understood their business and he was always prepared to walk away. He knew how to exploit their needs and desires to his ultimate advantage. He knew how to be a stubborn, confrontational hard-ass and make it work to his benefit. But he was about to learn how one man's greatest strength can be turned into a paralyzing weakness.

In the summer of 1981, as NBC languished in third place, Arthur Watson wanted to experiment with college football in prime time. It was a gamble, because no broadcast network had ever devoted the precious Saturday evening programming bloc to regular college football coverage, but NBC had very little to lose. Mired in an historic slump, the Peacock Network was desperate, so chairman Grant Tinker indulged Watson's unconventional thinking. Since the late 1960s, the NCAA had allowed ABC to turn a limited number of big games into prime time made-for-television spectaculars, and blockbuster showdowns like Pittsburgh–Penn State, Nebraska–Alabama, and Southern Cal–UCLA had produced some of the biggest Nielsens in series history. Even if football failed to generate blockbuster ratings every week, at least it would pull decent numbers while preventing the network from throwing millions upon millions into risky development deals for suspect comedies and dramas.

Who knew? The bold idea could turn into NBC's answer to *Monday Night Football*, which had once seemed like a ridiculous proposition for struggling ABC. Watson did not have to remind his boss that both CBS and NBC had passed on *Monday Night Football* before the NFL took it to ABC, or that perennial underdog ABC had exploited the landmark series in its unlikely climb to the top of the network ratings.

After offering the prime time slot to the NCAA, NBC started negotiating with the CFA, which was intrigued by the idea of Saturday night football. In mid-August, the CFA shocked the college sports establishment by announcing a four-year, $180-million deal with NBC—a direct challenge to the NCAA's authority that threatened to diminish and potentially destroy the ABC and CBS contracts. The pact was contingent on the participation of a large but unspecified number of the CFA schools, especially big-name programs like Notre Dame, Alabama, Nebraska, Georgia, and Texas.

Under the terms of the deal, teams participating in the CFA contract would grant NBC the rights to their home games, because home teams controlled the rights to television decisions. If the CFA and NCAA ended up competing, as most CFA officials expected, it was possible for CFA member teams to appear on the NCAA package during road games against schools not participating in the CFA deal.

The CFA leadership expected a large majority of the membership to sign up for their voluntary plan, which allowed four appearances per team each season and split all the revenue among sixty-one schools. Between 1978 and 1981, CFA schools appeared in 54.6 percent of the telecasts but collected only 48.5 percent of the revenue, a disparity the NBC contract would immediately end. At the same time, many CFA schools expected to be able to rake in additional dollars from cable, which was just reaching critical mass.

During the period, Oklahoma head coach Barry Switzer remarked, "People want to see good programs . . . and we have a marketable product." Like many of his colleagues, Switzer saw pay TV as a source of untapped wealth. "I've got to believe that people will pay $4 to sit at home and watch Oklahoma play," he said, anticipating $2 million annually in such fees.

CFA officials set a September deadline for members to approve or reject the NBC offer, but the vote was considered a mere formality.

Then the NCAA played a familiar card.

Stunned by the announcement, the NCAA Council, meeting at a resort in Oregon, issued a statement threatening to expel any school that participated in the NBC deal. Back at the home office near Kansas City, Tom Hansen issued a press release raising the specter of probation and expulsion if the CFA schools consummated the deal. Enforcement proceedings could begin soon after the CFA schools signed up for the contract, both Hansen and the chairman of the Committee on Infractions warned. "In this case, I wouldn't think it would take a great deal of work to discover whether or not they had violated our rule," Hansen said.

Thirty years after the NCAA used the members of the Ivy League to coerce Pennsylvania into abandoning its own television deal, the governing body was prepared to exploit the Big Bluff once more to threaten the vast majority of the major football schools into compliance. But this was not 1951, and the situation was much more complicated.

The talk of probation and bowl bans confronted three major postseason games with the potentially difficult choice of defying the NCAA or abandoning their conference partners. Mickey Holmes, the executive director of the Sugar Bowl, hosted by the SEC champion, pledged his commitment to the SEC and, by extension, the CFA. The Orange Bowl, hosted by the Big Eight champion, and the Cotton Bowl, hosted by the SWC champion, declined to take a public position, but both games owed their existence to CFA members. If the NCAA expelled the CFA rebels, the various other nonaligned postseason bowls, such as the Gator, Liberty, and Fiesta, would be forced to choose between NCAA certification and the participation of most of the sport's traditional powers. During the 1980 season, CFA members accounted for twenty-three of the thirty bowl teams.

If the CFA maintained solidarity during the crisis, many of their leaders believed, the NCAA would eventually cave. Expulsion was a dangerous option for the NCAA as well as the television rebels. After all, without the members of the Big Eight, SEC, SWC, ACC, and WAC plus major independents including Notre Dame, Penn State, Miami, and Florida State, the NCAA would be reduced to twenty truly major teams and several hundred small colleges. Next stop, NAIA.

Angered by the NCAA's decision to draw a line in the sand, the

CFA leadership reacted predictably. "There is a risk of being as hard-nosed at this point as the NCAA is," Big Eight commissioner Carl James told reporters. "I don't know what they hope to accomplish by using a big stick."

Fred Davison, the usually mild-mannered academician, found it difficult to contain his contempt. "Clearly, the NCAA and Walter Byers had forgotten who they worked for," he said. "At some point, Walter started confusing the NCAA with himself."

Peter Flawn, the University of Texas president, and William Banowsky, the University of Oklahoma president, discussed the situation on the phone and contemplated a response. "They had no right to threaten us," Flawn said. Banowsky said, "It is virtually impossible for us to overstate our resentment of the NCAA."

With the rest of the college athletics establishment—including the Big Ten and Pac-10—lined up behind the NCAA, the CFA was feeling pressure from several different directions.

"We thought what the CFA was doing was a wrong and a product of greed," Duke said.

In a memo to Flawn dated August 24, 1981, Texas faculty athletic representative Ronald M. Brown outlined his views on the situation and analyzed the NCAA's goverance problems:

> . . . The situation is analogous to state legislatures of 20–30 years ago, when the rural votes were controlling the destinies of the more populous cities; in this instance, however, one institution, one vote creates the inequity because of the broad variations in institutional size and, therefore, athletic programs . . .

As the two sides moved toward confrontation, ABC's Jim Spence was flooded with telephone calls. Most disturbing was a conversation with Joe Paterno, who vented for more than an hour about his frustrations with Byers and the NCAA. "I came away convinced the CFA people were serious, that they weren't going to back down," Spence said. Fearing for ABC's franchise, Spence immediately buzzed Arledge, the one man who could hold his own with the man from Kansas City.

The next morning, Spence and Arledge spent a lengthy telephone call trying to talk some sense into the head of the NCAA. They urged him to be smart and use some of his well-known negotiating acumen to broker a deal with the CFA people. "Walter pretty much blew us off," Spence said. "I don't think he understood the gravity of the situation."

At this critical juncture in the history of college athletics, the NCAA needed a dynamic leader who was not a captive of his own arrogance, a man who was not afraid to surrender an indefensible point in order to save his union. But unfortunately, the NCAA was stuck with Walter Byers, who stubbornly refused to concede the CFA schools' property rights claims and persisted in treating them less like constituents than like misbehaving children. He was a man of tremendous strengths who ultimately allowed his greatest achievement to be undermined by a rather prosaic weakness.

When NBC offered to pay half of any legal fees incurred by the CFA if the fight went to court, Byers lashed out publicly. "It's a sad day for college sports if athletic policy is to be dictated by a television network and educational institutions surrender their independence of action to NBC's corporate headquarters," he told reporters.

He thought it was much more appropriate for those educational institutions to surrender their independence of action to the NCAA, which did not strike him as the least bit contradictory or ironic.

Byers was conspicuously silent throughout most of the period. Many people advised him to pick up the phone and call the key CFA people, to try to broker a compromise, but that was not his style. He may have been the greatest negotiator in sports, but he did not know how to negotiate from a position of such weakness.

Usually, Byers dispatched associates such as Hansen, Hallock, and Dave Cawood to carry the NCAA banner, preferring to blend into the background of his bloated bureaucracy. Jerry McConnell, the Oklahoma City reporter, kept phoning Byers and leaving messages, but the calls were always returned by Hansen.

Finally, after yet another instance of the same routine, McConnell said, "Look, Tom, I really need to get a statement from Walter on this!"

"You just got one."

"I think Walter took the position that if they were dumb enough to think they had a better way he'd let them find out how wrong they were," said the NCAA's Cawood.


Inside his modest office in surburban Kansas City, Neinas spent most of his time burning up the phone lines, working with other CFA leaders to develop a strategy to deal with the situation. As the various CFA schools considered their options, Neinas took the NCAA's expulsion talk seriously. He started formulating rudimentary plans for CFA championships in several sports, should the CFA schools be kicked out of the NCAA.

"If we didn't have an NCAA, we would have to create one," said the SEC's McWhorter. "You have got to have some kind of national organization to control collegiate athletics. . . . But there is an honorable way to deal with membership in a voluntary organization, if indeed that is what [the NCAA] is. The decision is whether or not [there is] too big a price to pay to be a member of that organization."

At a mountain villa in Lago di Garda, Italy, where he was spending the summer with his brother, Father Joyce stayed informed on the situation by reading dispatches from Neinas and others. He knew what they were contemplating. "I was ambivalent about what they were talking about," he said. "We didn't want to be seen as the dogs in the manger, but we had to do something . . . "

The NCAA's outdated system of governance was never more

apparent than in the case of Charles Alan Wright, a University of Texas law professor who chaired the NCAA's Committee on Infractions. His decision to threaten CFA schools—including his own—with probation placed him in direct conflict with his boss, who was a strong proponent of the CFA.

"We did not see eye to eye on the subject," Wright said.

Three weeks after the NBC contract was announced, while preparing for a constitutional law class, Wright was startled when his secretary walked into his office with a process server. The document said the university was suing the NCAA in state court in an attempt to overturn the association's television monopoly. In the papers filed with the court, L. O. Morgan, chairman of the Texas Athletic Council for Men, said, " . . . the NCAA has been waging a campaign to coerce and intimidate CFA members to elect not to be bound by the CFA-NBC contract . . . " As an appointed NCAA official, Wright qualified as a representative of the governing body, which allowed his university to serve him—and for Peter Flawn to make a point about who represented the University of Texas.

"I thought the case had no merit," Wright said. "But it was still pretty unbelievable . . . to be served by my own employer."

Flawn realized it would be difficult to make a case that the NCAA had violated state law, but he felt the need to respond in some meaningful way. "We had to react," he said. "We had a situation where an outside bureaucracy was asserting itself into the business affairs of the university. We could not let that go unchecked."

Several hours later, the Board of Regents of the University of Oklahoma and the University of Georgia Athletic Association filed suit against the NCAA in U.S. District Court in Oklahoma City. The plaintiffs sought to overturn the NCAA's television controls as a violation of the Sherman Antitrust Act.

For months, some NCAA officials and allies had derided the CFA's television maneuvers as nothing more than a scheme to promote a hidden agenda: securing greater leverage to force further restructuring—which was at least partially true. The television dispute was a symptom of a chronic disease that had poisoned the CFA schools against the NCAA. It was inexorably linked to the frustrations caused by the parity legislation, which led directly to the formation of the CFA, which split major college football into two rival groups, which took on a life of its own and led inevitably to the television fight. But the Oklahoma-Georgia lawsuit proved the CFA schools were serious about the television issue for its own merits as well as for what it repesented about their relationship with the NCAA. By making a federal case out of the television dispute, the CFA schools were essentially calling the NCAA's bluff—demanding that the governing body prove that it had the right to force them to surrender their television rights under the threat of coercion.

"We got no real attention until the TV contract came up," Georgia's Davison said during the crisis. "And when we realized how little control we had over some matters, such as property rights, it made us all begin to think about how these things hurt us financially. We have to have more of a say, because Byers isn't going to come down here and bail us out if we fail."

Several weeks after the lawsuit was filed, Neinas moved his office from Leawood, Kansas—just a few miles from the NCAA headquarters in Mission—to Boulder, Colorado. "There was a lot of talk about it being just a personal dispute between Walter and me, and the board thought we needed to move out of the NCAA's shadow, which meant leaving Kansas City," Neinas said.

After dozens of long distance telephone calls among the various leaders, Oklahoma and Georgia agreed to file the suit on behalf of the CFA, whose members voted to share legal costs. Both Davison and Banowsky enjoyed the complete backing of their ruling bodies. Both men leaned heavily on distinguished professors of law in formulating the suit: Georgia's Ralph Beaird and Oklahoma's Dan Gibbens. Even among the CFA schools, the lawsuit was greeted with significant ambivalence.

Byers skillfully made many CFA schools think twice about the

NBC contract when he hastily arranged a special convention to consider the restructuring of the NCAA—set for early December in St. Louis. The apparent attempt at conciliation on the part of the governing body gave hope to some CFA fence-straddlers, who wanted to improve their television position but also desperately desired to avoid a nasty fight. If they could achieve meaningful re-alignment, many reasoned, the new structure would allow them to assume greater control of the NCAA television package, which meant they would not need to accept the NBC deal. Some schools harbored legitimate fears about being placed on probation or expelled from the NCAA, which was tantamount to being banished from big-time sports. Still others wanted to proceed with the NBC contract, regardless of the consequences.

When the votes were counted in late August—after the NCAA announced the special convention—the CFA membership approved the NBC package, but by a lackluster 33–20 majority, with eight abstentions. Neinas and his associates stalled the network for more time, believing they could change enough minds to make the deal work.

In mid September, Oklahoma president William Banowsky and his old friend Norman Topping, the former president of Southern Cal, bumped into each other in Los Angeles. With Marcus Allen and the Trojans set to meet Marcus Dupree and the Sooners at the Coliseum two weeks later in the seventeenth No. 1 versus No. 2 showdown in college football history, the two men exchanged the usual good-natured chest-thumping about the big game. Banowsky said he was looking forward to USC's visit to Norman in 1982.

"Well, you fellows are about to get out of the NCAA," Topping said.

Banowsky was dumbfounded. He said he harbored no such plans, but as the crisis unfolded, he didn't know how his university would ultimately respond to the NCAA's demands—or if the NCAA would act on its threats.

"We'll be there to play you unless the NCAA instructs us that we can't play you," Topping said.

. . .

When representatives from more than 800 NCAA member institutions arrived in St. Louis three weeks before Christmas, the NCAA Council publicly supported a plan to create a smaller and more cohesive Division 1-A. The membership, after substantial and sometimes heated debate, pared the football fast lane from 137 schools to 98, reversing the controversial Ivy League Amendment and banishing the Ivy League and several other conferences to Division 1-AA.

With no satisfactory way to classify big-time football schools competitively, the NCAA created a new kind of standard that reflected the sport's transformation into an entertainment business driven by box-office demands. In order to qualify for Division 1-A membership, universities were required to have averaged football attendance of at least 17,000 fans over the previous four years or to play in a stadium with a capacity of at least 30,000. At the time, nearly every team in the five most prominent conferences averaged more than 35,000 fans per game, and powers including Michigan, Tennessee, Ohio State, Penn State, and LSU routinely jammed more than 80,000 paying customers into their stadiums. The SEC and Big Ten averaged more than 60,000 fans per game, while some Division 1-A conferences struggled to reach 15,000.

It was not a perfect standard, and when the NCAA crunched the numbers, some marginal schools, including those in the Pacific Coast Athletic Association and Mid-American Conference, survived, clinging to Division 1-A membership like a life raft with a slow leak. The CFA's so-called Division IV concept, which applied a tougher standard to create a true super division of about eighty-one teams, failed to attract enough votes.

The elimination of the Ivy League was hailed as an historic triumph for the major schools, who considered the tradition-rich but obsolete conference the foremost example of the NCAA's structural flaws.

In an impassioned plea on the convention floor, Joe Paterno—once a halfback at Ivy League member Brown—crystallized the argument that had symbolized the frustrations of the major schools for years. "The Ivy League is in another world all their own," he said. "I'm in the real world."

Lamenting that "young football players have become commercial pawns," Harvard coach Joe Restic took the demotion like a slap in the face. "We were victimized by a war we aren't involved in," he said.

But even as the major teams achieved a greater measure of like-minded autonomy for football, the NCAA refused to allow the television issue to be brought before the convention. The CFA felt duped, especially after the NCAA announced that it would propose legislation strengthening its television controls at the annual convention a month later.

Angered by the rebuff, Oklahoma's Banowsky dominated a raucus postconvention meeting of CFA members. "That group [the NCAA] is going to correct a vulnerability [at the Houston convention] and give it the right to exercise controls," he said. He urged the others to join him in forging ahead with the NBC contract, which network officials believed could be salvaged with the participation of perhaps thirty schools, as long as the group included the most important powers, such as Alabama, Notre Dame, Oklahoma, Georgia, Nebraska, and Texas.

"Oklahoma will sign up, provided nine other CFA members join in, including one from our Big Eight conference and our close neighbor, Texas," Banowsky said.

"Don't worry about your friend across the Red River. We'll sign," shouted Texas faculty representative Ron Brown.

Clemson president Bill Atchley jumped to the floor and urged his colleagues to continue the fight. "Stand up and be counted!" he said. "The NCAA can't afford to kick us out!"

When the final deadline arrived about a week later, however, the CFA reluctantly abandoned the NBC contract. Not enough schools were willing to stick their necks out, especially with the

Oklahoma-Georgia lawsuit pending in the courts, which many believed would decide the issue once and for all or at least provide the leverage to make a deal with the NCAA.

On January 10, 1982, the first day of the annual convention in Houston, Texas president Peter Flawn obtained a temporary restraining order from a state judge in Austin preventing the NCAA from voting on the new television legislation. But the maneuver proved to be little more than an irritant. The NCAA's attorneys quickly found another state judge to vacate the order, and the association went about the business of strengthening its television hand.

By a vote of 631–178, the vast NCAA membership approved a regulation that represented a de facto codification of the powers that the governing body had been exercising for three decades, while also providing authority over the burgeoning cable television arena: "The telecasting, cablecasting, or otherwise televising of intercollegiate football games of member institutions shall be controlled by bylaws enacted by the Association." All sixty-one CFA schools voted against the measure—which affected them the most—but the outcome was never in doubt. Once again, the numerically superior smaller schools—most of them unaffected by the NCAA's TV procedures, some others bribed with guaranteed appearances—overwhelmed the major powers, rendering the December restructuring a victory of dubious worth.

If they could not control their own television rights, what good was realignment?

On the same day, the association threw a bone to the CFA forces by expanding the television committee from thirteen to eighteen members, reserving nine slots for officials from Division 1-A programs. But the move served only to remind the majors that despite all the talk of creating a more equitable system, schools like Penn State and Texas still carried no more weight on television affairs than Boise State and Whittier.

Byers hailed the legislative changes, which he said "provided a far more flexible TV procedure." He added that the struggle over

TV rights had proven "an extremely useful exercise that brought about an examination of our TV procedures."

The smug attitude displayed by the NCAA boss—who had used the NCAA's structural deficiencies to write himself a big fat blank check—served only to further infuriate some CFA leaders. Undaunted by the new NCAA legislation, Oklahoma's Board of Regents issued a statement condeming the NCAA's actions and reaffirming its "unstinting resolve to prosecute dilligently its suit" to "determine judicially the ownership of its television and cable-cast property rights . . . without fear of reprisals and sanctions" from the NCAA.

Dan Gibbens, who represented Oklahoma on CFA and Big Eight committees, is widely credited with suggesting the legal challenge to Banowsky and the Board of Regents. "We had no thought of a lawsuit until after [the NCAA] started threatening us with probation," he said. "After that, I thought we had two choices: go forward with the NBC contract or take it to court, where I thought our chances were good."

Several members of the Board of Regents pushed for the selection of Andy Coats, who was gearing up for a campaign for mayor of Oklahoma City, to head the legal team. He was joined in the effort by Clyde Muchmore, his colleague at the Oklahoma City firm of Crowe & Dunlevy. Phillip Hochberg, a specialist in communication law, represented the CFA and also played a major role in the suit.

"The NCAA's behavior was criminal," Muchmore said. "Their coercion kept the market from working, but no one had ever called them on it."

Rather than asking the court to invalidate the NCAA's controls on the property rights issue, which they considered risky, Coats and Muchmore decided to attack the NCAA in the context of the Sherman Antitrust Act. They built a strategy around what they argued were two violations of the code, a landmark statute passed late in the nineteenth century and designed to prevent the rise of anticompetitive monopolies. The plaintiffs argued that the NCAA artificially limited the number of games on the air which, coupled with the governing body's coercive tactics, represented a restraint of trade. They also asserted that price-fixing resulted from these practices, an important litmus test for proving antitrust violations.

"By the time we got to the trial, I realized the property rights issue had some problems, since the NCAA was a voluntary organization," Coats said. "But I thought the antitrust aspects were awfully strong in our favor. I really expected the NCAA to cut a deal."

But Byers and the NCAA were in no mood to compromise.

In fact, in the spring of 1982, the NCAA utilized its newly acquired authority over cablecasting rights to secure a two-year, $15-million supplemental package with WTBS, the Atlanta-based cable superstation.

By the time the trial convened inside the federal courthouse in Oklahoma City in June 1982, both sides had defiantly dug in their heels. Oklahoma and Georgia had filed the complaint in the federal court of Judge Luther Eubanks, but Eubanks, an Oklahoma graduate and well-known football fan, quickly recused himself. None of the local judges wanted to touch the case, so the Tenth Circuit appointed Judge Juan Burciaga of New Mexico to hear the case.

For seven days, Coats and Muchmore and NCAA counsels Robert Harry and Richard Andrews paraded their expert witnesses before the court. Coats attempted to prove that the NCAA wielded what is known in legal parlance as "market power"—which essentially meant that it was the only game in town and therefore enjoyed all the benefits of a monopoly, including price-fixing. Harry tried to prove that the NCAA was just another supplier of television programming, like Major League Baseball, the National Football League, and any number of Hollywood production companies. Advertisers, Harry told the court, enjoyed a multitude of choices.

But for all the complexity of the cumbersome antitrust law, the issue boiled down to several basic questions: Did the NCAA constitute a monopoly? And, if so, did the law apply to such an organization, with its supposed nonprofit, egalitarian aims? Anyone could see the NCAA was holding a very poor hand. While Coats methodically attacked the NCAA's practices—from its strong-arm tactics to its ability to set rights fees—Harry was left manning a defense built largely around a social argument. Aside from attempting to block Coats's monopoly assertions, he tried to prove that the NCAA plan was legal because it sought to minimize the effects of unrestrained television on attendance and on the competitive balance of the game. Clearly, these were among the foremost aims of the plan, but their legality had never been established.

Using the same defense Joseph Rauh had conceived three decades before, Harry maintained that the NCAA series met the "rule of reason" test established in antitrust precedent, arguing that the television plan was consistent with the organization's "educational, sports, and private association" purposes.

The pivotal moment in the trial was the reluctant appearance of Byers, who looked more than a bit perturbed, as comfortable on the stand as a king being cross-examined by his lowly subjects. Several times, Burciaga admonished him for trying to evade Coats's questions.

The lawsuit was limited to dealing with the specifics of the football television plan, and no one was attempting to overturn the association's right to control the TV contract for March Madness or shutter the enforcement division. But in a philosophical sense, the concept of the NCAA was on trial and so, by extension, was Byers. The mammouth bureaucracy created by the ultimate bureaucrat had gradually accumulated tremendous power on the basis of majority rule, and television was simply the most visible symbol of this flawed attempt at democracy. The lawsuit was about power and money, but it was also about the right to belong to a voluntary organization without being forced to surrender every last ounce of institutional autonomy.

During his cross-examination of Byers, Coats produced a

memorandum from Hansen to Byers concerning the establishment of rights payments. In part, it read: " . . . First . . . the (TV) Committee set the 1976–1977 rights fee at $501,538 for a national game and $380,000 for a regional game . . . "

The passage was underlined. In the margin, Byers had scrawled, "Do NOT use this language in inter-ofc [sic] memos, in minutes, in external communications. These are nec [sic] to ABC in response to their request for advice."

The implications were obvious. Anyone who had ever been involved with the television committee knew the NCAA routinely negotiated an aggregate rights payment with the network and then "recommended" how the network distribute the revenue in individual game rights fees. The recommendations were merely a formality, which appeared to prove Coats's assertions that the NCAA enjoyed price-fixing capabilities.

"Is it true," Coats asked Byers, "that most years, whatever the NCAA recommended, that's what the price was?"

"That's true, but ABC had the authority to change it," Byers said.

Of the memorandum from Hansen, which suggested that the NCAA had something to hide, Byers said: "I admonished him about the choice of words. I thought it inappropriate."

While the NCAA's counsel tried to prove that the colleges had the right to negotiate directly with the chosen network, Coats produced witnesses who refuted the notion. The NCAA could not provide any instance in which a college had negotiated directly with a network. Neinas related an exchange between ABC official Jan Sunberg and Alabama official Charlie Scott during a panel discussion about television during the 1982 CFA Convention in Dallas. According to Neinas, Scott—a past member of the NCAA Council—posed the following hypothetical question: Suppose Alabama and Georgia, who were not scheduled to play that year, were both undefeated at the end of the season and playing for the national championship. What if Alabama said it wanted $1.5 million for the showdown—instead of the $1.1 million rights fee paid for other games that season?

"Miss Sundberg indicated that individual game fees could not vary and that ABC did not want to get into a bidding contest for these games," Neinas said.

The plaintiffs scored further points by introducing evidence about the controversial "super regional" system. Witnesses testified that the 1981 Oklahoma–Southern Cal game, which appeared on 207 stations across the country, received the same rights fee as the Citadel–Appalachian State game, which was seen on four stations, and the Jackson State–Mississippi Valley State game, which was seen on two stations.

The plaintiffs produced witnesses who suggested competition would increase revenue for the major powers by letting free market forces work. However, Byers struck a much different chord. He predicted that saturation and overexposure would reduce revenue for most programs. He predicted that by deregulating the market, the networks would seize the advantage. He predicted a dramatic decline in attendance and the rise of "very narrow TV aristocracy."

On September 14, 1982, after two months of deliberation, Burciaga shook the college sports establishment by issuing a complete repudiation of the NCAA's television practices, branding the system a "classic cartel" and rejecting the social arguments proffered as justification for the monopoly. Burciaga agreed with the plaintiffs' assertion that televised college football constituted a relevant market of its own, rejecting the NCAA's contention that the sport was merely part of the larger relevant market of all televison programs. He also concluded that the association's television controls represented per se price-fixing and violated Section 1 of the Sherman Act. His action voided the NCAA's contracts with ABC, CBS, and WTBS and enjoined the association from entering into similar deals. In part, his decision read:

> . . . (the NCAA enjoys) almost absolute control over
> the supply of college football which is made available

to the networks, to television advertisers, and ultimately, to the viewing public. Like all other cartels, NCAA members have sought and achieved a price for their product which is, in most instances, artificially high. The NCAA cartel imposes production limits on its members, and maintains mechanisms for punishing cartel members who seek to stray from these production quotas. The cartel has established a uniform price for the products of each of the member producers, with no regard for the differing quality of these products or the consumer demand for these various products . . .

Several days later, Katz Sports, a television syndicator, struck a deal with Nebraska and Southern Cal to broadcast their upcoming game to an ad hoc network of 100 stations. But the Tenth Circuit Court of Appeals stayed Burciaga's decision pending appeal, which kept the NCAA plan in place for another season. The empire was shaken, but Burciaga could be reversed. Coats made an overture about a settlement, but the NCAA wasn't interested.

*Board of Regents v. NCAA* was supported by the members of the CFA, but it was a ripple that could not be contained to the CFA's end of the pond, and to the leaders of the Big Ten and Pac-10, this was not a comforting thought. They were happy with the status quo, and they resented the CFA's challenge. As the lawsuit moved through the courts, college football's rival camps grew ever more contemptuous of each other. In many cases, it strained friendships and further weakened the sport's ability to reach consensus on other major issues—including the festering problem of academic standards—but had no immediate discernable effect on the playing field. CFA teams continued to play Big Ten and Pac-10 programs during the regular season and in bowl games. Some coaches took the battle more personally than others who tried to pretend it was merely a dispute between administrators that did not affect them.

Before the television issue exploded, several days before Christmas in 1980, the Big Ten's Wayne Duke received a call at his Chicago office from Harold Emerson, the president of Ohio State, who was in Tempe, Arizona, for the upcoming Fiesta Bowl between Penn State and Ohio State. Enarson knew that Duke was about to leave for the Rose Bowl. Would he mind stopping in Tempe on the way to Pasadena? Enarson wanted to introduce Duke to Jack Oswald, the outgoing president of Penn State, who, as it turned out, was interested in speaking with the commissioner about joining the Big Ten. They talked, and over the next several weeks, discussions progressed on the subject.

But the lawsuit changed everything. Penn State lined up with the CFA, and the Big Ten lost interest in a hurry. The political rift prevented a potentially landmark conference realignment, and it would be a long time before the league started courting Penn State again.

The sport spent more than two years in limbo waiting for the issue to be settled. The total audience for televised college football soared to a new high under the NCAA's new three-network approach. With demand for advertising surging, the cost of a 30-second spot reached $57,000, a 137 percent jump in eight years. Rights fees jumped to unprecedented heights, too. Participating teams shared $1.2 million for a national appearance on ABC or CBS, $680,000 for a regional network game, and $475,000 for playing on WTBS's prime-time cable series. The networks kicked in another $250,000 as motivation for moving game dates. Even as they fought for their independence, many of the CFA schools saw their TV revenue increase sharply. Still, according to CFA estimates, their schools left about $15 million on the table during the two-year period.

As the case moved slowly through the court system, some of the major players changed. Between the trial and the appeal before the Tenth Circuit, the NCAA hired Frank Easterbrook, one of the nation's foremost experts on antitrust law, to take over the defense. In February 1983, as the game waited for the Court of Appeals to hear the case, Hallock retired from the Pac-10 and was succeeded by his old friend and long-time NCAA aide Hansen, who harbored no love for the CFA. The appointment of Hansen, who had been Byers's mouthpiece throughout the television dispute, further stratified the rival camps.

Several hours after arguing before the Court of Appeals in Denver, Coats bumped into Easterbrook at Ship's Tavern.

"Isn't there some way we can settle this?" Coats asked, nursing a drink at the bar as he waited for his table.

Easterbrook said he would talk it over with his client.

Even Coats was torn. He kept thinking—hoping—the NCAA would settle, because he understood how his clients benefited from some of the monopolistic tactics he was attacking and how perilous a completely free market might turn out to be. "I didn't want to go down in history as the man who ruined college football," he said.

After the Tenth Circuit affirmed Burciaga's decision by a 2–1 vote, the NCAA petitioned for a stay but was denied. U.S. Supreme Court Justice Byron White, the former all-American running back at Colorado known during his playing days as "Whizzer," saved the day for the NCAA. With the television plan in immediate jeopardy, the NCAA's attorneys located White on vacation and he granted a stay, which continued the monopoly through the 1983 season and allowed the governing body time to file an appeal to the nation's highest court. Four months later, when the Supreme Court announced that it would hear the case, the two sides started preparing for what promised to be the most important event in the history of college athletics.

For nearly two weeks in March 1984, Coats, Muchmore, and their legal partner Harvey Ellis huddled inside a suite at the J. W. Marriott Hotel, two blocks from the U.S. Capitol, to prepare for the oral argument before the Supreme Court. Day after day, with room service trays strewn around the room, Muchmore and

Ellis crammed with Coats on strategy and grilled him with questions they expected the justices to ask. All three lawyers felt confident in the case, but Coats—the newly elected mayor of Oklahoma City—was making his first appearance before the highest court in the land, and he could not help feeling anxious about the most important day of his legal career.

"I realized it was the chance of a lifetime," Coats said. "A friend of mine who had experience with the court had advised me to go to Washington and do nothing but prepare for a couple of weeks, and that turned out to be terrific advice. It allowed me to focus and get my game face on."

Several weeks before, the Justice Department had filed an amicus brief on the plaintiff's behalf, lending Oklahoma and Georgia moral support from the federal government, for whatever it was worth. On the night before the most important day of Coats's professional life, Solicitor General Rex Lee—who would argue in favor of the Board of Regents—stopped by Coats's room. Dressed in sweats and sneakers, he had been jogging around Capitol Hill. He told Coats not to be nervous.

As he sat before the court on the morning of March 20, 1984, waiting for his cue, Coats was dominated by one thought: Don't try to be funny.

At some point during the weeks prior to the argument, a prominent friend in the law had pulled him aside and given him a tutorial on Supreme Court etiquette. Coats was well known around Oklahoma legal circles for a rather easygoing, laid-back courtroom style, which often included cracking an occasional joke. Humor was a large part of his courtroom persona, so even as he endeavored to display a mastery of the sometimes complex facts in the case, Coats felt the need to moderate his own personality.

"I kept thinking that I had to walk a tightrope," he said. "I wanted to appear loose, but not flippant. The truth is, I was a little nervous."

Coats tried not to think about his butterflies as he listened to Easterbrook argue the NCAA's case. In the gallery, a small group of officials from Oklahoma, Georgia, the NCAA, and the television networks watched history unfold. Georgia's Fred Davison sat next to law professor Ralph Beaird and, at one point, feeling constricted by the tight quarters, Davison stretched his arm on the bench behind Beaird. A baliff quickly came up from behind and demanded, in a whisper, that Davison remove his arm.

"I had no idea that was against the rules," said Davison, who quickly placed his hands in his lap.

Although Easterbrook built his legal brief around seven specific points of law considered by the lower courts, he spent most of his allotted time before the justices dealing with the much-debated "market power" issue. The esteemed professor from the University of Chicago School of Law—subsequently appointed to the federal bench by President Reagan—hung the petitioners' case on the assertion that NCAA football did not represent a separate and distinct market, which meant it did not have the power to manipulate prices by artificially limiting production. Therefore, he said, the NCAA plan could not be considered a monopoly under the definition of the Sherman Antitrust Act.

"The court must address the question whether there is an ability to enrich the defendant's pockets by harming consumers," he said. "That in a word is our whole argument."

At both the district and appellate levels, the NCAA's attorneys had argued vehemently in favor of social aims as justifications for alleged monopolistic behavior, which met the so-called "rule of reason" test and prevented such tactics from constituting per se violations of the Sherman Act. Burciaga rejected these assertions and the Tenth Circuit affirmed his opinion, going so far as to equate the attendance defense with saying "competition will destroy the market," a position it found inconsistent with the Sherman Act. Instead of emphasizing the egalitarian aims of the plan, Easterbrook decided to play offense and not defense, attacking the lower courts' "different but equally erroneous approaches to the market power question."

Countering the Oklahoma-Georgia argument that the NCAA

plan exercised an artificial limitation on the number of televised games, Easterbrook told the court: "If the NCAA has no market power, then the plaintiff's argument that the NCAA is holding games off TV has to be viewed in one of two ways: Either the NCAA is cutting its own throat just by reducing the number of games and therefore getting its product shown to fewer viewers and therefore getting less total revenue, or there is something pro-competitive about these arrangments."

During his argument, Justice White asked Easterbrook why he did not include educational aims as a mitigating factor in his defense. While the court had held in the *Engineers* case that a for-profit association could not justify monopolistic practices, it had not established a similar precedent regarding nonprofit entities. Easterbrook feared that the court would reject such a posture, regardless of nonprofit status, and apply *Engineers*. "As we read this court's cases," he told Justice White, "goals other than economic are not reasons for monopolistic practices."

When Coats stood up to make his presentation, he was determined to keep his Oklahoma sense of humor in check. He looked around at the ornate, historic chamber and tried to remember where he was. During his opening statement, he discussed the assertions by Byers and others during the District Court trial concerning the limitations of televised games:

> COATS: . . . All said if we didn't have the plan all together, that the networks would grind down the prices . . . there would be lots and lots more games on television. And that's what the lower courts found . . . that there would be so many more games, mostly on the basis of local and regional circumstances.

> JUSTICE BLACKMUN: As long as Oklahoma's on every Saturday?

COATS: Well, it would be hoped, your honor, that the networks would want us. If we don't do better than we did last year, they may not.

The court erupted in nervous laughter. But the remark played well with the justices, and it chased his butterflies.

During his argument, Easterbrook had introduced the precedent established in the *Broadcast Music* case, in which the court ruled that an agreement among competitors (in this case, composers) does not necessarily represent an illegal cartel and in certain cases can constitute an exception to a per se violation of the antitrust laws. Easterbrook had emphasized the court's holding that Broadcast Music's behavior was legal in part because the organization performed other functions besides agreeing not to compete on a specific economic entity. Coats refuted Easterbrook's position by insisting that the NCAA plan failed to meet the standards of *Broadcast Music* because it precluded members from selling their games to other networks who were not party to the cartel:

> . . . We do not believe the court would have decided *Broadcast Music* as it had if all the composers had come together and agreed that they would sell only . . . to one or two networks. The reason the *Broadcast Music* exception to the per se rule came around was because there was indeed countervailing forces in the market, the ability of the composers to sell outside the package . . .

After addressing the parallels with free market televised college basketball and attacking Easterbrook's "market power" assertions, Coats stopped a few minutes short of his allotted time—an old law school trick designed to make him appear more confident in his performance. He felt good about his argument. Everyone among the Oklahoma-Georgia crowd seemed surprised by the relative simplicity of the court's questioning, which they took as a positive sign.

"The Tenth Circuit was much more rigorous," Muchmore said.

"The questioning by Clyde and Harvey back at the Marriott was tougher," Coats said.

The solicitor general offered a strong argument on the plaintiff's behalf. "Regardless of the path by which the result is reached—whether it's a per se violation, a full-blown rule of reason analysis or a more carefully tailored rule of reason middle ground—it should be apparent that the Sherman Act has been violated," Lee told the court.


Three months later, on the morning of June 27, Coats walked into his office in a bad mood. It was the day after a frustrating political defeat, and he was still feeling the sting. For months, the mayor had campaigned for a sales tax hike to fund a massive project to repair Oklahoma City's crumbling bridges and streets, but the voters had rejected his referendum. He was commiserating with a small group of city officials when his secretary burst into his office with the news.

"In a flash, I went from being sad over that sales tax defeat to being so elated that I forgot all about the election," said the mayor/lawyer/football revolutionary.

In a blistering rebuke of the NCAA, the court ruled by a 7–2 margin that the governing body's television controls represented a "classic cartel" that had "restricted rather than enhanced the place of intercollegiate athletics in the nation's life." Invalidating the NCAA's contracts with ABC, CBS, and WTBS and forbidding it from entering into similar monopolisic arrangements, the court sustained Burciaga's contention that the association maintained market power, which rendered its practices subject to, and in violation of, the Sherman Antitrust Act. Writing for the majority—which included Chief Justice Burger and Associate Justices Blackmun, Brennan, Marshall, O'Connor, and Powell—Justice John Paul Stevens said:

> . . . Because it restrains price and output, the NCAA's television plan has a significant potential for anticompetitive effects . . . Moreover, the Court found that by fixing a price for television rights to all games, the NCAA creates a price structure that is unresponsive to viewer demand and unrelated to the prices that would prevail in a competitive market. And, of course, since as a practical manner all member institutions need NCAA approval, members have no real choice but to adhere to the NCAA's controls . . . The NCAA's argument that its television plan is necessary to protect live attendance is not based on the desire to maintain college football as a distinct and attractive product, but rather on a fear that the product will not prove sufficiently attractive to draw live attendance when faced with competition from televised games . . .

In a dissenting opinion joined by Justice Rehnquist, Justice White clearly pined for a simpler era, before commercialism became such an undeniable fact of life in college athletics: "Although some of the NCAA's activities, viewed in isolation, bear a resemblance to those undertaken by professional sports leagues and associations, the Court errs in treating intercollegiate athletics under the NCAA's control as a purely commercial venture in which colleges and universities participate solely, or even primarily, in the pursuit of profits."

Several hours after the ruling was announced, NBC's *Today*

program located Dan Gibbens in Chicago, where he was attending an NCAA meeting. The producers wanted one of the architects of the lawsuit to appear on the news show the next morning, to help make sense of the situation.

Before dawn, Gibbens got up, showered, shaved, put on his best suit, and took the elevator to the lobby. But the limo was late. As the sun started to rise across the Chicago skyline, Gibbens kept looking at his watch, fearing that he was about to miss his first appearance on live national television.

Finally, the limo driver, who had gotten lost, arrived outside the hotel nearly an hour late and rushed him to the studio of the local NBC affiliate.

By the time Gibbens showed up on the set and settled in his chair in front of the camera, *Today* host Bryant Gumble had already started the discussion with television producer Don Ohlmeyer, who blamed the NCAA for "grossly mismanaging" televised college football.

After introducing Gibbens, Gumble asked: "Is oversaturation your primary concern now?"

"Well, I think that the main opportunity that we're looking for is to find out whether there is such a thing as oversaturation . . . "

He would get his answer rather quickly

Like many of his colleagues, Gibbens actually thought his side had won without losing.

# 10

## CIVIL WAR

**E**ven before the Supreme Court handed down the landmark *Board of Regents* decision, Gene Corrigan and several of his colleagues started planning for a new era. Corrigan spent several months trying to unite the members of the CFA with their rivals in the Big Ten and Pac-10. By joining forces, the Notre Dame athletic director argued, the two camps could present the networks with the most attractive features of the NCAA package while allowing the most popular teams to appear with greater frequency.

In the days immediately before and after the ruling, they talked peace. In late June 1984, a group including Corrigan, Father Edmund P. Joyce, and Chuck Neinas met with Wayne Duke and Tom Hansen inside a meeting room overlooking the United concourse at Chicago's O'Hare Airport. The atmosphere was tense. The Big Ten and Pac-10 had steadfastly refused to join the CFA for many years and they viewed the lawsuit and its architects with contempt.

"I think they merely feigned interest," Joyce said.

But Hansen insisted the linkage "was doomed to failure."

They talked about ways of subdividing the postregulation world so they could avoid butting heads, but the animosity and the complex calculus of slicing the coveted pie colored the discussions with a sense of futility.

"As soon as we started talking about appearance allocations, we could never reach an agreement," Hansen said. "Appearances meant money, and everybody wanted all of the exposures and all of the money."

Thirteen days after Justice Stevens's blistering rebuke of the NCAA's monopolistic practices, the governing body convened a special convention in Chicago. It was a desperate attempt to save the franchise. The Big Ten and Pac-10 sponsored legislation that would have created a less restrictive plan allowing more appearances by the major teams and featuring an open window concept that would have given conferences the freedom to assemble noncompeting regional packages. Leaders of the two leagues believed their plan would satisfy Judge Burciaga—who would have to sign off on any new NCAA television package—but their reasoning sparked heated debate. Most CFA schools thought they could do better on their own, and the proposal failed by a 66–44 vote of the Divison 1-A schools. After thirty-two years of dominating televised college football, the NCAA no longer had any authority on the subject.

Angered by the CFA's opposition, the Big Ten and Pac-10 abruptly abandoned the coalition and started formulating their own plan. For several days, no one knew if the CFA would hold together. Oklahoma tried to strike a separate deal but decided to stay with the CFA when the networks failed to meet the school's asking price. Turner Broadcasting's WTBS Superstation offered Notre Dame a bundle for exclusive rights to the Fighting Irish games, but Father Joyce said no. More than three decades after he first railed against the NCAA's television controls, like a voice in the wilderness, Joyce finally had the chance to place Notre Dame in a dominant position over the airwaves. But as one of the founding fathers of the CFA, he was determined to unify the group so they could keep the situation from splintering further.

One morning in July, with the season looming, leaders of the two rival factions bumped into each other in the lobby of Black Rock, the CBS headquarters in Midtown Manhattan. It was an odd scene, with looks of bewilderment all around. They nervously shook hands and exchanged pleasantries, as if they were not scheming and plotting against each other, as if their whole world had not been turned upside down.

The history of college athletics is strewn with the residue of intense turf battles and extreme divisions in philosophy. Through the years, the nation's football-playing colleges fought bitterly over issues as fundamental as financial aid and restructuring. More than intramural disputes, these periodic skirmishes reflected the decades-long struggle between higher education and commerce.

By the time the television war erupted in the early 1980s, the game was the center of a massive industry that in many ways rivaled the National Football League. The roughly 100 schools who played big-time college football in the most liberal interpretation of the term generated an average of $9 million per year from ticket sales, broadcasting rights, bowl games, alumni donations, and licensed products. The largest and most successful divisions of the college sports empire—including Notre Dame, Michigan, Penn State, and Ohio State—worked with budgets of $15 million or more, nearly all of the income produced by their football programs, although men's basketball generated significant income and, in some cases, turned a profit. Part big business and part benefactor, major college football was responsible for earning enough money to pay for its own existence—including scholarships for players, salaries for coaches, travel, and, in some cases, facility upgrades—as well as supporting large numbers of nonrevenue sports for both men and women.

As the common denominator in the transformation, television wielded more than a checkbook. It captured the excitement of the game and hooked millions of fans on the experience, many of them far removed from collegiate life and with no direct link to the institutions of higher learning behind their favorite teams. Just as television created a whole new context for news and entertainment, the medium crafted and sold a vision of big-time sports—placing college football alongside the NFL, Major League Baseball, the National Basketball Association, and, eventually, college basketball in the pantheon of games that matter to the American public.

The sport's television revolution did not occur in a vacuum. It was greatly influenced by the various eruptions that had divided the college sports establishment through the years, creating a climate of mistrust, rivalry, and personal animosity. It also was significantly affected not just by the financial and promotional power provided by television, but also by the impact wrought by decades of exposure to these addictive charms.

The *Board of Regents* decision was an earthquake in collegiate athletics, but it had been building under the surface since the days of Franny Murray. Over the next two decades, the television war would set the stage for the breakup and expansion of conferences and the transformation of the bowl system. It would become a catalyst for both competitive parity and financial disparity, forcing college administrators into a new array of choices and compromises while elevating the game on the field to an even greater level of exposure.

In the summer of 1984, however, no one was thinking about the long-term ramifications of the CFA-led revolt. The athletic officials scrambling around trying to sell the rights to televised college football were too busy learning some painful economic lessons.

For more than three decades, the NCAA had been able to exploit the power of exclusivity to win increasingly fat contracts from the networks. In 1983, the last year of the NCAA package, ABC and CBS paid a combined $66 million for the rights to college football. The NCAA's pacts with ABC, CBS, and ESPN would have generated $73.6 million in 1984.

When the Supreme Court created a free market, the networks quickly seized the advantage to divide and conquer. After the Big Ten/Pac-10 signed a deal with CBS for $10 million, the CFA had to settle for a $13 million contract with ABC. NBC, still stinging from the aborted CFA deal in 1981, declined to bid on either plan.

Freedom was costly for all concerned, even for those who

did not ask for their emancipation. In the first year of deregulation, as the supply of games soared and the demand crashed, college football's combined take from network television plummeted by more than 60 percent.

"It didn't take the colleges long to realize that they had killed the golden goose," said former ABC Sports executive Donn Bernstein.

The Supreme Court repudiated Byers, and justifiably so, but the free market proved that Neinas and his colleagues had greatly miscalculated. The CFA schools wanted control so they could place more games on the air and earn more money. They accomplished the former so well that the latter was rendered impossible. Many athletic officials had laughed at Byers when he suggested the breakup of the NCAA plan would allow the networks to drive down the prices, but he was right. He understood the market much better than the men who opposed him.

Cable and regional syndication helped the various leagues make up some of the shortfall but also contributed to the immense overexposure of the sport. Freed from the NCAA's tight controls but unprotected from their own hubris, the colleges competed against each other from noon to midnight, creating a viewing bonanza for fans but threatening the viability of the televised sport.

With three times as many games on the air, the college teams still earned $25 million less in the first year of their free market chaos than they had in the final year of Walter Byers's order. They had won, but not without losing.

Most frustrating for the leaders of the CFA was the memory of their unconsummated four-year, $180-million contract with NBC, which they had negotiated from a position of strength at the height of the market. Under the terms of that one-network deal, the members of the CFA would have split nearly $50 million in 1984, nearly two-thirds more than they actually earned from the combination of network, cable, and syndication.

With the ratings splintered, the price of a 30-second network spot crashed from $57,000 in 1983 to as little as $15,000 in 1984. All those choices for viewers and advertisers turned college football from a seller's market into a buyer's market overnight. Media buyers for the major sports advertisers—including auto makers, soft drinks, and beer—once felt the need to lock in coveted and finite time on the mega-rating ABC telecasts. But in the days after deregulation, buyers could pick and choose, often waiting until Friday afternoon when the networks started getting desperate to move the inventory. The colleges would be suffering the consequences of the saturation for years to come.

The Big Eight and the Southeastern Conference felt the full brunt of the market forces. In the first year of deregulation, the Big Eight's revenue fell from $6.1 million to $3.8 million and the SEC's from $11.2 million to $7.5 million.

All across the sport, the powers who had grown to depend on the fast-growing television revenue to help balance the books were stunned. Alabama's paycheck sank from $1.924 million to $764,000. UCLA's fell from $1.238 million to $735,317. Oklahoma's dropped from $1.276 million to $753,208.

Several weeks after the nationally televised Oklahoma–Nebraska game in 1982, the NCAA mailed a rights fee payment in the amount of $1.2 million to Robert Smith, the Sooners' athletic business manager. Someone at the governing body had made a mistake and shorted the check by about $200,000. The NCAA quickly sent a replacement check for the correct amount and instructed Smith to tear up the original, but he decided to keep it as a souvenir.

Two years later, when the Sooners, who led the rebellion, earned less from four appearances than for one Oklahoma–Nebraska game in the regulated era, Smith often found himself explaining the framed $1.2 million check that hung on the wall behind his desk. It was a vivid reminder of how dramatically things had changed.

Even before the new era began, the competing cartels allowed their greed and bitterness toward each other to push the rivalry to a new low.

As part of its deal with the CFA, ABC insisted that no CFA teams appear on CBS—even away games. But CBS, pointing to the tradition of home rule, believed its contract with the Big Ten and Pac-10 secured the right to telecast any of the member schools' home games—even those involving CFA institutions. Home rule had never been more than a gentlemen's agreement, however, and gentlemen were in short supply that summer.

In the tension-filled days of early August, the TV combatants met in Los Angeles and tried to settle the dispute. Charles Young, the chancellor of UCLA, demanded that CBS be allowed to televise the Bruins' home game against Nebraska. The CFA and ABC resisted. Also at stake was Notre Dame's visit to Southern Cal, one of the game's most traditional intersectional rivalries.

Unable to work out a satisfactory agreement, the Big Ten, Pac-10, and CBS filed suit against ABC, Notre Dame, Nebraska, and the CFA in Federal District Court, seeking to prevent the defendants from withholding consent to televise the two big games. With the season approaching and the survival of their respective contracts at stake, the two sides dug in their heels and waited for the court to rule on the matter.

On September 10, less than two weeks before the Nebraska–UCLA game, Judge Richard A Gadbois issued a preliminary injunction on the plaintiffs' behalf and ordered that CBS be allowed to televise both games. In his opinion, Gadbois opined that both sides would benefit from the airing of the two games while the plaintiffs would be harmed in the absence of such an order. ABC's attorneys had argued that the network would be adversely affected by allowing CBS to televise the two games, but Gadbois dismissed this line of reasoning. "By issuance of this order ABC and ESPN are not measurably harmed, other than by some perceived diminution of their ability quickly to dispatch CBS from the market for nationwide college football telecasts," he wrote.

With no real choice other than to abandon the CFA deal altogether or go forward within the parameters established by Gadbois—which essentially granted the home team wide authority over the disputed games—ABC allowed CBS to televise the two games and stuck with the CFA. The network continued to pursue the matter in the courts, however. Prior to the 1985 season, the parties reached a settlement that provided the home team and the home team's network with wide latitude concerning television rights in such "crossover" games, codifying the decades-old tradition of home rule.

"After going all the way to the Supreme Court to win their property rights, the CFA tried to tell us we didn't have the right to televise our home games," Hansen remarked. "I always found that terribly ironic."

Placing their faith in the free market, the CFA schools and their Big Ten/Pac-10 rivals abolished the old appearance rules.

In the new era, the members of the TV aristocracy—and some new initiates, including modern powerhouses Miami and Florida State—frequently appeared six, seven, eight times, or more per season.

Television officials gravitated to Notre Dame. During the regulated era, the Fighting Irish led the sport with seventy-eight appearances and drew huge crowds from coast to coast, including six of the twelve highest-rated games in college football history. After playing on TV the NCAA maximum of three times in 1983, Gerry Faust's team attracted the cameras eight times in 1984. In the first four years of deregulation, the Fighting Irish made thirty-seven appearances—more than every single team coached by Ara Parseghian, who led Notre Dame for eleven years.

Viewers who once gravitated to the single blockbuster game on an autumn Saturday afternoon and cherished the rare opportunity to see their favorite team in action quickly adjusted to a new era of abundance. Most markets wired for cable received about eight games each Saturday. Suddenly, football fanatics could flip on the tube before lunch and keep watching games all day and late into the night. Supporters of traditional winners such as Oklahoma,

Nebraska, Ohio State, Alabama, and Penn State could count on seeing the majority of their games on national or regional TV.

"We use that in recruiting," said Ohio State head coach John Cooper. "We're recruiting all over the country and it's nice to be able to go into somebody's home and say, 'You can turn on TV and watch the Buckeyes six to eight times a year.'"

But in contrast to what many of the NCAA's supporters predicted, the deregulated era was not limited to a powerhouse free-for-all. Viewer choice also extended to the variety of teams on the air. Thanks to the massive increase in the number of televised games, lesser programs who rarely appeared on the NCAA series—such as Ole Miss, Iowa State, Washington State, Indiana, and Oklahoma State—could be seen with much greater regularity under the new system. SEC lightweight Kentucky appeared on television nine times in the first two years of deregulation, which equaled the Wildcats' total number of TV games from the birth of the medium through the first year of the Reagan administration.

"Everybody talks about the money," Neinas told a reporter during the painful days after the red ink started to flow, when he attracted no small amount of the blame for the financial shortfall. "But no one seems to care about the football fan. He is the one who benefited from deregulation. And he isn't complaining."

With the Big Ten and Pac-10 sharing the exposures evenly on CBS, the initial year of the CFA plans on ABC and ESPN included the teams from the Southeastern Conference, Big Eight, Southwest Conference, and Western Athletic Conference and independents including Notre Dame, Penn State, and Pittsburgh.

The Mid-American Conference and the Pacific Coast Athletic Association—two leagues on the margin of the sport—were left without any national TV exposure. No one called the networks to complain about not being able to see Cal State-Fullerton, Kent State, and Central Michigan.

For many years, the TV powers had argued that the NCAA was unecessarily watering down the series by forcing the networks to carry unattractive properties. These forces took a certain amount of satisfaction when, in the days after the ruling, the NCAA attempted to sell the networks a package of Division 1-AA regular season and playoff games. No one was interested. Eventually, the NCAA bought time on a fledgling satellite channel and produced broadcasts of the Divisions 1-AA, II, and III championship games. Practically no one saw these small college super bowls.

CBS bought the rights to the Army–Navy game, a television staple since 1945, and placed it on against ABC's coverage of Alabama–Auburn, a high-pitched rivalry that had drawn the cameras eight times since 1964. Both had proven to be ratings bonanzas for television through the years, but when the fans were forced to choose, numbers for the two games tumbled to all-time lows. The same could be said of Oklahoma–Nebraska and Southern Cal–USC, forced to go head-to-head for viewers. Even the Nebraska–UCLA and Notre Dame–Southern Cal showdowns, considered important enough to spark another nasty court battle, failed to draw numbers even remotely comparable to the old days. The tradition-rich Irish–Trojans game followed the miracle victory by Doug Flutie and Boston College over Miami, but like the Hurricanes, CBS could not protect a lead. Forced to compete against Oklahoma–Oklahoma State, the sport's most important intersectional rivalry saw its audience fall to half of the previous season's level.

The colleges and the networks gradually awoke to an unsettling realization: The blockbuster was dead. With such a glut of games on the air, broadcasters could no longer count on attracting large national audiences of 15 million homes or more for big games, even when the national championship was on the line. Those days were over. The full measure of this unintended consequence of deregulation would not be appreciated for years.

One of the ways the colleges accommodated the demand for exposures was by creating the syndication window. After the Burciaga decision, Neinas realized the importance of preventing an antitrust backlash against any future CFA television plan. As he set up a mechanism for administering national network and cable packages,

Neinas formulated a concept for reserving a certain time during the day for the various conferences.

"Allowing the possibility for other markets for games to be sold automatically got rid of any possible antitrust problems," said CFA attorney Clyde Muchmore. "Plus, Chuck knew his membership wanted an open time where they could do what they wanted beyond the national package."

After the networks exercized the first selection in the process, which tended to place the most important games on ABC or CBS either nationally or regionally during midafternoon, the various conferences and independents placed many more games on television by creating their own supplemental plans starting at 12:30 eastern time. Suddenly, the landscape was flooded with many different groups selling game packages.

All of the major conferences—and some marginal leagues— signed with television production companies and started stringing together ad hoc networks of stations in their respective regions, which placed them in further competition for finite ad dollars. The Southwest Conference and Atlantic Coast Conference prospered by creating syndication plans through Raycom and Jefferson-Pilot, respectively. Notre Dame partnered with WGN, the Chicago-based superstation, to carry the games not picked up by ABC and ESPN. The Southeastern Conference signed a much envied deal with WTBS, the Atlanta-based superstation, basic cable's first and most widely distributed channel. At a time when SEC teams frequently appeared as part of the CFA plans on ABC and ESPN, the WTBS contract often placed the second or third best SEC game of the day on national cable.

"Regardless of what the network and ESPN were doing, you could turn on the television in any city in the country and see SEC football, and that set us apart," said former SEC Commissioner Harvey Schiller.

Many of the fledgling syndicators misjudged the market, however.

By the late 1980s, the Southern Conference—which could count on one or two big-payday appearances on the network in the old days as part of the NCAA's patronage game—started allowing a syndicator to sell its games without making a dime. "We just do it to promote our teams," said Commissioner Dave Hart.

No one fully appreciated it at the time, but the CFA's prime-time deal with the ESPN cable channel represented a major breakthrough for the entire sport. After years of steady growth, cable had reached a critical mass large enough for many major sports advertisers to take the medium seriously. The percentage of American households with cable had jumped from 13.6 percent when ESPN launched in 1979 to more than 40 percent by 1984. Even as the all-sports network struggled to overcome an image as the source for mostly marginal events like Australian Rules Football, college basketball was becoming a powerful draw for the channel. The prime-time CFA package, purchased for $9 million, would help take ESPN to the next level.

Syndication and cable broadened the sport's reach in the years after deregulation, but it would be a long time before the much-anticipated benefits of the free market translated into higher rights fees. College football spent the better part of the next decade trying to fight back to the high-water marks achieved in 1983. Using even the most conservative estimates, the game probably left at least $200 million on the table in the first ten years after the Supreme Court decision—if the NCAA package had remained in force and if it had continued to grow at the same rate. During the same period, contracts for Major League Baseball, the National Football League, and the National Basketball Association more than doubled. Measured against such deals, college football's losses seemed even more staggering.

By the late 1980s, with the number of games out of control and revenue still flat, some conferences started trying to arbitrarily limit their exposures in a futile attempt to reduce the inflation of their product. Everyone was talking about overexposure, but without the NCAA or anyone else to police the situation, no one could do much about it. Even with the dramatically reduced rights fees, the networks complained about losing money. Four years into the new era, the price of a network commercial on the Saturday games remained below 1979 levels, which prompted some talk that one or both networks might eventually be forced to abandon the college game.

"We're just trying to hold our own in what is a declining market," the SEC's Schiller told a reporter in 1987, when his league was filling the airwaves with games but still earning less than in the old system.

In 1988, after the CFA moved to CBS and the Big Ten/Pac-10 switched to ABC, a group working under the auspices of the National Association of Collegiate Directors of Athletics (NACDA) started trying to unite the rival factions under one umbrella. College athletics was hemorrhaging, and the leaders of the effort believed a single noncompetitive package could pump an additional $20 million per year into the system—and turn back the clock. The effort, led by Miami athletic director Sam Jankovich, eventually fizzled after the Justice Department cast a skeptical eye on the antitrust issue. It was probably doomed from the start. No one wanted to give up any power and no one wanted to trust the guy across the table, even if it meant ending what amounted to a civil war.

In the years after the Supreme Court dismantled one of the foundations of his empire, Walter Byers watched the unfolding battle for dollars and power with a sense of ambivalence. He detested everything the CFA represented, and friends say he took some measure of comfort in the comeuppance Neinas and his rebels experienced. But he loved college athletics. It was hard for him to look on as football suffered through such convulsions and not be able to do anything about it.

"I think he was quite devastated," Wayne Duke said. "He worked all those years to make the plan successful and then watched it be destroyed. He felt betrayed. He thought it was a big mistake. He was afraid of where it would lead."

For more than three decades, Byers defended the monopoly

primarily as a way to safeguard football attendance. But this was proven to be a myth. In the years after the Supreme Court decision, overall college football attendance remained fairly flat. In the first five years after deregulation, average Division 1-A attendance trended down slightly, from 42,162 to 41,454. Some schools experienced a tough time selling tickets in the face of all that football on free TV, but the quality of the competition remained a much bigger factor. In time, the sport would set all-time attendance records in the face of unrestricted TV.

The Southeastern Conference overtook the Big Ten as the perennial attendance champ not because the Big Ten dropped, but because several SEC schools enlarged their stadiums and started filling them to even greater capacity. In the first two decades after the television explosion, SEC attendance surged from 3.192 million in 1987 to 6.146 million in 2003, 97 percent of available capacity. Over the same period, the Big Ten and ACC also recorded significant increases. Dozens of schools across the country added seats. Despite the widespread availability of multiple televised games during every Saturday of the fall, millions of fans still spent their hard-earned money on tickets and headed for their favorite campus.

Although the television battle reflected a rejection of the NCAA's system of governance and the heavy-handed way it dealt with members, the association continued to dominate most aspects of college sports. The NCAA still aggressively investigated rules violators. Unable to use the weapon of television any longer, the Infractions Committee started punishing cheaters by taking away scholarships—a penalty that in some ways would prove more devastating. In the early 1980s, even as the *Board of Regents* case worked through the courts, the NCAA expanded greatly to assume control over the growing size and scope of women's athletics. By the middle of the decade the association was administering more than twenty different national championship events for men and women, and doing it quite well. After years of steady growth, the 64-team men's basketball tournament was exploding in popularity, thanks largely to television, which the

NCAA continued to control. In 1988, while the colleges were learning difficult lessons about supply and demand in football television, CBS signed a four-year, $163-million contract for the rights to March Madness—an 85 percent increase over the previous deal. Soon, NCAA television would help lead women's basketball out of the shadows as well.

The membership still used the NCAA as a forum for arguing about their problems and, in some cases, reaching consensus on solutions. In 1985, the newly formed Presidents Commission responded to the growing number of recruiting and academic scandals in big-time football and basketball by convening a special "Integrity Convention" in New Orleans. The movement led to the creation of the so-called "death penalty" legislation for habitual violators of NCAA rules, interpreted as a school that was placed on probation for serious offenses twice in a five-year period. Two years later, when a massive pay-for-play conspiracy was uncovered at six-time loser Southern Methodist University, the NCAA's Infractions Committee siezed the chance to make an example out of the Mustangs' football program. Using the "death penalty" rule for the first—and, to date, only—time, the association suspended the SMU team for one season. The ruling Methodist bishops, embarrassed by the headline-grabbing affair, later tacked on another year for good measure. SMU, which played in the Cotton Bowl and nearly captured the national championship four years before being hit with the unprecedented penalty, returned to the field of play in 1989. But it vanished from the national spotlight.

The nation's colleges also resolved to deal with the growing perception that big-time sports had become a haven for quasi-professional athletes unqualified and unmotivated for the rigors of academic life. Thirty years after the codification of the grant-in-aid, and in the shadow of the massive explosion of salaries in the NFL and NBA, many football and basketball players saw the college experience as little more than a pipeline to professional riches. As graduation rates for athletes sank lower and lower, the college establishment wrestled with a major public relations problem that reflected the inherent conflict between the traditional academic purpose of the institutions and their increasingly independent and contradictory big-time athletic programs. Feeling intense pressure to win, coaches recruited the best athletes—regardless of their academic abilities—and this left many college officials scrambling to play a popular game of justification and denial. Finally, in 1986, thirteen years after the NCAA effectively lowered the academic standards, the membership reversed course and raised the bar considerably. The passage of the controversial legislation known as Proposition 48 forced prospective athletes to meet a series of more rigid standards to qualify for admission. The satisfactory progress rule required student-athletes to pass a certain number of hours each year in order to be eligible. The combination of the two regulations gradually helped create better prepared student-athletes and improved graduation rates, but the movement had no effect on the larger issue driving the problem. Many football and basketball players still went to college dreaming of striking it rich in the pros, even though only a tiny percentage of college players ever make it to the NFL and NBA.

Even as the NCAA retained its historic role at the center of college athletics, the television revolution marked a turning point. Thirty years after the call to tame the beast of TV gave rise to the modern NCAA, the battle to control the medium slowly shifted a measure of power back to the conferences. Like the NCAA in the 1950s, the conferences soon would learn to use television not just as a programming delivery system, but as a tool to project and enhance their strength within the structure of college athletics.

By the time Byers retired in 1987, college athletics faced a mounting financial crisis. For years, administrators had watched with a sense of desperation while the cost of running the nation's athletic departments spiraled out of control. Big-time football's appetite kept growing, despite all the cost-cutting measures pushed through the NCAA conventions. The price of scholarships, salaries, travel, and all the rest kept rising, and when one school built an indoor facility or a fancy academic center or expanded its stadium, others felt the need to meet the competition in the athletic arms race. Demand for increasingly ambitious women's sports, protected by the 1972 federal law known as Title IX, placed even greater pressure on football and men's basketball to turn a profit. The mandate to achieve "gender equity" was widely supported but increasingly difficult to reach, given the growing disparity between resources and responsibilities. Within a few years, large numbers of men's nonrevenue sports—such as wrestling, swimming, and cross country—would be eliminated by cash-strapped colleges who were prevented by the courts' increasingly rigorous interpretation of Title IX from disbanding comparable nonrevenue women's sports.

Many of the college officials who had supported the television fight saw it as a way to help solve the funding problem.

"Title IX was beginning to put a pretty severe financial strain on our programs and others like it," said Fred Davison, the former president of the University of Georgia. "Football had to do it all, and football could only do so much unless we exploited it to a greater degree. I saw [free market television] as a way for us to alleviate some of the financial strain on our programs, especially in regard to the funding of women's sports."

Instead, the rights fee freefall made the situation even worse.

"The drop in TV revenues had a tremendous impact on college sports across the board," said Dick Schultz, the former Virginia athletic director who replaced Byers as the NCAA executive director. "It made the financial crisis even worse, and it didn't take long for everybody to wish we could turn the clock back to before 1984."

By the late 1980s, nearly half of all Division l-A programs were running deficits and desperately searching for creative ways to balance the books.

.  .  .

Ray Perkins, Alabama's athletic director and head football coach, called his business manager one afternoon in 1985 and asked how much money the Crimson Tide's sports program had in the bank at that precise moment. It was a simple question and Taze Fulford asked his boss to hold on as he shuffled through some papers near his desk. After a few moments, he found the figure, read it to Perkins, and went back to his work.

Several days later, perhaps by accident, perhaps by design, Perkins mentioned in public that his empire had $16 million in the bank. It was a statement that made all the papers in the state of Alabama.

"The figure was correct, on that particular day," Fulford said. "It was early in the fiscal year when we had collected most of our revenues but still had eight or ten months of salaries, scholarships, and other bills to pay. Yet people took that to mean that we had $16 million in savings, which simply wasn't true."

When legendary coach and athletic director Paul "Bear" Bryant retired after the 1982 season, he left behind one of the nation's most successful and financially vibrant athletic departments. Years of strong ticket sales, television fees, and bowl receipts had allowed the Crimson Tide to compete very effectively on the football field—capturing six national championships and thirteen SEC titles over the span of a quarter-century—while building a broad-based program of nonrevenue sports for men and women. Through the years, the thrifty Bryant managed to save $8 million in a rainy-day fund.

By the late 1980s, it was pouring in Tuscaloosa.

Like many major programs, Alabama was spending more money than it was making. In the fiscal year which ended in the summer of 1988, the Crimson Tide, a self-sustaining division of the university with nearly 100 employees, was forced to borrow more than $2 million from its reserves.

If television profits had merely continued their trend under the NCAA contract, Alabama—which appeared on TV seventy-six times during the regulated era from 1952 to 1983, second only to

Notre Dame—would have produced a surplus. Like many traditional powers, Alabama envisioned $3 million or $4 million paydays once it was better able to exploit the free market. But instead, in 1987 the Crimson Tide earned less than half what it had pocketed in 1983, which made the overall cash crunch even worse.

Alabama officials realized they needed to find a way to generate more money from the football program. The obvious answer was to launch a priority ticket system, which many other schools had adopted years before. Bryant had first recognized the need for such a change in the early 1980s, and Perkins set the wheels in motion. But the task of selling and implementing what became known as Tide Pride was left to the next athletic dirctor, former Tide quarterback Steve Sloan, who faced significant opposition and resentment from some alumni and fans who could not understand why Alabama needed to alter the decades-old ticket structure.

"So many fans still think we've got $16 million in the bank," Sloan told a reporter in 1988. "That's a common misconception, and it's really caused us problems. When we started Tide Pride, they would call us and say, 'But Perkins said you had this much money in the bank. What happened to it? Did the university take it away?' The truth is, of course, that money never existed."

A detailed financial analysis of the department revealed that revenues had more than tripled in a 10-year span—from $3,469,130 to $10,448,080—but the high cost of competing in football, the growth of women's sports—which cost $1,368,937 but generated only $20,591 in revenue—and significant staff additions teamed with rapid inflation in many areas to spend all the available cash and run the Crimson Tide into the red.

Football shouldered a tremendous financial burden, which placed even greater pressure on the Crimson Tide to win and keep the money flowing. The sport spent $3,020,850 directly on operations, including $299,523 for recruiting. But it gobbled up much more indirectly.

During the period, 'Bama officials felt the need to mount a massive capital improvement campaign to stay competitive with other teams in the SEC, including the construction of a lavish football office complex at a cost of $5 million and an indoor practice facility at a cost of $4 million. The department spent $14.5 million to modernize and expand Bryant-Denny Stadium by 12,000 seats, increasing the capacity to 70,000. It also spent more than $1 million renovating twenty-year-old Coleman Coliseum and purchased an eight-seat jet, used in recruiting, for $1.5 million.

To finance the spending spree, the Crimson Tide went more than $24 million in debt. In 1988, Alabama faced a debt service payment of $3.117 million—about 21 percent of projected revenues. 'Bama administrators saw the infrastructure improvements as a crucial investment in the future. They took on the debt and gambled that they could convince the university's loyal supporters to help pay it off.

"There is no way we could make it from now on without Tide Pride," Sloan said at the time.

For decades, many Alabama fans had been able to purchase season tickets for the face value of the seats. But Tide Pride altered the system by reserving the best seats for supporters willing to pay from $100 to $1,000 each to join the priority plan, which gave them access to purchase tickets. Sloan and his staff sold Tide Pride as a necessity for the future stability of the program, and more than 20,000 Alabama fans joined the program in the first year. Tide Pride pumped more than $7 million per year into the athletic department's coffers, helping the Crimson Tide meet its obligations and placing it on a more stable financial footing.

The program attracted criticism from some who believed it unfairly priced many fans out of the market for football tickets and others who lambasted it as yet another example of the megabucks business of college football trampling on the sport's innocence. But most fans accepted the change as a necessary compromise in the eternal struggle to field a winning team.

The rise of priority programs like Tide Pride represented a new level of incentive and risk for the nation's football programs. All those die-hard supporters who paid big bucks for the right to purchase good tickets felt less like visitors and more like share-holders in the corporation of their favorite team, and their de-mand for results loomed large over programs that feared nothing so much as the prospect of empty seats.

Faced with spiraling costs, administrators across the country struggled to find new sources of revenue. Many schools built high-priced luxury suites overlooking their stadiums, where the swells could enjoy the action and a catered lunch in air-conditioned comfort, surrounded by TV monitors. Others mar-keted corporate sponsorships—some going so far as allowing certain companies to "present" games. Still others aggressively ex-ploited their names through more inventive product licensing. Ea-ger to tap into the obsession shared by fans from coast to coast, Nike pumped millions into the sport by buying the right to place the sneaker maker's signature swoosh emblem on players' jerseys and coaches' shirts—so it could be seen on television.

An increasing number of athletic departments and conferences were led by people with experience in marketing and finance. They all knew their football and they all could speak with great passion and authority about the colorful characters of the past and the great rivalries of the day. But they also talked at great length about branding, corporate synergy, and the need to find new streams of revenue. They spent a lot of time talking about the need to reach consumers. In the old days, they called these people fans.

Desperate to feed the beast, college officials started pushing their conferences to devise new ways of generating income and granting them greater authority to structure more favorable deals with televison and bowl games.

# 11

# THE DEFIANT ONE

The college bowl games roared into the 1980s stronger and more popular than ever before, secure in the enduring power of their partnership with television. But even as TV pumped increasing millions into the postseason, the bowls remained captive to their own rigid caste system, which valued longevity more than performance, promoted safety at the expense of innovation, and discouraged all challenges to the established order. In those days, tradition was like a force of nature in the bowl business, as immutable as the wind.

The Chosen (Rose, Orange, Sugar, and Cotton) controlled the rights to the champions of the most important conferences and staged their games on New Year's Day, which set them apart in the eyes of the fans and the football establishment. The Big Four thought they owned New Year's Day. They believed it was their birthright. No one ever questioned their dominance of the sport's most important day or their monopoly on the final act in the annual national championship drama, because they were the pioneers who had invented the system. The Unchosen (all the rest) fought over the teams unworthy of playing on New Year's Day and held their games on various dates in December. Theirs was not a world of upward mobility. Ambitious little bowls were encouraged to know their place, to understand their limitations, to temper their dreams.

But Bruce Skinner was a rebel. He did not think these prevailing truths were self-evident.

After exploiting television to build the Fiesta Bowl into the most important "minor" bowl, Skinner quickly grew frustrated by the game's inability to shatter the glass ceiling that separated it from the annointed ones. He resented being made to feel like a second-class citizen, and he wanted more than the sport's crumbs. Tired of watching the Big Four use tradition like a weapon, Skinner started looking for a way to challenge the system and move the Fiesta Bowl to New Year's Day, college football's equivalent of toppling the Berlin Wall.

"Our goal was to put ourselves in a position to stage a game for the national championship," Skinner said. "But the only way we could possibly accomplish that was to move onto New Year's Day. You weren't anybody unless you played on New Year's Day, and we wanted to be somebody."

During the NCAA Convention in Miami Beach in January 1981, Skinner learned that the Sugar Bowl was planning to shift from early afternoon (where it played opposite the Cotton Bowl) to prime time (where it would compete against the Orange Bowl). He saw his chance to storm the gates. After securing the support of NBC, which recognized the opportunity to further dominate college football's signature day, Skinner took his plan to the members of the NCAA postseason football committe, who were stunned by the request.

After more than a quarter-century of overseeing the bowl system, the NCAA walked a fine line between the broad certification process and meddling micromanagement, holding the games to strict financial standards and exercising tacit control over playing dates. The governing body's ability to prevent other bowls from disturbing the tradition of the Big Four was, like the sanctity of the day, understood. New Year's Day was sacred, and by attempting to crash the party, Skinner was immediately branded a troublemaker with no appreciation for the importance of history and order.

"In no way did the NCAA want more than four games on New Year's Day," Skinner said. "They thought we had no right to challenge the system."

In the weeks after the Fiesta Bowl applied for the date change, the Big Four mounted an intense lobbying campaign to protect their monopoly. But even before the CFA challenged the football television plan, the NCAA was starting to come to grips with the limits of its authority.

"The attorneys advised us we would be treading on thin ice to try to keep the Fiesta off New Year's Day," said NCAA bowl liaison Dave Cawood.

After significant discussion and legal consultation, the committee reluctantly agreed on April 26—ten years to the day after the Fiesta Bowl's initial certification—to allow the game to move to college football's high-rent district starting in 1982, which marked a turning point in the history of the bowl system.

Over the next five years, the Fiesta Bowl assembled a series of high-quality matchups and posted consistently high ratings for NBC, which rewarded the game with increasingly generous rights fees—surpassing $1 million for the first time in 1984, a tenfold increase in less than a decade. However, the new kid on the block remained in the shadow of the Big Four, who maintained their dominance because they still controlled access to most of the important teams, which allowed them to pay higher appearance guarantees, which, in turn, gave them the leverage to keep the top leagues under contract.

But in 1986, all that security became a huge liability.

When independent powerhouses Miami and Penn State finished unbeaten and ranked 1 and 2 in the wire service polls, the whole world seemed to be clamoring for Jimmy Johnson's Hurricanes and Joe Paterno's Nittany Lions to settle the issue on the field. But the Big Four could not accommodate the highly anticipated event. The Rose Bowl was committed to Big Ten champion

Michigan and Pac-10 champion Arizona State. The Orange Bowl, hosted by Big Eight winner Oklahoma; the Sugar Bowl, hosted by SEC winner LSU; and the Cotton Bowl, hosted by SWC winner Texas A&M, could invite only one of the two teams, and since both Miami and Penn State desperately wanted a piece of each other, they started thinking outside the box.

Why not the Fiesta Bowl?

Seizing the opportunity to snare the biggest game of the year—and achieve real parity with the Rose, Orange, Sugar, and Cotton—Skinner made a pitch for Penn State and Miami to stage their national championship showdown in the Arizona desert. Although the bowl's television contract remained less lucrative than the other four New Year's Day games, the game had strengthened its financial position the previous year by signing a five-year, $7-million sponsorship deal with Sunkist, the citrus growers' cooperative. The newly christened Sunkist Fiesta Bowl launched a bidding war for Miami and Penn State, competing with the suddenly ambitious Citrus and Gator bowls for the right to host the big game while the Big Four looked on with a sense of frustration. Determined to win, Skinner and his associates convinced Sunkist to kick in an additional $1 million, bringing the Sunkist Fiesta Bowl's offer to $2.5 million per team—more than any other game except the venerable Rose Bowl. To sweeten the deal, NBC persuaded the bowl to play in prime time on January 2, where, instead of going head-to-head with the Cotton and Citrus, it would enjoy the nation's undivided attention.

When one of the biggest audiences in college football history watched Penn State upset Miami, 14–10, to clinch Paterno's second national championship, the bowl system changed forever.

The Big Four steamed as the Big Five emerged.

All across America, members of the Unchosen class started to think differently about their role in the system as the defiant Fiesta Bowl became the model for the new age bowl. No longer intimidated by the restraints of hallowed tradition, many officials started daydreaming about following the Fiesta Bowl's blocking all the way to the promised land. Suddenly, anything seemed possible.

"That was definitely a wake-up call," said Bud Dudley, the long-time executive director of the Liberty Bowl. "It signaled the birth of a whole new way of thinking."

By challenging the parameters of the NCAA's regulation of the bowl system and using sponsor money to land the big game, the Fiesta Bowl ushered in a new age.

"We changed the rules," Skinner said.

As television revenue continued to soar in the early 1980s, the bowl games used the bigger checks to dramatically increase their appearance fees. In 1985, the eighteen post-season games pumped $39 million into college athletics. Mandated by the NCAA to return 75 percent of their revenue to the participating schools, they also felt significant pressure to compete with each other. Every dollar mattered, because as the cash-strapped colleges grew addicted to the bowl money, payouts determined pecking order. Programs chose their holiday destinations for a variety of factors, but none loomed larger than the payout, which separated the bowls into a series of competitive tiers. Every year or two, the NCAA raised the minimum payout, which placed additional pressure on the least competitive bowls to meet the ante to stay in the game.

But the television money was a crutch and the bowls were heading for a tumble. Several factors roiled the system starting in the mid-1980s, transforming the postseason into a survival-of-the-fittest jungle.

Even though the *Board of Regents* decision directly affected only regular season football, the bowls also felt the downturn in rights fees. The glut of regular season games gave traditional bowl advertisers many more choices to reach the college football audience, which forced many bowl rights fees into the tank. Other factors conspired to push television revenue lower, including the three other games that followed the Fiesta Bowl's lead by crowding into New Year's Day.

The change diminished the cachet of New Year's Day. With the NCAA no longer able to preserve the purity of the day, the television networks started calling all the shots. No longer reserved for champions, New Year's Day mirrored the trend of regular season football: The big event atmosphere was diminished but in its place fans enjoyed a wall-to-wall bonanza of body-slamming, pass-catching delight, and the distinction was obscured in a blurr of remote-wielding gluttony.

Facing increased competition for playing dates from the NFL, many other games struggled to find good time slots. As a result, TV ratings tumbled by more than 20 percent over a three-year period, placing the bowl system on the wrong side of the supply/demand curve for the first time.

At the height of the market, the Liberty Bowl negotiated a five-game, $900,000 per year deal with the Raycom syndication company. Five seasons later, the bowl was forced to settle for $400,000 from ESPN.

Just about every bowl operator could share a similar tale of woe. Unable to raise ticket prices enough to make up for the shortfall, the various games faced the immediate dilemma of finding a significant new revenue source or reducing appearance fees and unleashing a doomsday scenario. Frightened by the prospect of a Division 1-A playoff—and believing the desperate colleges might be forced to pursue the lucrative option unless they kept payouts rising—many bowl officials followed the Fiesta Bowl's lead and turned to corporate America.

At a time when corporate sponsorship was already firmly established in the sports world—from NASCAR's Winston Cup to the Virginia Slims of Tennis and the Buick Open—the bowls represented an untapped, demographically desirable environment for many kinds of corporations who wanted to share the glow of an established brand with three hours of national television exposure.

By 1989, more than half of all the postseason games signed up title sponsors, including the USF&G Sugar Bowl, the Mazda Gator Bowl, the Sea World Holiday Bowl, the John Hancock Sun Bowl, and the Mobil Cotton Bowl. For fees ranging from $300,000 to more than $2 million per year, the bowls took on new partners who helped secure their financial stability.

"Once the Cotton, Sugar, and Fiesta all made title deals, we had to do the same in order to remain competitive financially," said Nick Crane, the former chairman of the Orange Bowl, which signed a four-year $10.5-million contract with Federal Express in 1989.

Some never negotiated the transition, however.

When Houston's Bluebonnet Bowl saw its television rights fee tumble by more than half and ticket sales plummet by more than 20,000, the game desperately searched for a title sponsor. But no one was interested. Unable to pay the bills, the bowl folded after twenty-eight years.

After promising a per team payout of $1.2 million—fifth among all bowls—the two-year-old Cherry Bowl became a victim of its own overheated ambition. When television revenue swooned and a title sponsorship deal with General Motors failed to materialize, the Detroit game wound up more than $1 million in debt. Organizers stiffed Maryland and Syracuse for several hundred thousand dollars each.

The Freedom Bowl premiered in 1984, during the most chaotic period in the television shakeout, and nearly sank after the syndicator Metrosports went bankrupt owing the game $340,000. Only a loan from the city of Anaheim kept the game afloat. Although the bowl's $515,000 payout ranked near the bottom of the system, officials stressed the importance of being able to live up to their obligations in a world made more cynical by the demise of the Cherry Bowl.

"That's something that's never going to happen to us," Freedom Bowl executive director Tom Starr told a reporter in 1988. "We've never promised anything that we couldn't deliver. We know our place, and our limits."

Four years later, the Freedom Bowl was dead, too, unable to survive without an infusion of corporate cash.

While most games eagerly pursued sponsors with little thought about surrendering a piece of their independence, the Rose Bowl steadfastly refused to consider the option, which was understandable under the circumstances. In 1988, ABC bucked the rights fee trend by stealing the Pasadena game away from NBC with a ten-year, $100-million deal, preserving the game's unrivaled financial dominance. ABC lost a bundle for several years, but the Rose Bowl was able to keep paying the Big Ten and Pac-10 more than $13 million combined per year without diluting its brand—flush with cash from TV and ticket sales.

Even as the system took on a Darwinian glint, with the various games competing vigorously for sponsors, television viewers, ticket buyers, and finite dates on the calendar, the bowl games used all the new corporate revenue to keep payouts soaring. The system generated $56 million in 1989—a 30 percent increase in five years.

Amid the flood of dollars, some bowl organizers faced painful, unanticipated compromises.

With a seating capacity of slightly more than 50,000 and a location far from major metropolitan centers, the Sun Bowl in El Paso relied even more than most postseason games on its worth as a television property. When CBS decreased the game's rights fee from $600,000 to $350,000 in 1986, Sun Bowl officials gladly accepted a deal with John Hancock Financial Services. The Boston-based insurance giant agreed to pump nearly $2.6 million into the event over three years in exchange for renaming it the John Hancock Sun Bowl, which bailed the game out of a jam and brought it a new level of financial security.

Like all such deals, the arrangement actually enhanced the importance of the game as a television property because the sponsor wagered a large percentage of its investment on the bowl's ability to achieve ratings and demographic success. For John Hancock, the deal represented more than advertising on a national television broadcast, however. The partnership allowed the company to tap into the goodwill associated with the Sun Bowl, to exploit the venerable brand of a college football institution as a way of raising the insurance company's profile in the consciousness of the nation's sports fans.

During the first three years of the deal, the company became increasingly disturbed by the reluctance among the media, and therefore, fans across the country, to refer to the game as the John Hancock Sun Bowl. Five decades of habits were tough to break. When the two sides gathered to negotiate an extension to the pact in the summer of 1989, John Hancock officials confronted the Sun Bowl organizers with a stunning ultimatum: Accept a generous 105 percent increase in the title fee—to nearly $9 million over five years—and change the name of the game to the John Hancock Bowl, or find another meal ticket.

The choice between independence and dependence was no longer the issue. Three years into the arrangement, the El Paso event was as reliant on sponsor money as it had once been on TV dollars. It was a matter of liberty or death, and with bills to pay and a whole city wrapped up in the game's existence, liberty seemed like a luxury the bowl could no longer afford.

"We had no choice," said Sun Bowl's executive director John Junker. "Without John Hancock, we wouldn't have been able to survive."

College football's rise as a big business evolved with a graduated momentum through the years, but few events symbolized the transformation as succinctly as the birth of the John Hancock Bowl.

Even as several games crashed and burned, the NCAA continued to certify new bowls, relying on the market to sort out the winners and losers.

"We're not in the business of determining how many games the market can support," explained NCAA executive director Dick Schultz. "From a legal standpoint, we have to allow a game to go forward as long as it meets the standard criteria."

Caught between the free market ethos inspired by the Fiesta Bowl and the tired vestiges of the old era, the bowl system entered the late 1980s struggling to maintain relevance with teams and the viewing public.

With the battle for the mythical national championship producing as much frustration as consensus in some years, the public's appetite for a major college playoff started gaining momentum. As the only NCAA sport without a national championship tournament, big-time football faced difficulty in explaining to fans, media, and its own players why it persisted in supporting the bowl structure instead of adopting a dynamic playoff system designed to crown a real champion on the field. Because the bowls had cultivated tremendous clout and loyalty among coaches and administrators, the concept remained mired in bureaucratic inertia, but the bowls knew their only sure defense against a playoff was to render it too big of a financial gamble.

With the Rose, Orange, Sugar, and Cotton bowls clinging desperately to the tradition of awarding automatic bids to the champions of the five most important conferences, the system seemed incredibly out of date. If the winners of the SEC and Big Ten finished unbeaten and ranked atop the wire service polls, their commitments to the Sugar and Rose, respectively, prevented them from meeting to settle the national championship. In fact, in most years, thanks to this structural handcuff, the big prize was decided not by a Number 1 versus Number 2 showdown on New Year's Day but by a series of good but not-quite-fulfilling matchups between contenders, sometimes resulting in controversial split decisions.

For years, teams and fans accepted such entanglements as a necessary flaw in the system—the price of giving the bowls, conferences, and television networks security. But the success of the Fiesta Bowl shined a spotlight on the blemish and proved another way was possible.

At the same time, the Fiesta Bowl's fingerprints were all over the intensified competition to fill the noncommitted slots every year. For decades, the NCAA maintained a rule prohibiting the bowls from issuing bids to teams prior to a certain date in late-November, which was intended to maintain a sense of order and prevent any one game from achieving an unfair advantage in the

selection of teams. But bid day was a joke by the late 1980s. No
one lived by the rule, which rendered it unenforceable and left the
various games scrambling to outfox each other and assemble
matchups weeks in advance. When one bowl brokered a surrepti-
tious deal, others were compelled to act quickly or risk losing access to the best teams.

No one was more frustrated by the chaotic system than the
leaders of the big conferences, and they were preparing to come to
the bowls' rescue. But first they needed to consolidate their power.

# 12

## AMERICA'S TEAM

Three years into Chuck Neinas's brave new world, most everyone involved in college football wanted to put the genie back in the bottle.

Network ratings had tumbled for two years and then bottomed out in the third. The glut of games available through syndication and cable left fans with a plethora of choices throughout the day, which mirrored the larger trend roiling the broadcast networks, who saw their share of total audience tumble from more than 90 percent to about 60 percent in the 1980s. The days of appointment viewing were over. College football suddenly was as accessible as *Headline News* and—like Peter Jennings—Keith Jackson was just another guy with a mike.

The uneven geographic distribution of the rival packages further complicated the battle between ABC and CBS. With the Big Ten and Pac-10 under contract, CBS scored well on the West Coast and in the industrial Midwest—the region with the second-highest concentration of TV sets—but ABC's CFA package—consisting of the SEC, SWC, ACC, Big Eight, WAC, and major independents including Notre Dame and Penn State—provided the network with greater balance across the country and much more relevance in the football-crazed Southeast.

In 1986, CBS strengthened its hand by securing a four-year, $60-million contract with the CFA starting in 1987. ABC responded by signing a four-year, $52-million deal with the Big Ten and Pac-10. The switch would allow CBS to take the lead in the fight for splintered ratings, but the whole market remained incredibly depressed. Four years into deregulation, college football's network earnings would still be down more than 50 percent from the record levels of 1983.

Unsatisfied with the status quo, Dennis Swanson, the newly appointed president of ABC Sports, decided to change the game. Swanson, a domineering former Marine captain, had risen through the ranks within the ABC station group before being chosen to succeed Roone Arledge, which was a bit like replacing Wilt Chamberlain in the paint. The business was changing as well. After Capital Cities Broadcasting purchased ABC for $3.5 billion—140 times Leonard Goldenson's original investment—the network was moving into an era of belt-tightening austerity. Feeling the pressure of replacing a living legend while casting a wary eye on the bottom line, Swanson was anxious to make his mark. He decided to divide and conquer.

Because college football occupies such a special place in Southern culture, the SEC is the center of the athletic universe for the vast majority of sports fans in the nine-state region. In 1986, it was also the lynchpin of the incredibly fragile CFA. In an effort to improve his prospects in the Southeast, Swanson was determined to steal the conference away from CBS. Without the powerful league, CBS would be significantly weakened and the CFA, which had survived mostly as an extension of Neinas's salesmanship and Father Joyce's goodwill, might collapse. He wanted the SEC. He needed the SEC.

After several weeks of discrete talks, Swanson flew to Birmingham to meet with a small group of conference officials at the Winfrey Hotel. They negotiated for several hours. After he offered the league a four-year, $24-million contract—considerably more than the teams were making with CBS—Swanson walked away believing they had a handshake deal. Donn Bernstein, ABC's director of college sports, rushed out of the meeting to find a pay phone and share the good news with network officials back in New York. On the plane ride home, Swanson and Bernstein celebrated their coup with cocktails and broad smiles. All that remained was for the lawyers to work out the details of the contract.

"We thought we had a deal—a huge deal," Bernstein said. "There was no question in our minds."

But Harvey Schiller later insisted the conference had not made a formal decision to accept the contract.

"We did not have an agreement," said Schiller, the commissioner of the SEC at the time and the former head of Turner Sports and the United States Olympic Committee. "If we had, we would have abided by it."

According to several college and network sources, the blockbuster agreement evaporated over the next several days as word began to spread among CFA members. Schiller reluctantly called Swanson to say the presidents had changed their minds.

Between the meeting and the telephone call, officials from other CFA colleges and conferences mounted an intense lobbying campaign on their SEC counterparts. Understanding how detrimental the league's defection could be to their shaky union, presidents and athletic directors put the arm on their colleagues. Martin A. Massengale, the Nebraska chancellor, proved especially convincing with his peers, filling the telephone lines with his understated academician's monotone, lecturing other administrators about unity, pleading for solidarity. Some of the officials were much less diplomatic—raising the specter of canceling games with SEC teams and boycotting the Sugar Bowl, hosted by the league's champion. Somewhere, Franny Murray was smiling.

In addition to the veiled threats, the CFA offered the SEC schools more exposures and corresponding revenue increases in their new deals with CBS and ESPN, which played a significant part in the reversal. But most officials close to the situation believe Father Joyce saved the union.

Joyce, who had never wavered in his preference for a unified national package, could say in all candor that Notre Dame had turned down several lucrative offers to walk away from the CFA. Everyone understood how Notre Dame's presence had significantly strengthened and perhaps preserved the CFA consortium in the chaotic days after the Supreme Court decision. When Joyce and athletic director Gene Corrigan pleaded with the SEC to maintain the group's unity, it carried the weight of prestige and the implication of shared sacrifice.

"I was furious when I heard about that deal," Corrigan said. "Everyone knew Notre Dame had turned down a big offer . . . that we could have gone out on our own at any point. Yet we thought it was better for everyone concerned if we stayed together."

During a combative, hastily arranged meeting with key SEC officials in Atlanta several days after the pact became public, Corrigan stressed the need for solidarity and the dangers of further disintegration. He pledged Notre Dame's commitment to the CFA plan, and as every member of the small, insular old boys network knew, Notre Dame's word was as good as a gentleman's handshake.

The Notre Dame mystique has been a powerful force in the sport since Knute Rockne built the dynasty in the 1920s. At a time when the nation's sporting landscape was still being formed, fawning newspaper coverage by sportswriters like Grantland Rice elevated Rockne and players like the Four Horsemen to national icons, transforming the Fighting Irish into the nation's most celebrated college football team. The national radio network assembled by Rockne enhanced the team's unique position, giving the school an unrivaled media presence for decades. Hollywood also played a role in creating a place for Notre Dame in the American cultural firmament. *Knute Rockne All American*, the 1940 motion picture starring Pat O'Brien and Ronald Reagan, lifted Rockne and star runner George Gipp to mythic status. Beginning in the 1950s, television coverage took the program to even greater awareness and stature, despite the rigid controls of the NCAA era.

Through the years, the national fascination with Notre Dame reinforced the dominance of the Fighting Irish. The sport's leading school in terms of victories, winning percentage, and national championships derived tremendous strength from the intense media coverage, which gave the Fighting Irish the pick of the best high school athletes from across the country. Many schools recruited nationally, but unlike Southern Cal or Nebraska, Notre Dame did not start with a base of instate talent. At any given time, the school's roster included players from dozens of states. Television was crucial in keeping the Fighting Irish front and center in the consciousness of the nation's athletes, coaches, and fans.

Notre Dame was college football's equivalent of the New York Yankees—beloved by many, hated by many others, and respected by all.

When the handcuffs came off, Notre Dame fans got the chance to see nearly all of the Fighting Irish games on television. Many of the big games appeared as part of the CFA's network and cable packages. The Irish also were seen on the Big Ten/Pac-10 series for crossover games like Southern Cal and Michigan—rivalries that flipped back to the CFA package when Notre Dame was the home team. Most of the remaining three or four games not picked up by the two major plans usually wound up on the school's supplemental cable deals—first WGN and later SportsChannel America.

Since Notre Dame Stadium's 59,000 seats had been sold out for decades, university officials did not worry about hurting the gate. They saw television as a way to promote the school and feed the insatiable appetite of their far-flung fans. All across the country, sports fans with no connection with the university—especially Irish Catholics—supported Notre Dame with an unsurpassed fervor. These so-called "subway alumni" rarely if ever visited the South Bend campus, but their passion and loyalty provided the university with tremendous clout.

Demand for coverage of Notre Dame games never waned in the early days of deregulation, even though the Fighting Irish were struggling through one of their most frustrating periods. Under onetime high school coach Gerry Faust, the most successful program in college history tumbled headfirst into mediocrity in the 1980s. In 1986, Notre Dame fired Faust and replaced him with former Arkansas and Minnesota coach Lou Holtz, who would quickly lead the Fighting Irish back to national prominence.

Several months after Holtz arrived, Father Joyce retired and Corrigan moved on to become commissioner of the Atlantic Coast Conference. The powerful pair were replaced by Father William E. Beauchamp, who had been groomed for the post during his three-year apprenticeship under Joyce, and South Bend banker Richard Rosenthal, a former Irish basketball player.

The forty-five-year-old Beauchamp, trained as a lawyer, was a precise, articulate representative of the Notre Dame empire. Most everyone called him "Father Bill." Genuinely well liked by his peers in college sports, he seemed at ease around both academics and athletic types, a rare quality and one vitally important in his fence-straddling role. Soon after his promotion to executive vice president, Beauchamp was appointed to several important college sports committees, including a place on the CFA's board of directors. He knew and everyone knew that in filling those positions he was not merely representing the nation's most important independent. He was inheriting Joyce's mantle of leadership.

Like Joyce, Beauchamp was sensitive about Notre Dame's unusual position within the college sports establishment, which engendered no small amount of jealousy and tension. "We don't want to be viewed as someone who is out there on their own," he said. "The more Notre Dame can be viewed as just another institution that's part of the NCAA is fine with me. The more Notre Dame is looked upon as something unique is distressing to me."

*Rudy*, the 1993 motion picture starring Sean Astin, raised the Notre Dame mystique to even greater heights. The movie, based on a true story, traced the unlikely journey of a small, untalented player who pursued the seemingly impossible goal of making the Notre Dame team with amazing tenacity. For Rudy Ruttinger, Notre Dame was not just the nation's winningest football program, it was a metaphor for the American dream. His experience transcended sports; it proved great things are possible if you have enough determination and heart. At the end of the movie, the whole country seemed to be shouting "Rudy! Rudy! Rudy"—even the millions of football fans from Michigan to Alabama who considered the Irish the enemy.

In the summer of 1989, as Notre Dame was preparing to defend its first national championship in more than a decade, the CFA began negotiating with ESPN to extend their contract. While the broadcast networks continued to battle for splintered ratings, which prevented them from paying higher rights fees, ESPN had been able to build its package of Saturday night games into a powerful new showcase for college football. The series drew a much smaller rating than the networks, but the growth of cable during the 1980s essentially cushioned the CFA's fall. Because ESPN was able to generate revenue from advertising as well as cable operators—who paid per-subscriber fees, which they passed on to customers—the channel was able to escalate rights fees, which reflected the rapid expansion of the cable universe. When the CFA signed a four-year, $110-million contract with ESPN covering 1991 to 1994—triple the original deal—members quietly rejoiced in what they saw as the long-awaited benefits of the free market.

In the days of the NCAA plan, the participation of the various schools was not a matter open for discussion. Several months before the governing body started planning a new contract, the membership was allowed to vote on the television committee's principles of negotiation, but given the makeup of the diverse body, the outcome of the vote was always a foregone conclusion. In the NCAA's view, approval of the principles of negotiation by a majority of the membership bound all schools to the resulting contracts.

The CFA operated much differently. Neinas and his television committee discussed their principles of negotiation among the membership and bargained with the networks based on those guidelines. Only after reaching a deal did the CFA bring it back to the members for approval. Each and every school reserved the right to participate or not.

In the fall of 1989, as Neinas and his committee finalized the ESPN contract and started working on a new network pact, Notre Dame's participation was assumed. On October 24, Beauchamp drafted a letter to Neinas:

> Dear Chuck:
>
> I know you have been anxious to receive from Notre Dame its commitment to participate in the ESPN package for the 1991 through 1994 football seasons. As I have indicated to you, the University was reluctant to make that commitment without knowing exactly what will be contained in the network contract, and we still have that reluctance.
>
> Thus, we are not willing to make an absolute commitment to participate at this time. However, I hope that the following will be helpful.
>
> Notre Dame is generally pleased with the agreement as negotiated with ESPN for 1991 through 1994. We note that an additional 5 percent of the proceeds of the contract will be paid to participating schools (25 percent v. 20 percent). Of course, this means that a small percentage will be available for game rights fees. Even though this potentially affects Notre Dame in a negative manner, we accept this because it is assumed that there will be more dollars distributed in total as games rights fees.
>
> You have indicated in your correspondence that you anticipate the network agreement terms (except for dollars) will be pretty much what is contained in

the current CBS contract. If that is true, I would expect Notre Dame to agree to participate in both the
ESPN and network agreements.

However, until such time as there is agreement
from a network on the network contract so that we
can look at the total package of the ESPN and network contracts combined, Notre Dame will not
make an absolute commitment to participate with
either ESPN or the networks.

Chuck, we will simply not lock ourselves into a
position that in the end might be harmful to our best
interests without having all the facts before us. As I
indicated above, Notre Dame fully expects to be a
participant in the network and ESPN agreements
with the CFA. But, the University will only agree to
such participation after they have seen the total
package as negotiated. Chuck, I hope you understand and appreciate our position.

If you have any questions, please do not hesitate
to let me know.

Sincerely,
(Rev.) E. William Beauchamp, C.S.C.
Executive Vice President

When he received the letter from Beauchamp instead of the anticipated consent form—which was sent to and received back from
all of the other member institutions—Neinas chose to interpret it as
a mere formality. He chose to condense the central point of the correspondence down to one line: ". . . Notre Dame fully expects to be
a participant . . . "

More than two years later, Beauchamp said, "Reading that letter,
it was reasonable to assume Notre Dame would participate. I had no
reason to believe we wouldn't participate, but I had a problem with

signing off on the cable deal before we had the network agreement in hand."

Neinas showed the letter to members of his television committee, but he did not provide it to ESPN or the broadcast networks. This was a huge mistake, a tremendous error in judgment. Neinas owed his television partners all the information available about the current mindset of the most important team in the cartel, especially such critical intelligence. Sharing the letter with the appropriate television officials would have significantly weakened his bargaining position—which is why he didn't do it—but he should have made it available regardless of the consequences. Not making the correspondence known to the broadcasters was like pretending that it meant nothing—and hoping and wishing and praying had no place in the serious business of negotiating multimillion-dollar contracts.

"Chuck knew he had a problem," said Ken Shanzer, executive vice president of NBC Sports. "He was scared to death of going to the networks and saying he had everybody except Notre Dame, so he assumed it would all work out. He took a calculated risk."

Neinas viewed the correspondence through the prism of Notre Dame's history of unswerving support for the CFA and his close relationship with Father Beauchamp. Rather than relying on the letter, Neinas chose to listen to the man. As secretary-treasurer of the CFA, Beauchamp played a significant role in developing both the ESPN and network contracts. Assuming that the man in the cleric's collar spoke for Notre Dame was hardly a leap of faith.


Six seasons after the Supreme Court ruling, college football's combined broadcast network revenue of about $32 million—50 percent below the final season of the monopoly—was a constant reminder of the disastrous effects of deregulation. Instead of using cable and syndication to rake in new millions for the football arms race and Title IX, the various conferences and independents had been forced to try to mine such sources simply to replace the dramatic network shortfall.

After the NACDA effort to bring the rival camps together fell apart in the summer of 1989, the Big Ten and Pac-10 renewed their deal with ABC for about $17 million per year. When the CFA entered the marketplace for a contract covering 1991 to 1995, CBS was anxious to extend its relationship with the sixty-three-team consortium. But after deeming an initial offer of $150 million over five years unacceptable, the CFA television committee—including Beauchamp—gave Neinas the go-ahead to gauge the interest of ABC and NBC. NBC made an offer, but it was similarly unappealing.

However, the CFA's contract was more valuable to ABC than CBS because, by adding the cartel to its existing Big Ten and Pac-10 deals, the network could end the broadcast competition and presumably increase ratings and ad rates. ABC officials crunched the numbers and made a series of educated guesses. Then they presented the CFA with a stunning bid of $210 million over five years—50 percent more than CBS.

ABC's offer included a very big catch. Because of its preexisting Big Ten/Pac-10 deal—which guaranteed those conferences at least one game each Saturday to be seen in at least 50 percent of the country—ABC wanted to pursue predominantly a regionalization approach. Otherwise, it could never get all the games on the air.

The choice was clear: revenue versus exposure.

The CBS and NBC deals would allow the CFA schools to maintain their national network window. But the ABC bid represented significantly more money.

"We had been very pleased with CBS," Beauchamp said. "We went in with the hopes of continuing with CBS. But CBS wasn't offering enough money."

Given the choice between an exclusive national window and more money in exchange for sharing a window, the CFA chose ABC for strictly financial reasons.

The deal represented a financial breakthrough. In 1983, the CFA schools received about $37 million from the network package.

With ABC's offer, the cartel would in 1991 earn about $42 million. Eight seasons after deregulation, the consortium finally would surpass the high-water mark achieved by the NCAA. Finally, after nearly a decade of red ink and finger pointing.

The sport's total take from the broadcast networks still fell short of the final NCAA package, counting the Big Ten and Pac-10 packages. Not to mention the effects of inflation. Or what might have been.

During an explosion in sports pricing—when the NFL's television contracts nearly tripled—college football was a conspicuous exception to the trend. Had the monopoly remained in place and benefited not only from its own success but also from the rights fee spiral, the colleges might have earned $125 million or more per year from the networks by the early 1990s. No one could say for certain.

But in the context of the new era of lowered expectations, the ABC gambit represented a significant achievement.

On the morning of January 17, 1990, after listening to the final proposal by ABC officials, Neinas convened a conference call of the CFA's television committee. The group included Syracuse athletic director Jake Crouthamel, Alabama athletic director Hootie Ingram, Brigham Young athletic director Glen Tuckett, Texas athletic director DeLoss Dodds, and Big Eight commissioner Carl James. He explained the merits of the offer and asked the board to vote whether to recommend the deal to the membership. The result was unanimous. Everyone seemed delighted with the offer, including Beauchamp.

His yes vote would come back to haunt him.


Seventeen days after the vote, Neinas received a telephone call from Father Bill, who wanted to know if the CFA executive could meet with him and Dick Rosenthal the next day at Denver's Stapleton Airport, located less than an hour's drive from the organization's Boulder office. Neinas gladly agreed without asking what it was about. A few minutes later, he called Beauchamp back.

Neinas knew Rosenthal owned a cabin in the area, so he thought the two administrators were stopping by on their way to the ski slopes.

"Would it be better if I just meet you at the cabin?" Neinas asked.

No, Beauchamp replied. The airport would work fine.

Naturally, Neinas was a little curious. But he didn't press the matter.

When the three men sat down in a private room inside the Red Carpet Club the next morning, Neinas asked innocently, "Are you guys going up to the mountains?"

"No" Beauchamp said. "We just came to see you."

Over the next hour, Beauchamp and Rosenthal told Neinas in great length of their serious concerns about the CFA's network package with ABC. They discussed their dissatisfaction with the regionalization concept, which would prevent Notre Dame from making its usual number of national appearances. They explained how national television was the key to Notre Dame's football recruiting and a vital part of the overall university's public relations.

Then they hit him with the bad news: NBC had made Notre Dame a generous offer, and they were considering it.

Painfully aware of Notre Dame's enormous importance to the CFA television deals, Neinas tried to disuade his two colleagues. He pleaded with them much as Father Joyce once had pleaded with the leaders of the SEC.

"Father Bill knew his big games against Miami, SC, whoever, would be national," Neinas said later.

He was prepared to guarantee whatever they wanted, but Notre Dame's position seemed irreconcilable with the new CFA contract.

"Chuck kept saying, 'Tell me what you need [to stay within the CFA plan] and I'll take care of it,'" Beauchamp said. "But it wasn't that simple. We told Chuck that he couldn't make a separate deal for Notre Dame. There was already enough resentment of Notre Dame by some of the schools. If the CFA had made a separate deal with us, that would have made the situation even worse."

Less than a week later, Notre Dame announced an exclusive $38-million contract with NBC, covering thirty Irish home games from 1991 to 1995. At a news conference in South Bend, Rosenthal tried to explain the school's position. "We face a demand for television exposure of our games from fans and alumni all over the country," he said. "And after reviewing the details of the ABC contract, we felt it in the best interests of Notre Dame to seek a contract that would offer our fans more opportunities to see Notre Dame football."

The news hit the rest of CFA like a punch in the stomach.

Notre Dame? Notre Dame had done this?

More than a few people who had opposed the Oklahoma-Georgia lawsuit took a measure of smug satisfaction in the decision. Upon hearing the news, Wayne Duke, the recently retired commissioner of the Big Ten and a steadfast supporter of the NCAA plan, placed a call to Walter Byers. When his old boss answered the phone, Duke attempted to disguise his voice, but Byers knew it was him almost immediately.

"Walter, this is Father Joyce," Duke said, trying not to laugh. "We finally got you sons of bitches!"

"Yeah," Byers snapped back, "but it took you forty years to do it."


Like every other CFA official on the line, Father Beauchamp voted to approve the ABC contract and recommend it to the membership during their January 17 teleconference. He never voiced a word of dissent. He never uttered a syllable about Notre Dame's dissatisfaction with the deal. While his vote did not bind Notre Dame, it carried the implication of Notre Dame's consent.

"Father Beauchamp never raised a concern about the ABC deal," said BYU's Tuckett. "He voted yes like all the rest of us. We all thought it was a good deal. We assumed his yes vote was a yes vote from Notre Dame."

Beauchamp, who was directly involved in the negotiations, insisted that the committee members read too much into his affirmative vote.

"In my opinion, it was clear that this was the feeling of the committee . . . to take the contract to the membership," he said. "As the secretary-treasurer of the CFA, I felt that I had to vote in the best interests of the membership. I didn't think it was my place to say no. My vote wasn't an approval from Notre Dame."

In a legal sense, of course, he was right. But everyone on the telephone line assumed—and quite logically so—that Beauchamp spoke for Notre Dame. Who wouldn't make such an assumption? Father Bill's presence on the committee was a confirmation of Notre Dame's importance to the package as well as a safeguard to make sure America's Team was satisfied with the resulting plan. A man of Beauchamp's savvy and intellect should have known how his vote was being perceived.

Beauchamp vehemently denied that he intentionally misled his colleagues. "At the time of the vote, I did not have any intention of striking a separate deal," he said.

No evidence exists that Beauchamp was secretly negotiating the NBC deal prior to the teleconference, but some leaders of the CFA later insinuated as much. "Most disconcerting to me were the absolute lies and falsehoods made about me," Beauchamp said. "The suggestion that while I was involved with negotiations on behalf of the CFA, I was really negotiating with NBC on behalf of Notre Dame! That is simply not true. We were not out looking for our own network."

According to Notre Dame and NBC officials, the idea of a separate contract grew out of a trip to New York in the middle of January by Rosenthal, who stopped by the networks while in town for a basketball game. At NBC, he met with Shanzer and expressed, in what Shanzer described as a "casual conversation," his problems with the impending CFA deal with ABC. Two days later, Shanzer said, he called Rosenthal in South Bend and asked if, under the circumstances, Notre Dame was free to discuss an indepedent deal. The athletic director said he would have to call him back. After conferring with Beauchamp, Rosenthal told Shanzer Notre Dame would like to talk about a separate contract.

Excited, Shanzer walked over to the office of his boss, NBC

Sports president Dick Ebersol—one of the industry's most influential figures, the visionary who helped give birth to *Saturday Night Live*—and stuck his head in the door. "I think we might have a chance to catch lightning in a bottle," he said.

On January 24, Shanzer flew to South Bend and met Rosenthal and Beauchamp at the athletic director's house, because all three men wanted to keep the talks hush-hush. They discussed what Notre Dame desired in terms of guaranteed national exposures, consistent starting times, and promotion. They never talked about money.

About a week later, Rosenthal flew to New York and started talking numbers with NBC. It didn't take them long to reach the framework of a deal. "There are only two people who know what really happened: Dick Rosenthal and me," Shanzer said. "There were absolutely no discussions about a contract between NBC and Notre Dame until the CFA deal was completed. There was no collusion."

Considering Notre Dame's pivotal role in the CFA television plan, Beauchamp's approval of the package and his silence at the time of the vote seem unfathomable. For Beauchamp to say the school had signed with NBC because the ABC deal that he had approved had been "unacceptable" was difficult to reconcile with the facts. Not only had he never given the CFA a chance to fix the problem, he had never given the other leaders of the organization any hint that there was a problem—notwithstanding the months-old letter, which was overshadowed by his more recent actions.

Beauchamp's silence allowed him to use the resulting plan as an excuse to take Notre Dame to NBC, which represented a failure of his fiduciary responsibility to the CFA and a betrayal of the university's long and distinguished tradition of ethical leadership. He acted more like a lawyer than a priest.

Against the backdrop of Notre Dame's history as a staunch supporter of CFA solidarity—and the university's role in preventing the SEC from bolting three years before—the resulting outcry against the program was understandable. Many of Beauchamp's colleagues felt blindsided. "Father Joyce never would have let that happen," some said privately.

But despite the controversial way Beauchamp handled the matter, one fact remains unassailable: Notre Dame had every right to make the deal.

In the days and weeks after the blockbuster announcement, many college officials wallowed in hypocrisy while deriding the pact as a cynical money grab. Some people had very short memories, including Georgia head coach and athletic director Vince Dooley, who railed against the act of "ultimate greed."

The television rebels failed to understand that there was no such thing as a little freedom. They were frustrated because they had launched a process that they could no longer control. The same emancipation that had allowed the whole sport to break away from the oppressive NCAA monopoly also provided Notre Dame with the right to flee a CFA package that no longer fit its needs.

The sanctimonious critics of the Fighting Irish needed a mirror. For the Notre Dame deal and all of the madness to follow, the CFA schools ultimately had no one to blame but themselves.

# 13

## MUSICAL CHAIRS

The day after Notre Dame's blockbuster announcement, Chuck Neinas flew to New York and tried to convince ABC and ESPN he could hold the fragile CFA coalition together. After quickly renegotiating the two contracts for a combined $45-million rights fee reduction—assuming the participation of all sixty-three remaining teams—Neinas made a bold promise: He would have every school signed up within seventy-two hours. The network executives were supportive but skeptical.

When he returned to his Boulder office, with his empire teetering on the brink, Neinas relentlessly worked the phones. He gently warned the various administrators and coaches about the perils of further splintering the television situation and bluntly explained how the demise of the CFA plan could prevent some teams from accessing the TV audience at all. He sold hard and well. By Thursday afternoon, with a deadline of noon eastern time Friday looming, only the SEC remained undecided.

For five days in February 1990, the CFA package survived only on the hope—not so much the belief, but the hope—that the SEC would not follow Notre Dame out the door. The SEC's value to the cartel was lost on no one. Without the SEC and its powerhouse teams—including Auburn, Tennessee, Alabama, and Florida—the

ABC and ESPN contracts were worth much less, perhaps zero in the eyes of the network number crunchers. While the SEC was being courted by CBS, Turner Broadcasting's TBS superstation, and syndicator Jefferson-Pilot, the other members of the alliance held their collective breath. If the SEC bolted, the CFA was DOA.

"Notre Dame pulling away forced us all to look at the situation and decide what was in our best interests," Alabama athletic director Cecil "Hootie" Ingram later explained. "There were other folks offering us pretty good deals to go out on our own. We had to look out for ourselves."

Without the SEC, the other fifty-three commitments seemed as valuable as Confederate money. Concerned—like Notre Dame—by the practical application of ABC's regionalization concept, the SEC athletic directors seriously considered several hastily assembled proposals from other television entities but eventually voted to stay with the CFA if they could win a very big concession.

"We would like to remain within the CFA," LSU athletic director Joe Dean said, fresh from a Thursday afternoon conference call of league athletic directors, "but we have to have some assurances."

During the first six years of the CFA plan, the SEC schools, who represented 16 percent of the membership, had appeared in 26 percent of all broadcast network telecasts, a testament to the league's popularity and clout. The regionalization concept, complicated by the presence of the Big Ten and Pac-10, threatened to undermine the SEC's traditional dominance in this calculus, potentially costing the conference money and exposure. The SEC demanded a guarantee of at least 20 percent of the exposures in the new plan, and after some back and forth, Neinas agreed.

On Friday morning, however, SEC commissioner Roy Kramer, one of the saviest deal-makers in the history of college sports, called Neinas and said the SEC needed 24 percent in writing. Or it was good-bye.

"I told him there was no way I could authorize that," Neinas recalled later. "But I said, 'I'll tell you what I'll do. I'll unilaterally go to 22 percent and hope I can get the blessing of the [television] committee.'"

Kramer, who knew he controlled the CFA's future, took the compromise and sealed the deal, which represented a guarantee of at least $7.9 million per year from the network package.

"Those were uncertain times and it was important that we try to work together as we figured out where everything was heading," Kramer said.

The tense week was a wake-up call for the SEC and the other major players in college athletics. Even as they guaranteed the CFA's survival for another five years, the college football leadership started preparing for a future without the cartel.

During his tenure as SEC commissioner in the late 1980s, Harvey Schiller spent significant time concentrating on marketing issues. With his ten institutions facing tremendous financial pressures, the retired Air Force colonel was determined to more effectively exploit the league's brand and find new ways to generate revenue. Under Schiller's leadership, the SEC aggressively courted corporate sponsors, creating a lucrative partnership program soon copied by other conferences.

During discussions with various business leaders, Schiller discovered a fundamental weakness in his league's appeal. Corporations as diverse as Regions Bank and Chick-fil-A saw tremendous benefit from tapping into the frenzy associated with the SEC teams, but many other sponsors and advertisers who wanted to connect with fans in the Southeast also craved access to other areas of the South without SEC teams, especially Texas, Arkansas, and South Carolina. The SEC's area of dominant influence fell short of the footprint desired by many consumer-oriented corporations.

"There was also the concern among marketers," Schiller explained, "that even by advertising on an SEC program in the state of Florida, they were missing something by losing the Florida State and Miami fans."

The key, he quickly realized, was TV sets. The greater number of television homes a conference could claim within its domain, the more clout it could wield with television networks and advertisers. About the same time, Schiller discovered an obscure NCAA rule allowing conferences with at least twelve members to hold a championship playoff, which he saw as a way to generate tremendous additional revenue—especially as a TV property—while heightening the level of fan excitement in the mold of the league basketball tournament.

Out of an ongoing discussion with various officials, Schiller started pushing the SEC leadership to consider expansion by at least two teams.

"I was convinced [expansion] could take us to the next level as a conference," Schiller said.

"Harvey is the one who put the notion in everybody's mind," said Big East commissioner Mike Tranghese.

Less than a month before longtime Vanderbilt athletic director Roy Kramer replaced Schiller—who took over the U.S. Olympic Committee—in January 1990, the presidents of the Big Ten extended an invitation to independent powerhouse Penn State. The admission of the Nittany Lions was held up indefinitely after the conference's athletic directors rebelled because they had not been consulted on the decision, but it forced everyone—especially the SEC—to start thinking about expansion more seriously. Although the Big Ten presidents chose to add Penn State to the family primarily for academic reasons, the impact on the league's television footprint was impossible to deny. Bringing several million East Coast television sets into the Big Ten's domain further strengthened the conference with the networks and immediately devalued the CFA, which lost its second most important independent.

The future of the two major television cartels was also being threatened by the government. Six years after the Supreme Court invalidated the NCAA monopoly, the Federal Trade Commission (FTC) was investigating possible antitrust violations by the CFA and Big Ten/Pac-10 plans, a fishing expedition that assumed greater urgency after ABC brought the factions back together under one roof. The CFA unwittingly played into the FTC's hands by signing the more restrictive but more profitable contract with ABC.

Notre Dame's Father Beauchamp saw it coming even before the Irish bolted the CFA package. "Putting [college football] all on one network, it seemed to me, would exacerbate the situation with the FTC," he said.

If the CFA package was dismantled by the government, every conference would be forced to deal directly with the networks. Some were more prepared for this possibility than others.

The combination of Notre Dame, Penn State, and the FTC colored the college sports landscape with a tint of uncertainty and vulnerability in the spring of 1990.

When SEC officials gathered for their annual meeting in Destin, Florida, at the end of May, they felt compelled to act to strengthen their hand. The league's presidents and athletic directors authorized the conference to explore with all deliberate speed expansion to as many as sixteen teams. Their wish list included Miami, Florida State, Texas, Texas A&M, Arkansas, and South Carolina. All of the schools seemed compatible with the current SEC members and all had expressed some level of informal interest in joining the conference.

Most important, however, any combination of two or more would allow the league to launch a megabucks playoff game and significantly enhance its television clout.

"The Notre Dame decision and Penn State's moving to the Big Ten sent us a signal," said former Georgia athletic director Vince Dooley. "The train was leaving the station. If we were going to be prepared to negotiate our own television contracts in the future, and hold a championship game as we'd talked about, we needed to move to strengthen our television base."

Kramer, who led the effort, told a reporter at the time: "We don't know what the college football television landscape will look like in five or ten years, but we have to be ready to go it on our own. Maybe the CFA will be around, maybe not. But we have to be prepared."

Less than a week later, the Big Ten formally admitted Penn State.

Spurred by the combination of combustable situations—and inexorably linked to forty years of prerequisite events, especially the Oklahoma-Georgia lawsuit—the entire college athletics establishment caught realignment fever in the summer and fall of 1990. Anxiety was high, and in order to protect their self-interest in a future full of unknowns, the colleges started plotting and scheming with each other and against each other, determined to enhance their strength with regard to television, scheduling, marketing, and competitive balance.

After decades of stability, every league in the country appeared to be in play. The Big Eight and SWC talked about a merger. The Pac-10 considered issuing invitations to several teams, including Colorado from the Big Eight, Brigham Young from the WAC, and Texas and Texas A&M from the SWC—half a continent away. The ACC joined the SEC in expressing interest in Miami and Florida State. After some debate, the Big Ten voted a moratorium on further expansion—saddling the league with 11 teams and a name that defied logic—but that didn't stop representatives from Big Eight members Nebraska and Missouri and independent Syracuse from placing discrete calls to Chicago.

Some officials not directly involved in the drama watched in amazement from the sidelines, the smart ones realizing that no big-time program could avoid being caught up by the historic tide. "The paradigm of college athletics is changing before our eyes," lamented Navy athletic director Jack Lengyl. "The future is being driven by economics, by television."

With the various independents feeling especially vulnerable, Raycom, the Charlotte-based television syndicator, floated a proposal to create a massive new football league using the shell of the Metro Conference, which sponsored major basketball and other sports but not football. The planned sixteen-team league—to include Miami, Florida State, Syracuse, and West Virginia, among others, with a footprint from Boston to New Orleans—could command as high as 35 percent of the nation's television households (nearly twice the size of the mammouth Big Ten). The proposal also featured a twelve-team basketball league split into two divisions.

"Television sets mean power," said Raycom vice president Ken Haines, perfectly capturing the spirit of the day.

Several teams on Raycom's list played all sports except football in the Big East, which made the leaders of the powerful basketball conference nervous.

"There was a certain amount of fear driving the whole process," said Big Ten commissioner Jim Delany. "You had a lot of activity and you had a lot of talk, and it created a feeling of urgency."

It was like a high-stakes game of musical chairs. And no one wanted to be left without a seat when the music stopped.


As the realignment frenzy gathered steam, the nation's coaches were preoccupied with one of the greatest threats ever to confront the sport. Bowing to legal pressure, the NFL reversed its decades-old gentlemen's agreement with the colleges and began drafting underclassmen who had completed three years of college, which fostered tremendous resentment toward the pro league.

In the first year, thirty-eight juniors made themselves available for the draft, throwing away their final season of college eligibility in the process. Only eighteen were drafted, including eight of the first twenty-five selected overall.

The lure of NFL riches was nothing new, and the common denominator was familiar. It was the power of television dollars that made pro football such an irresistible force for college players, especially student-athletes from impoverished backgrounds, and it was the power of television promotion that made some campus stars—including Illinois quarterback Jeff George—instantly marketable commodities for NFL teams.

Even as the colleges maneuvered to exploit television on the re-alignment front, the medium was exploiting college football in a profoundly different way.

After years of allowing lowered academic standards and the lottery atmosphere of the NFL to conspire to create a generation dominated by unqualified, unmotivated student-athletes—including many who saw college as little more than a launching pad for the pros—coaches felt frustrated and helpless. Even as the movement to raise the bar academically created more pressure than ever to graduate student-athletes in some reasonable comparison to the larger student body, the pressure to win mounted with equal force. Coaches were held accountable for both standards, despite the inherent conflict between the two.

The drafting of underclassmen increased the burden on both fronts. By raiding some of their best athletes at the peak of their playing ability, the league could decimate a powerful college team, as in the case of Southern Cal, which lost four juniors in 1990. By removing such players from the classroom before their fourth year—and planting a seed in the minds of their peers—the league further undermined the academic mission and left college coaches to deal with the consequences and the all-too-public statistics.

"We understand the NFL's situation with regard to the antitrust laws," said UCLA head coach Terry Donahue. "But they have to realize they are placing the college game in a very difficult position."

As the relationship between college and pro football sank to an all-time low, the members of the CFA voted to ban NFL scouts from their practices.

"We have a real problem with graduation rates and the NFL is only making it worse," Neinas said.

The colleges could not escape their role in creating the situation. Even as it caused them problems through the years, the tug of NFL fame and fortune became a selling point for many recruiters who could not resist pointing out how many players their program had sent to the pros—or recognizing the reality that many young athletes chose colleges based on such considerations. They used the NFL as surely as the NFL used them. It was a two-way street.

"It's hard to blame these poor kids from looking at college football that way," said former Tennessee and Pittsburgh head coach Johnny Majors. "They come from nothing and they have skills that can make them rich overnight. How can we as coaches steer them away from chasing that dream?"

By allowing their sport to slowly assume elements of a big business, the colleges had unleashed market forces that eventually overwhelmed their ability to insulate the game. After many years as an enabler of a hypocritical process, the NFL suddenly became more of a direct competitor for the services of the most outstanding college players. In the years ahead, college coaches would be forced to adjust to an ironic new era when the strongest teams were also the most vulnerable.

As the colleges shifted to chase multimillion-dollar television deals, the concept of amateurism, under assault for decades, seemed increasingly out of date. Even as scholarship athletes were being pulled between the traditional academic mission and the NFL, the value of the grant-in-aid no longer included the full cost of attendance, thanks to NCAA cost-cutting and antiabuse legislation in the 1970s and 1980s. Meanwhile, the pressure on players continued to increase—pressure to win in order to fill seats, land television appearances, and secure bowl bids.

The once proud, once powerful Southwest Conference limped into the 1990s, crippled by several major recruiting scandals—including the pay-for-play conspiracy that led to the "death penalty" for SMU—and the growing disparity in resources and commitments among its members. The elite programs—Texas, Texas A&M, and Arkansas—were feeling restless even before the music started blaring. They drew huge crowds and provided the lion's share of the league's television and bowl money, but the lower rung teams like Rice, TCU, and SMU—who shared the bounty—brought much less to the table. The SWC had the look of an old married couple who had grown apart. No one wanted to be the first to use the word "divorce."

After the Destin meeting, the SEC's Kramer tried to camouflage his list of expansion possibilities, but it was a tough secret to keep. By courting Texas, Texas A&M, and Arkansas, the SEC was effectively declaring war on the SWC, which marked a turning point in the history of college athletics. Never before had one league so audaciously pursued teams from a rival conference. Never before had one league's actions so clearly endangered the survival of another.

Without its three most important teams, the SWC would be rendered irrelevant in the context of major football, major basketball, and other sports. Losing Texas, Texas A&M, and Arkansas would drain the rest of the league of prestige, television revenue, the most powerful draws for in-stadium attendance, and, undoubtedly, its host relationship with the Cotton Bowl.

When the SEC started flirting with the three schools, the Pac-10 and Big Eight took notice and started sniffing around, too. Everyone could count. Twelve teams suddenly loomed as a magic number for conferences wishing to follow the SEC's lead to a championship game, and the desire to acquire more television homes overshadowed the geographic weakness of some expansion scenarios.

"It's all one big grab of television homes—that's all," said Pac-10 commissioner Tom Hansen. "It's not like-mindedness. It's solely a television-driven activity, and when one conference expands, it has an effect on everyone else. Everyone has to look at expansion. We really don't have a choice but to consider it."

The Pac-10 presidents eventually voted to stand pat for the forseeable future, but the fear of their action helped fuel the process.

With the SEC lusting after his three most powerful teams, SWC commissioner Fred Jacoby was privately criticized by his members for failing to stem the invasion. "We're not panicking," he said. "The worst thing we could do is throw out a knee-jerk reaction."

Kramer and his colleagues did not have to work very hard on Arkansas athletic director Frank Broyles, who led his school's decision to join the SEC starting in 1992. The longtime Razorbacks' coach, who steered the program to six SWC titles and one national championship before retiring in 1976, thought his program fit much better in the SEC. Frustrated by the weaknesses of the SWC, Broyles bought into Kramer's vision of creating a conference with the power to negotiate its own lucrative television deals and culminate its season with a profitable championship game. The switch would immediately pump about $1 million more into Arkansas's athletic coffers, and the future offered even greater possibilities in terms of television and bowl revenue. The Razorbacks also would be able to trade dates with poor drawing teams like Rice and Houston for games with powerhouses like Tennessee and Georgia, who routinely attracted more than 80,000 fans.

"We enjoyed a long and fruitful association with the Southwest Conference," Broyles explained. "But you can't sit still. Change is inevitable. Joining the SEC was the best thing for Arkansas, and we had to look out for our own best interest."

After luring the Razorbacks, SEC officials expected Texas and Texas A&M to fall like dominos. Joining the SEC made sense for both schools. After all, the Longhorns and Aggies had a lot more in common with Alabama and Tennessee than TCU and Rice. Before the Razorbacks jumped, Texas athletic director DeLoss Dodds told a reporter: "We would be very cognizant of what that means to us. We would protect the University of Texas however we had to."

Texas and Texas A&M officials underestimated the political will rising up across the state to stop the defection and save the SWC. Texas legislators who wanted desperately to see the SWC survive threatened to suspend state funding for the schools if they jumped to the SEC—though no formal invitation had been extended. State

Representative Robert Junell, a Democrat from San Angelo, introduced a bill requiring any school bolting from the SWC to forfeit half of its television revenue. Whether such laws were enforceable was not the point. Some lawmakers acted like they were rallying around the Alamo, and the public pressure to maintain the venerable, if wounded, Texas institution was enormous.

Both schools reluctantly committed to stay with the SWC in the short term. "I can't say what we might do two or three years from now," Dodds warned.

In many cases, the power of free market television predictably reinforced the dominance of the traditional powers. But deregulation also gave less powerful leagues much greater access to the nation's football fans, especially the Atlantic Coast Conference.

Throughout the 1960s and 1970s, the ACC toiled in the shadow of the five premiere conferences. Rarely was it mentioned in the same breath with the Big Ten or the SEC. Widely considered the nation's toughest basketball league, the ACC was much less competitive in football. A good year for the ACC champion was to finish in the latter half of the top 20 and play in the Gator Bowl.

During the regulated era, the NCAA and ABC considered the ACC an afterthought. When North Carolina, Duke, Maryland, and the rest played before the cameras, they often were seen before tiny audiences. In 1971, ACC members played before regional audiences two times on a total of twenty-six stations. The SEC, by comparison, earned seven appearances that season—five of them national—on an aggregate of 1,198 stations. National appearances were rare. In the entire history of the NCAA series, Texas A&M alone played on national television more than every ACC team combined.

Some respect started to flow to the conference after Danny Ford led Clemson to the 1981 national championship, but it was more of a fluke than a trend. At the dawn of the deregulated era, the ACC was still considered an inferior football league.

The conference moved quickly to assemble a syndication package after deregulation, creating a television footprint from Atlanta to Baltimore. After selling a plan directly to the networks in 1984, it subsequently joined the CFA plan and slowly began to gain more national exposures and revenue. In the first year after the Supreme Court decision, the teams of the ACC played on TV nearly as many times as in the entire decade of the 1970s.

"For the ACC, the lawsuit was the best thing that ever happened," said Gene Corrigan, who became commissioner in 1988. "We were so rarely on the NCAA package. We never would have had our syndication package without the lawsuit, so from that standpoint, it was a good thing."

When the expansion sweepstakes began in 1990, the ACC remained a step below the most important conferences in terms of football. But Corrigan saw his chance. He knew one team could change the perception and reality of ACC football in the blink of an eye.

For decades, Florida State languished in the shadows of major college football, a lowly regarded Spoiler dominated by the University of Florida and ignored by most everyone else. Then Bobby Bowden turned the Seminoles into one of the game's strongest powers—a prize worthy of being courted by the SEC, ACC, and Metro Conference at the same time.

"I had been after our people for a while to look at expansion," Corrigan said. "But most of the presidents were reluctant. Then all the stuff started happening and they saw the handwriting on the wall. I had to do a whale of a selling job, but there was just the feeling that this was the right time and Florida State was the right institution to help us get to the next level."

When talks between the SEC and FSU broke down over scheduling issues, Florida State joined the ACC in the fall of 1990. The Seminoles, who started ACC play in all sports in 1992, immediately changed the complexion of the league. FSU raised the quality of competition, forcing every other team to measure up to a higher standard. The expansion gave the ACC access to millions of television homes in Florida and allowed its teams to recruit more effectively in the talent-rich state. The move gave the ACC a much greater level of clout with the networks and bowl games.

Florida State made the ACC a big-time football conference. Not the SEC. Not the Big Ten. Big big-time—a player capable of competing routinely for the national championship and worthy of full access to the sport's spoils.

Television played a central role in the Big East's meteoric rise as the most successful basketball conference of the 1980s. But the television-driven realignment for football nearly destroyed the league in the summer of 1990.

With the three Big East members who played Division 1-A football as independents—Boston College, Pittsburgh, and Syracuse— feeling threatened by the changes roiling the sport, the possibility of one or all three defecting to another all-sports league, such as the Big Ten or the supercharged Metro, or forming an entirely new conference of Eastern independents loomed large. Some ACC officials favored approaching the three schools as football-only members.

"We started to believe that independence in football might not be a viable option in the very near future," said Syracuse athletic director Jake Crouthamel. "Change was in the air, and we all felt the need to do something to protect ourselves in terms of television and scheduling."

Several days after the SEC launched its expansion drive, Big East founder and commissioner Dave Gavitt retired, leaving the conference without a pilot at the most precarious time. Mike Tranghese, his longtime deputy, knew the Big East was imperiled.

"We were seeing a new day dawning in college football," Tranghese said. "Everybody felt they had to go out and protect themselves. Without some sort of alliance, our football schools could have become nonentities, with television and everything else."

During his interview for the commissioner's job, Tranghese was blunt.

"I told [the selection committee] we had to go after Miami," Tranghese said. "If they weren't prepared to get Miami and build a base for our football schools, we were going to be out of business. It was that simple."

Tranghese scared the hell out of his interviewers, but he was absolutely right. He got the job and then went about the business of saving the Big East.

Once lowly Miami, which seriously considered dropping football in the late 1970s, morphed into the sport's most powerful program in the 1980s, capturing three national championships in seven years. Under Howard Schnellenberger, Jimmy Johnson, and Dennis Erickson, the Hurricanes became a huge television draw, attracting viewers from coast to coast with a high-powered passing offense and a defiant attitude.

By attracting Miami, Tranghese reasoned, he could keep his football schools from bolting, strike a devastating blow against the rival Raycom plan, and create a competitive base worthy of attracting other football independents.

The SEC and ACC also wanted Miami, but in the end, the Hurricanes chose the Big East primarily because the league offered a more favorable financial package. Miami, which earned a reported $5.4 million from football television and bowls in 1989, would be allowed to keep the majority of such revenue for several years while gaining access to the Big East's lucrative basketball distribution.

After Florida State and Miami landed, the Raycom deal collapsed, which left several other Eastern independents searching for a home, including West Virginia, Rutgers, and Virginia Tech, who eventually joined the new Big East football conference.

In swiftly responding to the volatile climate, Tranghese became one of the architects of the new era of college football. His bold action fundamentally altered the structure of the game. Without him, the Big East probably would have disintegrated, forcing the the league's football playing members to seek shelter elsewhere or risk an even more dubious future as independents. He understood how to leverage Miami's clout with the networks, bowls, and other programs to the advantage of the entire conference. His decision to go after the Hurricanes not only saved the Big East, it created a framework that empowered those eastern football schools to an unexpected degree—giving them a seat at the table for the coming feast.

After failing to land several of its most coveted teams—although none were ever extended formal invitations—the SEC looked to some like a loser in the expansion wars. Not only was it unable to annex the state of Texas into its television domain, the conference suddenly found itself forced to share the state of Florida with the ACC and Big East.

But going for the long bomb didn't prevent the SEC from scoring big. In time, it would be clear that the SEC was the most prodigious winner of all in the realignment game.

When South Carolina accepted an invitation to join the conference in the fall of 1990, the SEC suddenly consisted of an even dozen teams, which allowed the league to split into two divisions and stage a championship game.

"We set out to make ourselves stronger and I'm convinced we did that," Kramer said after the expansion binge took a breather.

Kramer, who enjoyed a successful career as a football coach at Central Michigan before moving into administration, placed an indelible stamp on college athletics by leading the SEC through the turbulent period. Over the course of his tenure, Kramer transformed the SEC into an unrivaled financial powerhouse—generating more than $70 million per year from television and bowls by the end of his run.

Some college officials were skeptical about the playoff concept, often derided as a gimmick that could not possibly be worth the trouble of expansion, a regional enterprise that could never attract a big national audience. But they were wrong. The SEC Championship Game, launched in 1992, proved to be one of the most revolutionary innovations in college football history.

In addition to creating a tremendous level of season-ending excitement among fans throughout the region, the title game immediately became a financial bonanza. In its first five years, the playoff—quickly copied by three other leagues—generated nearly $40 million. After drawing an average of more than 10 million homes, the game's television rights fee tripled over the same span. By the late 1990s, the SEC was earning more from the championship game alone than it had pocketed from a season full of televised games in the early days of deregulation.

"The SEC Championship Game has proven to be one of the smartest ideas in the history of televised sports," said CBS Sports vice president Len DeLuca.

The combination of the expansion and the playoff made the SEC much stronger for television, which gave the league leverage and options heading into the new era.

When the FTC filed suit against the CFA and ABC in October 1990, justifying the colleges' fears about their vulnerability regarding the antitrust laws, no one was surprised. After careful consideration, the Big Ten and Pac-10 contracts were not challenged. The commission charged that the CFA had "entered into restrictive telecast agreements, much like those condemned in *Board of Regents* . . . through collusion with and among its members." The suit sought to invalidate the network agreement, scheduled to begin in the fall of 1991.

The same weapon the CFA had used to wrestle control away from the NCAA suddenly was pointed at Neinas's jugular. Somewhere, Walter Byers was having a good laugh.

"The members of the CFA have absolutely no relationship to each other," explained Steve Riddell, the FTC staff attorney who led the investigation. "The only reason for those colleges to get together is to pool their games and drive the price up."

No one could argue that point. The only question was whether the combination met the parameters of the *Board of Regents* decision, and the courts would be dealing with that matter for another two years.

The CFA's decision to choose ABC's more limited plan gave the FTC an easier burden to prove, but the deal turned out to be tremendously rewarding for the sport. With ABC pursuing the new regionalization approach, ratings soared 30 percent in the first year and kept climbing. With nearly all of college football on one broadcast network—except for NBC's Notre Dame package—the sport slowly evolved from a buyer's market to a seller's market for the first time since deregulation, simultaneously proving the FTC's point and enhancing the game's clout.

As the cable universe continued to expand, ESPN's importance to the sport experienced a quantum leap. In many ways, the all-sports channel supplanted ABC as the network of college football during the Clinton years, redefining the meaning of the term. ABC still carried the biggest games but ESPN's intense coverage of the sport on Saturdays produced a more intimate relationship with the fans, feeding their frenzy from the *Gameday* preview show in late morning through the highly rated prime time game hosted by Ron Franklin and Mike Gottfried, the signature voices of the new age. When the *Gameday* gang—Chris Fowler, Lee Corso, and Kurt Herbstreit—started taking their act to campuses around the country and found fans standing for hours in all kinds of weather just to whoop and holler at their commentary and predictions, ESPN executives knew they had struck a chord that transcended the Neilsen overnights. The ESPN brand's hold on the college football audience was further strengthened with the launch of ESPN2 in the early 1990s, which doubled the number of games the ESPN juggernaut could accommodate.

The CFA's decision to experiment with Thursday night games was widely dismissed but the package slowly built an audience. In the early years, most of the matchups consisted of lesser teams desperate for TV exposure, but eventually even the biggest powers warmed up to the idea of rearranging their schedules to secure a prime time national window without competition. The Thursday night franchise would prove to be one of the most important innovations in the history of the sport, expanding the college football franchise beyond Saturday for the first time—all because of the power of ESPN.

"We see the Thursday package as a mini *Monday Night Football*," says Dave Brown, ESPN's director of programming and acquisitions. "It's a great showcase that everyone involved with the game is watching, and it's like the unofficial start of the football weekend."

During the same period, the scope of coverage also expanded. Television and other media began to pay enormous attention to the recruiting wars, lifting the national signing day in February to a new level of publicity and scrutiny in the mold of the NFL's draft day frenzy. When prized running back Emmitt Smith held a news conference to announce he had chosen to attend Florida, local TV stations carried it live and ESPN treated it as big news on *SportsCenter*. In time, local, regional, and national outlets would launch programs devoted to the contentious battle for talent, epitomized by the highly rated *Countdown to Signing Day* on Fox Sports Net. But the colleges sometimes wished they could turn off the spotlight, which also accentuated the sport's flaws. Problem athletes who might have gone unnoticed in a less media conscious world often became public relations nightmares for the football powers, proving there was a price to pay for all the money and attention created by television.

When Rupert Murdoch's upstart Fox network stormed into television sports by spending $1.58 billion to purchase the rights to the NFL's NFC package in 1994—leaving CBS without football for the first time since the early days of television—the Tiffany Network suddenly found itself flush with cash and in desperate need of fall sports programming. CBS subsequently dangled a five-year, $85-million contract under the SEC's nose, an offer the conference found irresistible.

It was a landmark deal for the SEC and the entire college sports establishment. After years of struggling to mop up the red ink caused by deregulation, the CBS contract represented the first significant payoff of the free market at the network level, allowing the SEC to more than double its CFA earnings.

Even as the CBS deal vindicated Neinas's strategic vision, it killed the CFA television plan, forcing the conferences to fend for themselves and launching another round of musical chairs.

The Southwest Conference was relegated to the trash heap after the Big Eight expanded to become the Big XII with the addition of Texas, Texas A&M, Baylor, and Texas Tech. The remaining SWC schools, unwanted by the Big 12, wound up scattered among the expanded WAC—a sixteen-team monster stretching across five time zones—and Conference USA, a new league of misfits, cast-offs, and strong basketball schools like Louisville, Tulane, and Memphis.

The process rendered Houston, TCU, SMU, and Rice losers in the television-driven war, forcing their programs into arenas where they would be much less competitive in terms of TV, bowl games, ticket sales, licensing, and, ultimately, the field of play. In a world where success is determined not only by your own identity but also by who your friends and neighbors are, the four schools could not be blamed for feeling a bit lost. Houston—which captured four SWC championships over a fifteen-year period, playing in the Cotton Bowl as recently as 1985—ended up living down the street from UAB, a former Sun Belt Conference basketball power whose fledgling football program could be traced all the way back to the first Bush administration. Lowly Rice certainly had more in common with new WAC mate Texas-El Paso than Texas, but it was a long road trip from Houston to San Jose State.

The effects of the reshuffling cut both ways, representing equal parts perception and reality: Virginia Tech suddenly was defined less by its mediocre past than by its association with Miami in the new Big East. The Hokies, who finished 8–3 in 1990 but could not land a bowl bid, would no longer face such a problem. When the

Hurricanes struggled after being placed on NCAA probation, Virginia Tech filled the vacuum and became an even more powerful force in the conference. But no amount of television money and exposure could make the world believe that lowly Temple belonged in the same league as Miami and Virginia Tech. Even as the Owls saw their program elevated only because they gave the Big East access to the huge Philadelphia television market—a dubious proposition at best, given the vast number of Penn State fans in the area—traditional winner Brigham Young slipped a notch because it was no longer part of the CFA television plan. South Carolina grew tremendously in stature by joining the SEC, even though through the years the Gamecocks had been less competitive than fellow independent Southern Miss, which wound up in Conference USA.

Even the MAC, forever hugging the margin of the big-time game, expanded to twelve teams, gained some stature by adding former Division 1-AA powerhouse Marshall, and joined the SEC and Big 12 in staging a championship playoff game.

The ranks of the major college games swelled as several former Division 1-AA teams—including South Florida, UAB, Northern Illinois, Central Florida, and Boise State—crashed the party. Most would up in the MAC and C-USA. The Big West—successor to the lowly regarded Pacific Coast Athletic Association—struggled through several plusses and minuses before losing all of its Division 1-A football teams. The Sunbelt reinvented itself as a home for former 1-AA programs, including Troy State, Arkansas State, and Louisiana-Monroe.

By the time the music stopped, more than forty schools had changed affiliations in a period of structural upheaval unprecedented in the history of college athletics. The football-led realignment also caused significant change in the landscape of college basketball, dramatically altering the shape of prominent hoops leagues like the Big East, ACC, and Big 12 and forcing a chain reaction that diminished and in some cases killed other non-football conferences, including the Metro, whose schools defected to form the core of Conference USA.

In the new world that began in 1996, the SEC's attractiveness as a television property placed it in a league of its own. The other CFA conferences fought over significantly less revenue and exposure at the network level, and the impact of their maneuvering was unmistakable. The Big 12 and ACC signed with ABC, sharing the national window with the Big Ten and Pac-10. The contracts called for the Big 12 to earn $57.5 million and the ACC $54 million, respectively, over five years. The Big East inked a five-year, $56-million deal with CBS, sharing exposures with the SEC. ABC, CBS, and NBC—which continued to carry Notre Dame— paid more for the leagues separately than their combined properties had earned under the CFA banner during the 1991 to 1995 period, but probably significantly less than the CFA would have been able to demand during the same negotiating cycle, given ABC's successful regionalization approach and the overall health of the advertising market.

All of the most prominent leagues also cut lucrative cable deals—most with the Disney ESPN/ESPN2 powerhouse—sister networks of ABC. The SEC, ACC, and others continued to rake in additional millions from regional syndication.

Unable to attract any interest at the network level, the rest of the conferences were left to deal strictly with cable. In fact, they were lucky ESPN and ESPN2 had so much time to fill. Otherwise they might not have been able to generate any national television exposure. The WAC, which once gained stature and guaranteed national network exposure as part of the CFA package, ended up settling for leftover time slots and meager rights fees with the ESPN networks, alongside C-USA and the MAC. The best games from these lower-rung conferences fought for finite cable air time with the second- or third-best games from the SEC, Big Ten, Big 12, and ACC. The Pac-10 could be seen nationally on the series of regional cable channels eventually known as Fox Sports Net. The lesser Division 1-A conferences and some Division 1-AA leagues also brokered low-dollar deals with the regional cable networks, filling the airwaves with more games than ever before.

. . .

In the years after the new alignments took effect, the structural changes quickly spread to the field of play.

After splitting into two divisions, the SEC adopted a new eight-game conference rotation, which forced the end of several annual games, including the tradition-rich Tennessee–Auburn rivalry. At the same time, the new organization of teams placed Tennessee and Florida in the Eastern Division and they started playing every year. Overnight, the game grew into one of the most heated and important rivalries in the league as Philip Fulmer's Volunteers and Steve Spurrier's Gators annually battled for SEC supremacy.

With so many tough conference games to play, SEC teams felt less inclined to futher complicate their schedules with difficult intersectional showdowns.

"All of a sudden, because of the new conference rotation, Alabama can't play the kind of schedule it should be playing," said Cecil "Hootie" Ingram, the Crimson Tide's athletic director at the time of the expansion. "I think it's bad for us and bad for the conference. It doesn't make as much sense for us to play people like Penn State and Notre Dame now because we're already playing eight tough conference games, plus hopefully the conference championshp game and a bowl game. That's a negative for our program, because we should be playing those kinds of teams."

Instead, teams from the SEC and the other major conferences started scheduling more games against marginal programs like Northern Illinois, Colorado State, and Louisiana Tech, guaranteeing huge paydays for what in most cases turned out to be easy victories. The games provided an unprecedented opportunity for such schools—once completely isolated from the big-time sport—to crash the party in a more fundamental way. When some of the lesser teams started pulling the occasional upset, proving the gap between the haves and have-nots was not insurmountable, the impact of the scholarship limitations was visible for all to see.

Dissatisfaction over scheduling concerns caused an immediate rift in the expanded WAC. Original members including BYU, Air Force, and Wyoming resisted losing some of their most cherished traditional rivalries. Four years after the league expanded, the eight original members split off to form the Mountain West Conference, knocking the WAC down another notch in the world of big-time football.

Critics predicted the SEC Championship Game would prevent the conference from competing effectively in the national championship wars. After all, the prized event essentially placed a roadblock on the way to the Sugar Bowl, forcing the best SEC teams to survive yet another difficult test on the road to glory. But the threat was overblown. Through the years, the title game proved more often than not to strengthen rather than cripple the best SEC teams. In the first twelve years of the event, four different schools—Alabama (1992), Florida (1996), Tennessee (1998), and LSU (2003)—used the playoff as a springboard to the national championship.

But the concept of divisional play and championship games was not universally appreciated. The Big 12 coaches opposed the establishment of a title game but were overruled by their presidents, who said they needed the estimated $7.5 million payday to fund gender equity. In 1996, Tom Osborne's Nebraska Cornhuskers appeared headed for the Nokia Sugar Bowl against Florida with the chance of capturing a third straight national championship. But because of the new North–South divisional format, the Cornhuskers first had to pass through St. Louis and the premiere Big 12 Championship Game, where they were upset by an underdog Texas team with four losses.

In the summer of 1996, as the members of the CFA prepared to launch their own competing television deals, the rebel organization voted itself out of existence.

After nearly two decades at the center of the struggle for the major schools to control their own affairs, the CFA suddenly seemed like an anachronistic organization, a relic from another age. After leading the fight for television rights, higher academic standards, restructuring, and other issues, the CFA was no longer needed by the members who once invested it with such enormous authority and hope. Just as the CFA collapsed as an institution, the NCAA took steps to grant the major schools a greater level of legislative independence—the seemingly quixotic idea on which the union had been founded.

The very moment the CFA seized the issue of television property rights, the organization inevitably sealed its own demise. It was always only a matter of time. Even Neinas instinctively understood he was building a fleeting empire, because the spoils of the free market were destined to drive a wedge between the various factions, convincing some and then all to be motivated less by the collective good than by greed and self-interest. When Neinas and his organization were discarded with as much haste as they had once dismissed Walter Byers and the NCAA, many of the officials who opposed the Oklahoma-Georgia lawsuit considered it poetic justice. But the demise of the CFA was even more fundamental. Capitalism worked for the CFA and then it worked against the CFA, but once the market was allowed to function legally, it always empowered the schools with the marketable products to sell, and this will remain the CFA's enduring legacy.

"We have become a victim of our own success," Neinas said wistfully.

# 14

## THE BCS

When the long-suffering University of Virginia football program climbed to the top of the national rankings in 1990, George Welsh, the Cavaliers' dour, no-nonsense head coach, suddenly found himself barraged with holiday invitations.

With the sport's postseason games competing vigorously for sponsorship deals, television ratings, and ultimately, the most desirable teams, undefeated, unattached Virginia was a hot commodity coveted by all. Because the ACC—still struggling to escape its Spoiler heritage—didn't have the clout to arrange a permanent bowl destination for its champion, Welsh's team entered November as the most likely contender up for grabs. Feeling pressure to lock up a quality opponent to face the SEC champion—and, in the process, outperform the Rose, Orange, Cotton, and Fiesta in the battle for viewers on New Year's Day—the Sugar Bowl—ignoring the routinely abused bid day rule—unofficially invited the Cavaliers when they were 7–0 and on a collision course with the national championship. Then the other bowls hurried to fill their available slots, creating a chain reaction driven by equal parts fear and ambition.

But at the Sugar Bowl people watched in horror. Virginia lost three of its last four games and tumbled out of the rankings, providing a cautionary tale for a system increasingly paralyzed—and imperiled—by the mounting tension between the rival forces of sacred tradition and unbridled, free market zeal.

While eventual ACC champion Georgia Tech accepted an invitation to the less prestigious Citrus Bowl and knocked off Nebraska to capture the UPI national championship, Virginia limped into New Orleans and lost to Tennessee, finishing a four-loss season as the only unranked team in modern Sugar Bowl history.

"It would be great if we could wait till the end of the season to choose our teams, but that isn't the reality of the situation," said longtime Sugar Bowl executive director Mickey Holmes.

The bowl system desperately needed to be saved from itself.

Even as the bowls kept printing money for the cash-strapped colleges in the early 1990s, they were constantly forced to play defense—against their frustrating inability to guarantee an annual showdown for the national championship; against the growing perception that the whole system was a meaningless, anticlimactic relic; against their unwillingness to police themselves or reach any consensus on how to improve the structure; and ultimately, against the tantalizing—and, for the games themselves, surely fatal—lure of a lucrative and dramatic Division 1-A playoff.

In the shadow of this dilemma, the power structure of big-time college football was experiencing historic change as the sport came to grips with the full ramifications of the CFA-led television revolt. Empowered by the *Board of Regents* decision, the most prominent conferences were using television as a strategic tool to enhance their clout within college athletics, and as the various leagues maneuvered to make themselves stronger for television during the realignment frenzy that began in 1990, the major commissioners quickly emerged with newfound authority and influence. Television gave men such as the SEC's Roy Kramer, the Big 12's Steve Hatchell, and the ACC's Gene Corrigan a power base much greater than their predecessors', and as surely as control of broadcast rights had once enhanced the stature of Walter Byers and Chuck Neinas, it helped extend the reach of the new age commissioners.

Even as the biggest conferences schemed and plotted against each other in the zero-sum game of regular-season television, they began to talk about how to harness their collective strength to enhance the postseason structure.

"We were in a situation where the bowl system was under assault on several fronts," said the ACC's Corrigan. "The selection process was out of control, which was contributing to the larger problem, which is that we couldn't seem to find a way to have a national championship game. The fans were griping, and the playoff talk was getting louder. Everybody knew we had to do something."

The first step was tentative and wobbly, but it was progress. The original Bowl Coalition, which took effect during the 1992 season, marked a turning point in the history of college football, because it was the first time a group of bowls and conferences had resolved to work together to try to make the postseason more relevant.

Under the terms of the new order, the Cotton, Sugar, Orange, and Fiesta—in partnership with the SEC, Big Eight, ACC, Big East, SWC, and Notre Dame—agreed to abide by a format intended to end the chaotic selection process and increase the possibility of a legitimate showdown for the national championship. It achieved mixed results. Despite ending the much maligned process of backroom deals and setting up the Alabama–Miami national championship battle in the 1993 Sugar Bowl, the plan was widely criticized for relying entirely on the Associated Press media poll, for retaining the system of automatic qualifiers, and for not including the Big Ten, Pac-10, or the Rose Bowl, who declined to participate.

When the Cotton Bowl bypassed third-ranked Florida State in favor of fifth-ranked Notre Dame—violating the spirit of the system, if not the fine print—Seminoles fans complained that it cost their team a shot at the national championship. But the Dallas game chose the Fighting Irish because they represented a stronger TV draw, which forcefully demonstrated the bowls' resistance to surrendering their independence in the process.

"The best interest of the coalition was getting one and two together. It doesn't say anything about three or four," said a defiant

Jim "Hoss" Brock, the Cotton Bowl's executive director. "If that's what they want, then they should make it a rule."

With the major bowls increasingly anxious about their future, the clamor for a Division 1-A playoff reached a fever pitch in the early 1990s. Dick Schultz, the NCAA executive director, used his annual address to the membership at the 1993 Convention to tout the issue. "Ultimately, the playoff issue will be decided on its financial merits," Schultz predicted.

With the costs associated with running big-time programs soaring, administrators started taking the playoff concept more seriously. Even longtime playoff opponent Charles Young, the UCLA chancellor, conceded the need to consider all options. "Money's tight and we have to look at all possible sources of new income," said Young, who chaired an NCAA committee which determined that a sixteen-team playoff could generate as much as $200 million.

Nike, Disney, and the QVC home-shopping network all floated lucrative national championship tournament proposals, but in the end, the movement failed to generate necessary NCAA approval, at least partially because the major powers were reluctant to give the have-nots—who dominated the NCAA in a numerical sense—a slice of the pie. While many coaches embraced the playoff idea, most presidents opposed the concept, which they saw as yet another high-profile surrender to commercialization. However, the fear of the playoff option gave the major commissioners even greater leverage with the bowls, who eventually felt motivated to act in self-preservation.

Two years after they joined forces with the first Bowl Coalition, the commissioners of the SEC, Big East, ACC, and the newly formed Big 12 (which supplanted the SWC and Big Eight) along with Notre Dame took control of the process and changed the game. Roy Kramer, Mike Tranghese, and Gene Corrigan devised a revolutionary plan intended to exploit the televison and sponsor situation to maximum advantage while crowning a champion on the field. Determined to create a bold new structure and generate significant new revenue, the alliance opened the process to bids—forcing the bowls to compete for the three seats on the jet to the future.

Requiring participating bowls to abandon their ties to individual conferences, the new format sought to guarantee a number one versus number two game—as long as those teams didn't belong to the Big Ten or Pac-10—while also matching number three versus number five and number four versus number six from among the champions of the four conferences and Notre Dame, if it qualified according to a predetermined formula. The national championship game would rotate among the three chosen bowls, giving all three a stake in the success of the new system. Conference champions earned automatic bids, leaving room for two at-large teams.

"The desire to maximize revenue is central in this," said Corrigan. "We're looking for the best deals."

Even if it had accomplished nothing else, the commissioners' decision to end the practice of tying their champions to specific bowls represented a major breakthrough. With the Sugar, Orange, and Cotton bowls no longer dominating certain spheres of influence, the new creation could match the two top-ranked teams, which had been possible under the old system only if one of the contenders was an independent (or the member of a nonaligned conference, like the ACC) without a predetermined holiday destination. This required a greater level of risk for the bowls and the conferences, but they understood the overarching need to be able to guarantee a national championship game trumped all other considerations, and in the context of their timid, security-conscious past, this strategic change marked a tremendous victory for the sport.

The networks enthusiastically embraced the change. Buffeted by the steady expansion of the bowl system (which featured a total of twenty-three games by 1996), the soft sports advertising market exacerbated by the plethora of choices, and the perception of an overabundance of relatively meaningless games, television executives saw the new format as a way to energize the postseason experience and bolster sagging ratings. It was not quite a playoff, but it was a much more TV friendly alternative for several reasons, especially because it offered the opportunity for the networks to achieve much greater predictability in terms of hosting a big game.

When CBS Sports offered a combined $300 million over six years if the Federal Express Orange Bowl, OS/2 Fiesta Bowl, and Outback Steakhouse Gator Bowl were chosen to head the alliance, Robert Dale Morgan, executive director of the Peach Bowl, steamed. His game competed for one of the coveted spots but never had a prayer. "[CBS's bid] is nothing more than a TV network trying to buy college football," he grumbled.

Rick Catlett, executive director of the Gator Bowl, who also bid to be part of the coalition, was more realistic. "The commissioners realize that money is the only thing that matters in this process," he said.

Barely a decade after the Fiesta Bowl overturned the old order, the new world it helped to create was reflected in the supercharged Bowl Alliance, inspired by the tradition-smashing nerve of Bruce Skinner, empowered by the nascent free market landscape he left behind.

Believing that the new structure would generate a much greater level of interest, enthusiasm, and ratings, the networks and corporate sponsors dug even deeper into their pockets than the commissioners had anticipated. The Sugar, Orange, and Fiesta committed a combined $135 million over three years to win the coveted sweepstakes—increasing overall bowl revenue by more than 30 percent and silencing, at least for the moment, the chatter about a big-money playoff.

Several bowls were crushed to lose the auction, but none took the defeat harder than the Cotton Bowl. Left without a seat at the head table, the tradition-rich Dallas game—already reeling from the demise of the SWC—was automatically devalued, rendered a loser in the chase for television and sponsor money.

While the new Big Three took centerstage, the remaining

bowls also prospered from the conferences' new assertiveness. In contrast to the previous era, when the various minor bowls were forced to scramble for teams on a yearly basis, most games cut long-term deals with the major leagues, who devised predetermined formulas to distribute their teams who didn't qualify for the Bowl Alliance. Games like the Citrus, Gator, Cotton, and Alamo benefited from an orderly process that allowed them to market themselves with greater consistency, and the conferences guaranteed holiday trips for a large number of their teams, which represented millions of dollars in locked-up revenue.

The SEC led the way in signing up bowl deals—such as the arrangement with Atlanta's Peach Bowl, where the fourth- or fifth-best team from the SEC annually faced a comparable team from the ACC—and the Big Ten, Big XII, Pac-10, and others quickly followed. Soon, lesser leagues such as C-USA, the MAC, and the WAC struggled to place their high-achieving teams in a system where all the participating slots were spoken for, leading to further expansion of the post season, which grew to twenty-eight destinations by the dawn of the new century, with games such as Motor City Bowl, the Humanitarian Bowl, and the Las Vegas Bowl.

Like the regular-season TV packages, the number, combined payout and relative prestige of the bowl partnerships—closely linked to the value of the various television contracts—reflected the clout of the individual conferences. It was yet another way to project and enhance their power and marketing strength. The formal links between the minor bowls and the conferences represented a new level of business integration at the highest stratas of college football, giving the partners an unquestioned stake in each other's success.

The Bowl Alliance, which took effect with the 1995 season, represented another positive step in the evolution of the major games. But the system could not escape its fundamental flaw: The absence of the Big Ten and Pac-10, who clung to the megabucks Rose Bowl and felt no need to participate in the process. Without the two powerful leagues, the Bowl Alliance lacked complete legitimacy, and instead of quelling the call for a real playoff to decide the national championship on the field, it gave voice to the critics who derided it as a meaningless half-measure.

In 1995, Nebraska and Penn State finished the regular season as the top-ranked teams in the wire service polls. However, because Penn State was committed to the Rose Bowl as the Big Ten champion, the nation's only undefeated teams could not battle for the title. When both schools won their bowl games and Nebraska was awarded the controversial national championship, public dissatisfaction with the system intensified. Two years later, Michigan and Nebraska shared the national title because the sport could not find a way to put them on the same field.

Through the years, fans, media, and teams had grown accustomed to the concept of a split championship. Nearly a dozen times during the wire service era, the Associated Press media poll and the coaches poll—sponsored by United Press International, and later *USA Today*—awarded their trophies to different teams, reflecting the fickle nature of an incredibly subjective process. But the climax to the 1995 title chase gave birth to a new kind of frustration, as the Bowl Alliance tried to sell its big game as the definitive battle despite the murky reality caused by what essentially represented a political division between two rival camps. The public was not buying this convoluted logic. Even the fans who believed Nebraska was the better team and the poll voters who awarded the Cornhuskers the championship felt shortchanged by the process. After all that bother to tear up the old bowl structure and start anew, what should have been decided on the field once more came down to a vote which left much of the country demanding a recount.

Suddenly, the stubborn isolationists from the Big Ten and Pac-10 faced a defining choice: Join the Bowl Alliance and reap the benefits, including the ability to play for uncontested national championships and collect even bigger paychecks, or stay on the sidelines while attempting to maintain the primacy of the long-dominant Rose Bowl, which continued to win the ratings war and pay $13 million per year combined to the two leagues.

It should have been a no-brainer. But it wasn't.

Although the CFA played no role in the formation of the Bowl Alliance, the postseason consortium had been created by the same conferences who had once made the CFA such a powerful force—the same conferences who had once used television as a battering ram against the NCAA and, by extension, the governing body's allies in the Big Ten and Pac-10. Even as the CFA collapsed as an organization in the mid-1990s, the sense of division it represented lived on in the two leagues' resistance to the Bowl Alliance.

The situation was further complicated by the intense rivalry between CBS and ABC. CBS owned the rights to the Orange and Fiesta, but ABC controlled the Sugar and Rose Bowl, held virtual veto power over any change in the format of the Grandaddy of Them All, and was in no hurry to help enhance a series of games that would also benefit CBS.

However, soon after Joe Paterno's Nittany Lions lost the chance at the big prize, the leaders of the Big Ten and Pac-10 privately started high-level discussions about joining the alliance. They understood that they could no longer sit by while the other leagues dominated the postseason in terms of revenue and promotion, nor could they prosper by effectively isolating their teams from the national championship process, even if it was devalued by their absence. Still, without several prerequisite events—including the decision to pit a Big Ten team against an SEC team in the Citrus Bowl, and the mid-1990s efforts by most of the major conferences to cooperate in fostering NCAA realignment—the historically insular presidents of the two conferences might never have taken the plunge.

"There were a whole series of things that helped us make that transition," said Big Ten commissioner Jim Delany, who replaced longtime CFA antagonist Wayne Duke in 1989. "It came to the point where it was the right thing for the Big Ten and the right thing for college football. It wasn't healthy for the Big Ten and the Pac-10 to be separated" from the rest of the major college establishment.

The decision by the Big Ten, Pac-10, and Rose Bowl to join the system starting with the 1998 season symbolized the reunification of big-time college football after a quarter-century of political division, the end of a cold war waged over NCAA micromanagement, the formation of the CFA, Division 1-A restructuring, and the Oklahoma-Georgia lawsuit. It was a period placed emphatically at the end of an era, and it gave the two leagues a full stake in shaping the future of the bowl system. For all the flaws of the Bowl Alliance, its ultimate victory was not so much crowning national champions as in succeeding well enough in that endeavor to force the Big Ten and the Pac-10 to the table—making it unacceptable for the two conferences to remain on the outside looking in. The move was a concession by two holdout organizations that the outcry of the fans and teams carried significant weight—which some in their ranks had tried to deny—and that, for all their high-minded talk, they could not allow the other major football institutions to maintain such a huge financial, recruiting, and competitive advantage. Joining the Bowl Alliance was the price of remaining a vibrant and competitive component in major college football, and the two leagues' decision represented a calculated choice to meet the ante of a game with ever increasing stakes.

Although the commissioners created the framework, the driving force of the new partnership was ABC.

For more than eight decades, the Rose Bowl had towered over the postseason landscape, a position secured by the game's close ties to the Big Ten and Pac-10, which guaranteed it competitive security and unrivaled clout in the television marketplace. As the Bowl Alliance gathered steam in the mid-1990s, it was understandable for some within the organization to view it as yet another troublesome trend that the Rose Bowl could avoid because of its unique position in the sport's establishment—just as it had stubbornly avoiding diluting its brand during the title sponsor craze. Like their Big Ten and Pac-10 partners, the leaders of the game were institutionally averse to surrenduring any measure of autonomy to a larger entity, which often struck other bowl executives as a smug superiority complex.

But ABC executives, who saw the Rose Bowl as their ace

against CBS and the rest of the alliance, spent several months lobbying the Pasadena folks to become the fourth bowl in the rotation and eventually committed more than $500 million over seven
years to usurp CBS and lock up the rights to the Rose, Orange,
Sugar, and Fiesta—which allowed the games to elevate the per-
team payouts to more than $12 million per year.

Without ABC's intervention and deep pockets, the new
partnership—rebranded as the Bowl Championship Series (BCS)—
could not have been created. For the first time, thanks to the
network's pivotal leadership, college football would be able to
guarantee a national championship game sanctioned by all of the
nation's major programs.

A generation after Ed Scherick gave birth to ABC Sports by
landing the NCAA game-of-the-week, the division he left behind
played an undeniable role in shaping a new age in college football.

With the six most important conferences finally pooling their
teams, the commissioners, led by the SEC's Kramer, faced an even
more daunting problem: How to determine the contenders for the
big game, as well as the participants in the other three bowls. It
was easy for the sport's leaders to promise a showdown for number
one, but except in those rare instances when the whole country
united behind the only two undefeated teams at the end of the
season, the process was inevitably burdened by subjective factors.

No matter what kind of formula they devised, the BCS would
never be able to escape the central flaw that connected it to every
other national championship process ever conceived: It was only
human. It wasn't fifty guys in a room choosing teams, but it was,
nevertheless, a small group of insiders establishing a criteria and
then arbitrarily deciding how much weight to apply to the various
statistical components.

Determined to mitigate the subjective aspects of the selection
process—and avoid the widely criticized overreliance on the Associated Press media poll during the first permutation of the
consortium—the commissioners created a formula to determine

their own BCS rankings, utilizing the traditional media and coaches' polls but also encompassing strength of schedule, won-lost records, and computer rankings. In response to fan and team objections, the makeup of the various contributing factors would be altered several times over the first few years of the system.

"Everybody wants the same thing," observed Kramer, the co-ordinator of the unofficial group. "We all want to ensure as much fairness as possible in the selection process, so that we have the two most qualified teams deciding the national championship. But you're never going to get to perfect."

The BCS rankings attracted controversy from the start. When the numbers were crunched at the end of the 1998 season and once-beaten Florida State was chosen over once-beaten Ohio State to face undefeated Tennessee for the big prize in the Tostitos Fiesta Bowl, the howls from Columbus were predictable and even justifi-able. After Philip Fulmer's Volunteers knocked off Bobby Bowden's Seminoles in the much-hyped first "unified national championship game," fans of the Big Ten champion Buckeyes could not help won-dering what might have been. The non-title games in the rotation also attracted their share of criticism, especially from supporters of Kansas State, which failed to receive an at-large BCS bid in 1998 despite finishing ranked fourth with a single loss. Sometimes, the empirical formula favored the wrong teams, such as when Nebraska lost its final regular-season game in 2001 but still earned a bid to the national championship game. Meanwhile, an 11-1 Oregon team was shut out of the process. In 2000, the system favored once-beaten Florida State over once-beaten Miami, even though the Hurricanas handed the Seminoles their only loss.

But as Kramer and his associates liked to point out, the contro-versy surrounding the process fueled a new level of interest and excitement in college football, and the release of the weekly rank-ings gave the sport a jolt of urgency way beyond the old days of the wire service polls. The complex nature of the calculations re-quired to produce the rankings imbued the process with an aura of mystery and intrigue. It gave fans, media, coaches, and players something to argue about. At any given time, somebody had a beef with the system, and if the BCS rankings were undoubtably riddled with unintended biases, the nonstop debate was mostly good for college football because it injected the national championship race with a profound sense of graduated drama and meaning.

"It's hard to argue that this setup isn't a great improvement over what we had," said Florida State head coach Bobby Bowden, whose Seminoles captured the 1999 national championship after defeating Virginia Tech in the Nokia Sugar Bowl. "Some people are going to talk about a playoff regardless of what we do, but all I know is getting the top two ranked teams on the same field at the end of the season strikes me as real progress. What more can you ask for?"

The BCS started out as a way to reward achievement, but it soon began affecting the game on the field. Because strength of schedule was factored into the rankings, ambitious programs were forced to consider playing more games against tougher nonconference opponents, and conference rivals suddenly felt a new stake in the relative success of their league opponents. In the new world of the BCS, a team was only as strong as its weakest opponent. Because some of the computer rankings that were utilized in the formula emphasized margin of victory, many title-chasing teams had a new reason to run up the score. The system also altered the effect of late-season losses. During the wire service era, the human polls tended to reward teams for rebounding from an early-season loss and punish them for stumbling late in the season. Without any way to quantify such a distinction, the BCS treated one loss with equal weight, regardless of the timing involved, which effectively reversed the traditional belief that teams should be judged most critically on how they finish the season.

The BCS placed even greater emphasis on the emerging series of conference championship games, especially the climactic events of the SEC and Big 12, and late-season traditional rivalries such as Ohio State–Michigan and Florida–Florida State. Because the final BCS rankings could not be completed until after the championship games, which helped to determine who qualified for the BCS games and who would be relegated to the lesser bowls in the domino-tumbling process of prearranged, overlapping deals, they became closely watched elimination rounds on the road to the postseason.

Although it was intended solely as a solution to the glaring problems associated with the bowl system, the BCS quickly took on a life of its own. Almost overnight, the BCS became the context for everything, morphing into an unofficial super division within Division 1-A football, a sixty-two-school club that empowered members with legitimacy and financial riches while relegating the fifty-five excluded programs to irrelevance and relative poverty.

After three decades of struggling to separate themselves within the structure of the NCAA, the members of the BCS conferences managed to achieve something even more powerful and profound. The BCS emerged as a marketplace validation of the concept and characteristics of big-time college football, a closely guarded and widely coveted stamp of approval.

"I don't think any of us saw that coming," said Big Ten commissioner Jim Delany. "We never anticipated that the BCS would become such a powerful brand, that it would get to the point where even university presidents would start referring to themselves as 'BCS presidents,' which strikes me as a bit ridiculous."

As the new bowl structure created a new paradigm for the sport, it became the most stratifying force in the history of college football. But it also accurately reflected not only marketplace viability but historical reality.

Throughout the television age, the members of the present-day BCS—the SEC, Big 12, Big Ten, Pac-10, Big East, ACC, and independent powerhouse Notre Dame—have dominated the national championship race, the bowl selections, the Heisman Trophy winners, the NFL draft picks, and all other statistical measures of achievement in big-time college football. In fact, since World War II, only one non-BCS team—Brigham Young, in 1984—has captured the national championship, and even Cougars fans would have to concede their team's coronation that year benefited from a series of very unusual circumstances.

Teams from the MAC, present-day Conference USA, and now-defunct Big West always struggled to land bowl bids, until the power of television led to the expansion of the postseason in recent years. None of those teams ever contended for the national championship, rarely even finished in the top twenty of the wire service rankings, and earned television appearances only as part of the NCAA's patronage game. Most were major teams with an asterisk, clinging desperately to their precious Division 1-A membership but all too aware of their perceived inferiority.

The rise of the ACC and the fall of the WAC—and its offspring, the Mountain West Conference—proved the possibility of both upward and downward mobility, and the birth of the Big East showed how a small number of elite teams could lift an entire conference.

But the establishment of the BCS marked the dawn of a new era in major college football. The BCS took on the look and feel of a permanent wall between the sport's haves and have-nots, creating a division in which the chosen members felt significant incentive to protect their lofty status.

While teams from the non-BCS conferences were provided an opportunity to win their way into the postseason rotation by earning at-large bids if they finished among the top six teams in the final BCS standings, the anti-BCS forces argued that the structure was weighted against them. In 1998, critics howled when Tulane finished unbeaten and won the Conference USA championship but was excluded from the system. While both sides danced around the vagaries of the mathematical formula, the reality was that even in the days before the BCS, the Green Wave probably would have been ignored by the big bowls because of the relative weakness of their schedule as well as television and ticket sales considerations. Those who suggested that going 11–0 in C-USA was comparable to achieving the same record in the Big Ten or SEC were living in a fantasy world, and the fact that once-beaten

Florida State represented a much stronger draw for both TV and tickets was hardly a revelation.

"The BCS inherited a system," said Big East commissioner Mike Tranghese. "The only difference is how the participating schools are chosen."

The BCS reflected the already huge financial disparity between the haves and have-nots. While SEC teams like Alabama, Auburn, Tennessee, and Georgia averaged more than 80,000 fans per game and split more than $70 million per year from the league's lucrative television and bowl contracts, MAC teams like Toledo, Kent, and Northern Illinois attracted fewer than half as many paying customers and shared less than $10 million per year from TV and bowls.

But the BCS also exacerbated the dominance of the big conferences. Over the first five years of the BCS, the big four bowls pumped more than $450 million into the big six conferences, a huge windfall which they used to compete more effectively in big-time football while also paying the freight for broad-based men's and women's nonrevenue sports. Even though none of their teams participated in the series, the five lesser leagues split $17 million from the BCS, which was seen in some quarters as a kind of hush money.

The financially strong programs could afford to compete at a much higher level, spending lavishly to modernize facilities, recruit, and compensate their coaches and other staff. After leading LSU to the national championship in 2003, Nick Saban signed a contract guaranteeing him a record $2.3 million annually—more than ten times the average salary of his counterparts in the MAC or WAC.

As the BCS became a shorthand for the truly major schools, it also emerged as a powerful symbol of the growing commercialization of the sport, which reflected the immense power exerted by five decades of intense television coverage. It was difficult to separate the big business of college football from the game's headline-grabbing excesses and abuses, such as the all-too-frequent recruiting scandals that produced one black eye after another—personified by the Alabama booster who alledgedly paid a high school coach $125,000 to deliver a promising player—and the well-publicized student-athlete problems that mocked the academic mission and the concept of amateurism, such as the case of Ohio State running back Maurice Clarrett, who was suspended after failing to cooperate with a school investigation and subsequently abandoned his college career to challenge the last vestiges of the NFL's draft restrictions.

When the University of Oregon's faculty senate passed a resolution condemning the Ducks' $80-million stadium expansion in the face of massive campus salary cuts and criticized the decision to reschedule the game against archrival Oregon State during the dead week prior to exams—to accommodate television—the leaders of the effort defiantly invoked the name of the BCS, as if it were some sort of disease infecting the university's institutional integrity.

In the context of the historic struggle between higher education and commerce, it was impossible for the organizers of the BCS to contain the impact of the series to the climactic bowl games it produced. Inevitably, it was seen by many as a powerful symbol of the compromises required to play football at the highest level.

For the unannointed, the effect of the BCS loomed bigger even than the major bowl games and the huge paychecks they produced. Cast as outsiders, as less than worthy and therefore unable to effectively battle for the national championship and the other spoils, they saw their exclusion as a kind of self-fulfilling prophecy that diminished their recruiting efforts, inhibited their ability to compete, and trapped them in a Division 1-A no-man's land.

"The BCS has created the perception that some teams are second-class citizens in the world of college football," said MAC commissioner Rick Chryst. "And nobody wants to feel like a second-class citizen."

. . .

The competition for teams reached a new level of intensity and bitterness in the summer and fall of 2003, when the ACC raided Miami, Virginia Tech, and Boston College from the Big East. The move, which consolidated the ACC's rise from onetime lightweight to football powerhouse, dramatically increased the league's clout with regard to competitive strength, regular-season television, minor bowls, and the BCS, and allowed the new twelve-team conglomeration to start planning a megabucks playoff game, to premiere in 2005. After inviting Miami and Virginia Tech, the ACC presidents initially stalled on Boston College, but eventually invited the Eagles to join under pressure from the league's budget-conscious athletic directors, who insisted they needed the estimated $8 million annual payoff from a conference championship game (which required twelve members) to balance the books and make the expansion work financially.

Many inside and outside the conference decried the unmistakable impact on the ACC's unique brand of basketball competition, but the grab for money and power trumped the desire to preserve the sanctity of Tobacco Road's most treasured tradition. The expansion was strategically timed to be completed before the league started negotiating a renewal of its ABC/ESPN contract, and before the commissioners created the framework and the television deal for the next BCS contract. The addition of the three teams—especially perennial national championship contender Miami—allowed the ACC to grow TV revenues by more than 50 percent—to $258 million over seven years. The expansion also significantly increased the chances that the ACC could routinely earn a second bid to the BCS—in addition to the automatic berth awarded to the league champion—worth at least $13 million in additional revenue for the cash-strapped schools. It also meant the possibility of further minor bowl bids, giving the league the ability to lock up even more postseason revenue.

"This was all about the desire to grow and become stronger as a conference," said ACC commissioner John Swofford. "I think this will put us in a position to better influence the future direction of intercollegiate athletics. I think it puts us on par with any other league in terms of football."

While the expansion elevated the ACC to virtual parity with the SEC, Big Ten, Pac-10, and Big 12, it decimated the Big East. Left without three of its most important football programs, the conference built on basketball but saved in the harrowing days of 1990 by Mike Tranghese's nimble response to the first waves of football-television-driven realignment, teetered once more on the brink.

Once again, Miami was the pivotal player. The Hurricanes' decision to join the Big East in 1990 had allowed Tranghese to build a viable base for football, eventually giving the league the clout to cut its own regular-season television deal and making it a full partner in the BCS. The presence of one of the game's strongest powers raised the level of competition—and commitment—throughout the league. Thirteen years later, Miami's decision to chase a bigger split of a bigger pie in the ACC played an undeniable role in the defection of Virginia Tech and Boston College. In addition to the various attractive features of the ACC, the two universities were motivated by the knowledge that, without Miami, the Big East would be significantly weakened in terms of television, the BCS and everything else.

Feeling duped, four of the remaining Big East football schools—Connecticut, Pittsburgh, Rutgers, and West Virginia—filed suit against Miami and the ACC, seeking unspecified damages as compensation for the millions they had spent upgrading their football programs. Calling the actions of Miami and the ACC a conspiracy to destroy the Big East, the plaintiffs insisted that they had made significant investments in their programs on the assumption that Miami would remain in the conference. A state court judge in Connecticut later dropped the ACC from the suit, which paved the way for the league to court and eventually consummate the relationship with Boston College.

The unprecedented battle for teams produced a kind of rancor reminiscent of the bitter days of the CFA's television revolt against the NCAA. Officials from the two conferences traded jabs in the press and in many cases stopped talking with each other altogether, which placed them in a difficult position because they were simultaneously forced to work together as partners in the BCS.

Swofford defended the ACC's actions as "all about freedom of choice and the ability of institutions to decide where they best fit," but Tranghese clearly felt betrayed, not only by the institutions who left but by the leaders of a conference who had essentially declared war on his league.

With the future of the Big East in serious jeopardy, Tranghese moved quickly to secure five new teams for the league, including three Divison 1-A football institutions: Louisville, Cincinnati, and South Florida, all lured from Conference USA. But the new teams, who joined Pittsburgh, Connecticut, Rutgers, West Virginia, and Syracuse, left the Big East in a significantly diminished position heading into the renegotiation of its four year, $60-million contract with ABC and ESPN. The result of all the shuffling also left the Big East struggling to defend its position in the BCS, which was facing trouble on two different fronts.

Even before the major conferences' postseason scheming matured into the BCS, discontent among the excluded schools captured headlines. After Brigham Young was denied a place in the Bowl Alliance despite finishing 13–0 and ranked fifth in 1996, players and coaches appeared before Congress and tried to make a federal case against the structure.

"As a team, we just wanted what we thought was a fair shot" to compete against the nation's top programs, testified BYU tight end Chad Lewis.

Wyoming wide receiver Richard Peace told sympathetic senators that being denied a place in the bowl system "took away not only part of our season, but part of our lives . . . a part that can never be replaced."

"The most powerful conferences and most powerful bowls have entered into agreements to allocate the postseason market among themselves and to engage in a group boycott of non-Alliance teams and bowls," charged Senator Mitch McConnell (R-Ky). "The result of these agreements is to ensure that the strong get stronger, while the rest get weaker."

The criticism intensified when the Big Ten and Pac-10 joined the system. But despite all the carping, the outsider institutions who felt victimized by the process seemed absolutely powerless to storm the gates. After all, the BCS was devised outside the structure of the NCAA. It was a creation not just of the big six leagues but of the free market, of television, and while the marketplace had lobbied long and hard for the inclusion of the Big Ten and Pac-10, the marketplace could live without the WAC, MAC, C-USA, Mountain West and Sunbelt, who had traditionally been shunned by the big bowls anyway.

When Tulane University president Scott Cowen started making noise about breaking into the elite club in early 2003, practically no one took him seriously. The BSC conferences and the outsider five had been talking informally for months, trying to tweak the formula, but the man from New Orleans turned it into a public squabble. Admired by some and vilified by others, Cowen may go down as one of the most important figures in recent college football history, because he forced a compromise that could have a profound impact on the sport.

By uniting the outsider conferences under one umbrella—dubbed the Coalition for Athletics Reform—Cowen skillfully worked the media, Congress, and the BCS member leagues while attacking the BCS as an "unjust and unjustifiable . . . unnecessarily restrictive and exclusionary system that results in financial and competitive harm" to the unannointed. Placing the prestige of his office behind the effort, Cowen convinced both the United States Senate and House of Representatives to hold committee hearings on the subject, producing a flurry of soundbites and headlines at a critical juncture. "The BCS has created a system of haves and have-nots," Cowen said. "Now, I don't believe it was some sort of conspiracy. But the reality of it is, five years, into this, there have been significant unintended consequences."

Even as the BCS conferences struggled to resist any outside in-
terference, Division 1-A college football was being roiled by two
powerful, countervailing forces. While the BCS and all it represented exacerbated the massive financial disparity between the two
levels, making it much harder for the have-nots to compete against
the truly major schools, the long-term effects of the scholarship
limitations, which divided the NCAA in the 1970s, brought such
marginal programs a limited measure of on-the-field parity. The
competitive gulf between the Big Ten and MAC was huge, and in
the vast majority of cases, the big leagues dominated the lesser
conferences. But in the age of eighty-five scholarships, it was no
longer unthinkable for MAC teams to dream about pulling the occasional upset.

On one memorable Saturday in September 2003, just as the
outsiders were preparing to make their case before Congress, the
often ridiculed MAC stunned the college football world. Marshall
knocked off fifth-ranked Kansas State from the Big 12. Toledo
stunned ninth-ranked Pittsburgh from the Big East. Northern
Illinois upset twenty-first-ranked Alabama from the SEC, three
weeks after the Huskies had shocked fifteenth-ranked Maryland
from the ACC. "After a day like that, it's hard to say our teams
don't deserve the chance to compete in the BCS," said MAC commissioner Rick Chryst.

One major contributing factor in the relative rise of the
MAC was free market television. After the major conferences
filled the airwaves with games starting in 1984, the marginal
leagues were largely shut out of the national television picture.
The MAC went thirteen straight years without a regular-season
national TV appearance, and the college football audience barely
noticed. No one in Dallas was demanding, "Get me Toledo!" But
when the cable networks, with many hours to fill, started looking
around for additional product, the MAC was able to sign a deal
placing several games per year on ESPN—including the league
championship game—which brought the conference new revenue
and allowed its teams to recruit more effectively. "Television has

played a significant role in our growth as a conference," Chryst said. "It has given our teams more of an identity across the country."

At the same time, however, several MAC teams faced the prospect of losing their Division 1-A status. Tougher standards, enacted by the governing body in 2001 and due to take effect in 2004, required member schools to average at least 15,000 fans in home attendance every season. Six of the eleven schools that failed to meet the criterion in 2003 belong to the MAC, including Buffalo (which drew 9,414 fans per game), Kent State (10,546), and Eastern Michigan (11,260). The new rules also specified that members should award at least 90 percent of the NCAA-mandated limit of eighty-five football scholarships (at least seventy-six, and offer a minimum of sixteen sports and at least 200 scholarships overall. Left undetermined was how the NCAA might deal with non-qualifiers, which forced the MAC as well as the Sunbelt to lobby fellow members for some sort of mercy.

The larger issue driving the BCS controversy and the move toward tougher Division 1-A standards was the seemingly incessant debate over what constitutes a big-time football program. Half a century into the national television age, the line between on-the-field and marketplace strength has blurred beyond distinction. It is virtually impossible for a college football team early in the twenty-first century to compete effectively between the white lines if it cannot attract a large following, especially through television. Thanks largely to the effects of TV, the definition of a big-time program is now shaped to a great degree by marketplace acceptance.

Is Notre Dame big-time because it wins? Or is Notre Dame big-time because millions of people care deeply whether the Fighting Irish win or lose? The truth lies somewhere in between, and the people in South Bend understand that. In addition to attempting the difficult and sometimes impossible task of remaining true to their academic mission, they are marketing an entertainment product competing in a choice-filled world for hearts, minds, and dollars.

At the opposite end of the spectrum, tiny Rice University, the smallest institution in Division 1-A, struggled to remain competitive on the field and in the marketplace. The link between the two was undeniable. Unable to attract more than about 20,000 fans per game for football, trapped in a marginal conference without big-time television or bowl contracts, Rice faced a $10 million athletics deficit in 2003. The Owls' inability to attract more of a following exacerbated their struggle to compete on the field and forced the university's administration to subsidize the overall sports program in a time of widespread academic austerity. After considering several options—including eliminating the football program or dropping down to Division II—the university's leadership decided to continue swallowing the losses as the price of retaining their Division 1-A membership, which they considered a valuable asset in the overall branding of their institution.

The core members of the major college football community have always been easy to identify, but the debate over where to set the boundaries assumed a new level of urgency—and, in many cases, defensiveness—as the spoils associated with the game and the financial responsibilities of maintaining a broad-based program multiplied to unimagined levels.

For Cowen and his allies, the BCS was more than the megabucks next generation of a system that had always ignored the marginal teams. They saw it as an attempt by the powerful leagues to *move* the margin, and in a way, it was. By lobbying for inclusion in the BCS, the outsiders believed they were fighting to retain their stake in big-time college football. In reality, many of their programs were trying to grab a piece of something they never had in the first place.

Striking a hard line, Cowen raised the possibility of challenging the BCS on antitrust grounds or seeking congressional action, which spooked his presidential counterparts. He deftly applied political pressure both in Washington and at the grassroots level, painting the members of the BCS as an exclusionary old boys' club determined to protect their monopoly while deserving teams were shut out of the process. Antitrust experts disagreed on whether the BCS could be vulnerable on the issue, but the BCS presidents were in no mood to allow their structure to be placed under the legal microscope. "The threats of political intervention or taking us to court were particularly galling," said University of Oregon president Dave Frohnmayer. "We were trying to work through the situation and find a solution, and that wasn't helpful. It created some amount of animosity."

Burdened by a series of headline-grabbing scandals—including the sordid affair involving the alleged rapes of several University of Colorado coeds and the alleged sexual misconduct involving several recruits—the presidents of the BSC conferences were determined to avoid another public relations disaster. Cowen and his allies maximized their limited amount of leverage in the situation, and after two meetings between the rival forces, the presidents representing the BSC conferences agreed to a landmark settlement granting the lesser leagues greater access and a corresponding share of the television-dominated revenue while adding a fifth game to the system. "This has been a difficult and contentious issue to deal with," Cowen said. "But we came together as a group of presidents . . . and did something that was incredibly positive for higher education and for our student-athletes."

At the same time, the weakened Big East successfully lobbied the other members of the big six to retain its automatic bid to the BCS. But it was living on a prayer. Without Miami, Virginia Tech, and Boston College, the league faces an uncertain future. Unless Louisville, Cincinnati, and South Florida can dramatically enhance their programs quickly, the Big East will risk its stake in the powerful partnership in the years ahead.

As the entire sport seemed focused on maneuvering to project strength in the context of the BCS, the system failed miserably in 2003, undermining its credibility with teams and fans. When Oklahoma was crushed by Kansas State in the Big 12 championship game but still wound up ranked first in the BCS standings and playing for the national title in the Nokia Sugar Bowl, critics howled. It made a joke of the entire process. LSU knocked off the Sooners to capture the BCS portion of the championship, but undefeated Southern Cal—ranked first in both human polls but denied a shot at the officially sanctioned title game—was awarded a share of the crown by an Associated Press media survey after winning the Rose Bowl.

After overcoming significant obstacles to create the framework to stage a unified national championship game, from the inertia of the old automatic qualifier system to the political residue of the CFA-led television revolt, the BCS stumbled over a math problem. The complex formula utilized to rank teams failed to recognize what many ten-year-old fans understood instinctively: that LSU and Southern Cal deserved to play for the championship.

Mindful that ratings are the ultimate barometer of marketplace acceptance, the coalition of leagues were concerned to see the audience for the official national championship game tumble 14 percent, a number that could weaken the group's leverage with networks and advertisers. Sophisticated fans could see they were being sold an illegitimate conclusion to the national sweepstakes. However, the debate over LSU and Southern Cal fueled even greater interest in the Rose Bowl, whose ratings soared 23 percent. "Controversy isn't the worst thing in the TV business," said ABC senior vice president Loren Matthews.

Embarrassed by the debacle and well aware that they must zealously protect their credibility with the viewing public, BCS officials vowed to tweak the formula once again. The new criterion was expected to place less emphasis on the computer rankings and more on the human polls, which, for all their subjectivity, never rewarded the victim of a season-ending blowout with a No. 1 ranking.

But as the commissioners ran the numbers on several different formula variations, they were preoccupied with an even more daunting task: how to enlarge the BCS without destroying it.

The presidents' determination to keep peace in the family led them to dump a very big problem at the doorstep of the major commissioners. Even as ABC and the bowls themselves expressed serious reservations, the commissioners were forced to figure out how to add a fifth game and lower the standards of admission, which was both a testament to the success of the series and a threat to its future viability.

Six years after pulling a very big string, ABC executives were forced to come to grips with the limits of their power. "We do write a pretty big check, and we'd like to think they're listening," said ABC's Matthews. "But ultimately, it's [the conferences'] ball-game, and they set the rules."

Struggling to live up to the parameters of the brokered deal while trying to protect the BCS as a television property, the commissioners considered several options during the spring of 2004. Facing a deadline of early June—when ABC was scheduled to begin negotiations on the next round of its Rose Bowl contract—the conferences vigorously debated how to model the next round of the system, to begin after the 2006 season.

"Everybody is obligated to a good-faith effort to try to make this work," said the Big Ten's Delany. "But ultimately, whatever we come up with, we have to take to the marketplace and see what happens."

"The BCS commissioners have been put in a very difficult position by the presidents," said Matthews. "They have to do what they have to do, and I understand that. But they sure aren't doing this for television."

For several weeks, the commissioners argued over whether to add a new bowl to the system or to allow one of the four incumbent bowls to host an additional game every fourth year. Both options presented problems.

Bringing a new game into the mix held the potential for diluting the power and financial strength of the Rose, Orange, Sugar, and Fiesta, who took the risks to build the system and were understandably protective of their sweat equity. Title sponsors Frito-Lay,

Nokia, FedEx and AT&T, who committed at least $8 million per year to associate their products with the big games and trade on the corresponding national television exposure, resisted any change that would reduce the value of their sponsorship packages.

Rotating another game among the current lineup represented a different kind of threat to the existing Big Four. Because the presidential deal essentially guaranteed a berth for one of the outsider conferences under certain conditions; the possibility of being compelled to host a game including a team with limited television and fan appeal struck many of the bowl officials as a potentially devastating drain on their tradition-rich brands. The proud Rose Bowl, which could always spurn the BCS and go back to matching the Big Ten and Pac-10 champions every year, bristled at the thought of allowing the game's storied history to be sullied by lightweights like Miami (Ohio), Central Florida, or TCU.

Twelve bowls presented bids to join the system, but the commissioners and the existing Big Four ultimately chose to rotate the new game among the current organizing groups in New Orleans, Tempe, Pasadena, and Miami. With many details still to be worked out as they headed into the summer, the commissioners announced that the Rose, Orange, Sugar and Fiesta would host their traditional bowls as usual, to be followed by the national championship game about a week later, which would continue to rotate on a four-year cycle.

But as the BCS prepared to enter negotiations with ABC in the fall of 2004, the sport faced a defining moment. Concerned that the expansion of the system could dilute the powerful BCS brand without adding significant value, the commissioners waited nervously for the marketplace to react to the changes. Television made the BCS possible, and television would have the final say on whether the larger and more inclusive BCS worked financially.

"This whole thing is about creating access to something that has proven successful," said the Big East's Mike Tranghese. "But what happens when you create access that the marketplace doesn't embrace? What then? We don't have an answer for that."

The commissioners insisted they were creating a solution that needed to be tested in the marketplace, and no one could say exactly how ABC would respond to the new model, whether another network might make a run at the package; whether the major conferences were prepared to walk away from their forced solution if television failed to adequately value the new system; or whether the public would enthusiastically embrace the altered series in the years ahead.

With the major schools desperate to hold on to one of their biggest revenue sources, the outsiders struggling for a piece of the action and the legitimacy it represented, and the public continuing to push for a full-blown playoff system, the stakes seemed enormous. It was a maneuver certain to affect the future look of conferences, the ability of the colleges to fund Title IX, and the very definition of a big-time football program. The rise or fall of the BCS seemed destined to exert tremendous influence in shaping college football for years to come, empowered by the seductive charms of television.

# SOURCE NOTES

Unless otherwise indicated, all direct quotes were taken from interviews conducted by the author.

1 "We are dealing with a terrific force": Transcript of 45th Annual NCAA Convention, NCAA Archives, Jan. 11, 1951.

7 "Television does have an adverse effect": Transcript of 45th Annual NCAA Convention, NCAA Archives, Jan. 11, 1951.

8 "It is the near-unanimous opinion": Transcript of 45th Annual NCAA Convention, NCAA Archives, Jan. 11, 1951.

9 "I think we are being a little shortsighted": Transcript of 45th Annual NCAA Convention, NCAA Archives, Jan. 11, 1951.

10 "carry on as an obligation": *The New York Times*, June 7, 1951.

11 "Central control is a kind of disease": *The New York Times*, June 7, 1951.

11 "By breaking away": *The New York Times*, June 7, 1951.

12 "We have the firm intention": *The New York Times*, June 16, 1951.

12 "If these powers are permitted": *The New York Times*, Jan. 16, 1951.

25 "The networks would love to have Notre Dame": Minutes of TV Committee meeting, Asa Bushnell Papers.

26 "One is safe": Minutes of TV Committee meeting, Asa Bushnell Papers.

33 "There is such a thing as minority rights": Transcript of Keep Posted program, Jeff Coleman Papers.

33 "We are trying to save the game": Transcript of Keep Posted program, Jeff Coleman Papers.

84 "Are you really going to abandon": Roone Arledge, *Roone* (New York: HarperCollins, 2003).

88 "Moore suggested that the two parties": Minutes of TV Committee meeting, NCAA Archives.

111 "I don't know anything about hockey in Minnesota": *Birmingham Post-Herald*, Aug. 16, 1975.

112 "[The legislation] was more of an attempt": Deposition of Board McWhorter, *Board of Regents v. NCAA*, Feb. 19, 1982.

112 "That was a symbolic piece of legislation": *The Atlanta Constitution*, Aug. 15, 1975.

114 "No longer will the little guys": *The New York Times*, Aug. 7, 1973.

115 "The issue of whether institutions wish to give up": *The Atlanta Constitution*, Aug. 15, 1975.

116 "It is disappointing to study": Minutes of TV Committee meeting, April 23, 1969.

126 "It is important that the NCAA Committee on Infractions": Minutes of Congressional hearing.

127 "I'm upset about things": *The Atlanta Constitution*, Aug. 17, 1975.

127 "We support Coach Bryant": *The Atlanta Constitution*, Aug. 17, 1975.

128 "The Hennessey Court found that the limitations": Correspondence files, NCAA Archives.

129 "We have not made congressional protection": Correspondence files, NCAA Archives.

129 "Whether the NCAA needs": Correspondence files, NCAA Archives.

136 "A vote for the principles": *The Daily Oklahoman*, May 3, 1981.

136 "The NCAA legal counsel's position": *The Daily Oklahoman*, May 3, 1981.

136 "The NCAA would consider that to be": *The Daily Oklahoman*, May 8, 1981.

137 "The drift of the NCAA plan": *The Daily Oklahoman*, May 10, 1981.

137 "When you belong to a democratic organization": *The Daily Oklahoman*, May 10, 1981.

137 "These arguments demonstrate a lack of understanding": Correspondence files, NCAA Archives.

137 "I have some difficulty": Correspondence files, NCAA Archives.

138 "The principles are no longer principles": Wiles Hallock Papers.

140 "No, you know what the number is": Jim Spence, *Up Close and Personal: The Inside Story of Network Television Sports* (New York: Atheneum, 1990).

144 "There is a risk of being as hard-nosed": *The Daily Oklahoman*, Aug. 20, 1981.

144 "It is virtually impossible for us to overstate": Deposition of William Banowsky, *Board of Regents v. NCAA*, Dec. 21, 1981.

144 "The situation is analogous to state legislatures": Correspondence file, NCAA Archives.

145 "It's a sad day for college sports": *The Daily Oklahoman*, Aug. 20, 1981.

146 "If we didn't have an NCAA": Deposition of Boyd McWorther, *Board of Regents v. NCAA*, Feb. 19, 1982.

148 "We got no real attention": *Sports Illustrated*, Oct. 12, 1981.

149 "Well, you fellows are about to": Deposition of William Banowsky, *Board of Regents v. NCAA*, Dec. 21, 1981.

151 "The Ivy League is in another world": *The New York Times*, Dec. 5, 1981.

151 "Young football players have become commercial pawns": *The New York Times*, Dec. 5, 1981.

151 "That group [the NCAA] is going to correct a vulnerability": *The Boston Globe*, Dec. 8, 1981.

151 "Oklahoma will sign up": The *Boston Globe*, Dec. 8, 1981.

152 "The telecasting, cablecasting or otherwise televising": *The New York Times*, Jan. 13, 1982.

152 "provided a far more flexible TV procedure": *The New York Times*, Jan. 13, 1982.

153 "unstinting resolve to prosecute diligently": Minutes of University of Oklahoma Board of Regents Meeting, Jan. 14, 1982.

156 "Is it true": *The Daily Oklahoman*, June 11, 1982.

156 "Miss Sundberg indicated": *The Daily Oklahoman*, June 11, 1982.

157 "[the NCAA enjoys] almost absolute control": Federal District Court opinion, Sept. 15, 1982.

162 "The court must address the question": Transcript of U.S. Supreme Court argument, *Board of Regents v. NCAA*, March 20, 1984.

163 "If the NCAA has no market power": Transcript of U.S. Supreme Court argument, *Board of Regents v. NCAA*, March 20, 1984.

163 "As we read this court's cases": Transcript of U.S. Supreme Court argument, *Board of Regents v. NCAA*, March 20, 1984.

163 "All said if we didn't have the plan": Transcript of U.S. Supreme Court argument, *Board of Regents v. NCAA*, March 20, 1984.

164 "We do not believe the court would have decided": Transcript of U.S. Supreme Court argument, *Board of Regents v. NCAA*, March 20, 1984.

165 "Regardless of the path": Transcript of U.S. Supreme Court argument, *Board of Regents v. NCAA*, March 20, 1984.

166 "Because it restrains price and output": Majority opinion, U.S. Supreme Court, *Board of Regents v. NCAA*, March 20, 1984.

166 "Although some of the NCAA's activities": Dissenting opinion, U.S. Supreme Court, *Board of Regents v. NCAA*, March 20, 1984.

167 "Is oversaturation your primary concern": Transcript, *Today*, NBC television network, June 28, 1984.

175 "By issuance of this order": Federal District Court opinion.

210 "Dear Chuck": Personal correspondence file, Father William Beauchamp, University of Notre Dame.

237 "entered into restrictive telecast agreements": Federal Trade Commission complaint.

249 "The best interest of the coalition": *The Atlanta-Journal Constitution*, Dec. 7, 1992.

266 "As a team, we just wanted": *The Atlanta Journal-Constitution*, May 23, 1997.

266 "Took away not only part of our season": *The Atlanta Journal-Constitution*, May 23, 1997.

266 "The most powerful conferences": *The Atlanta Journal-Constitution*, May 23, 1997.

267 "Unjust and unjustifiable": Oral testimony, Senate Judiciary Committee, Oct. 29, 2003.